CHANCELLORSVILLE

AND

GETTYSBURG

BY

ABNER DOUBLEDAY

BREVET MAJOR-GENERAL U.S.A., AND LATE MAJOR-GENERAL U.S.V.;
COMMANDING THE FIRST CORPS AT GETTYSBURG

 LONGMEADOW PRESS

1996

A Platinum Press Book

This special reprint edition originally published
in 1882 is now republished by:

Longmeadow Press
201 High Ridge Road
Stamford, CT 06904

in association with

Platinum Press Inc.
311 Crossways Park Drive
Woodbury, NY 11797

Library of Congress Cataloging-in-Publication Data

Doubleday, Abner, 1819-1893.
   Chancellorsville and Gettysburg / by Abner Doubleday.
      p.   cm. — (Campaigns of the Civil War)
   "A Platinum Press book."
   Originally published : New York : C. Scribner's Sons, 1882.
   Includes bibliographical references and index.
   ISBN 0-681-21631-X
   1. Chancellorsville (Va.), Battle of, 1863 — Personal narratives.
   2. Gettysburg (Pa.), Battle of, 1863 — Personal narratives.
   3. Doubleday, Abner, 1819-1893. I. Title. II. Series.
   [E475.35.D685 1996]
   973.7'349 — dc20   95-52202
                                                                      CIP

Cover design by James C. Romano II

ISBN: 0-681-21631-X

Printed in USA

First Longmeadow Press Edition 1996

0 9 8 7 6 5 4 3 2 1

PREFACE.

In writing this narrative, which relates to the decisive campaign which freed the Northern States from invasion, it may not be out of place to state what facilities I have had for observation in the fulfilment of so important a task. I can only say that I was, to a considerable extent, an actor in the scenes I describe, and knew the principal leaders on both sides, in consequence of my association with them at West Point, and, subsequently, in the regular army. Indeed, several of them, including Stonewall Jackson and A. P. Hill, were, prior to the war, officers in the regiment to which I belonged. As commander of the Defences of Washington in the spring of 1862, I was, owing to the nature of my duties, brought into intimate relations with the statesmen who controlled the Government at that time, and became well acquainted with President Lincoln. I was present, too, after the Battle of Gettysburg, at a very interesting Cabinet Council, in which the pursuit of Lee was fully discussed; so that, in one way and another, I have had better opportunities to judge of men and measures than usually fall to the lot of others who have written on the same subject.

I have always felt it to be the duty of every one who held a prominent position in the great war to give to posterity the benefit of his personal recollections; for no dry official statement can ever convey an adequate idea to those who come after us of the sufferings and sacrifices through which the country has passed. Thousands of men—the flower of our Northern youth—have gone down to their graves unheralded and unknown, and their achievements and devotion to the cause have already been forgotten. It is, therefore, incumbent upon us, who were their comrades in the field, to do all in our power to preserve their deeds from oblivion.

And yet it is no easy task to relate contemporaneous events. Whoever attempts it must be prepared for severe criticism and the exhibition of much personal feeling. Some of this may be avoided, it is true, by writing a colorless history, praising everybody, and attributing all disasters to dispensations of Providence, for which no one is to blame. I cannot, however, consent to fulfil my allotted task in this way, for the great lessons of the war are too valuable to be ignored or misstated. It is not my desire to assail any of the patriotic men who were engaged in the contest, but each of us is responsible for our actions in this world, and for the consequences which flow from them ; and where great disasters have occurred, it is due both to the living and the dead that the causes and circumstances be justly and properly stated.

Richelieu once exclaimed, upon giving away a high appointment: "Now I have made one ingrate and a thousand enemies." Every one who writes the history of the Great Rebellion will often have occasion to reiterate the statement; for the military critic must necessarily describe facts which imply praise or censure. Those who have contributed to great successes think much more might have been said on the subject, and those who have caused reverses and defeats are bitter in their denunciations.

Nevertheless, the history of the war should be written before the facts have faded from the memory of living men, and have become mere matters of tradition.

In a narrative of this kind, resting upon a great number of voluminous details, I cannot hope to have wholly escaped error, and wherever I have misconceived or misstated a fact, it will give me pleasure to correct the record.

A. D.

New York, January, 1882.

CONTENTS.

PAGE

LIST OF MAPS, ... vi

CHANCELLORSVILLE.

CHAPTER I.

THE OPENING OF 1863—HOOKER'S PLANS, . . . 1

CHAPTER II.

FRIDAY, THE FIRST OF MAY, ... 11

CHAPTER III.

THE DISASTROUS SECOND OF MAY, ... 20

CHAPTER IV.

THE ROUT OF THE ELEVENTH CORPS, ... 25

CHAPTER V.

JACKSON'S ADVANCE IS CHECKED, ... 85

CONTENTS.

CHAPTER VI.

SICKLES FIGHTS HIS WAY BACK—ARRIVAL OF THE FIRST CORPS, ... 41

CHAPTER VII.

THE BATTLE OF THE THIRD OF MAY, ... 45

CHAPTER VIII.

MAY FOURTH—ATTACK ON SEDGWICK'S FORCE, . . 63

CHAPTER IX.

PREPARATIONS TO RENEW THE CONFLICT, . . . 75

CHAPTER X.

BATTLE OF BRANDY STATION (FLEETWOOD), . . . 81

GETTYSBURG.

CHAPTER I.

THE INVASION OF THE NORTH, ... 87

CHAPTER II.

HOOKER'S PLANS—LONGSTREET OCCUPIES THE GAPS IN THE BLUE RIDGE—ALARM IN RICHMOND—HOOKER SUPERSEDED BY MEADE, ... 98

CHAPTER III.

STUART'S RAID—THE ENEMY IN FRONT OF HARRISBURG —MEADE'S PLANS, ... 117

CONTENTS.

CHAPTER IV.

PAGE

THE FIRST DAY OF THE BATTLE OF GETTYSBURG,
WEDNESDAY, JULY 1, 1863, ... 124

CHAPTER V.

BATTLE OF GETTYSBURG—THE SECOND DAY, . . . 156

CHAPTER VI.

THE BATTLE OF THE THIRD DAY—JOHNSON'S DIVISION
DRIVEN OUT, ... 186

CHAPTER VII.

GENERAL RETREAT OF THE ENEMY—CRITICISMS OF DIS-
TINGUISHED CONFEDERATE OFFICERS, . . . 204

APPENDIX A, ... 211
APPENDIX B, ... 222
INDEX, ... 227

CHANCELLORSVILLE

LIST OF MAPS.

	PAGE
FIELD OF OPERATIONS IN VIRGINIA,	1
OPERATIONS ON THE FIRST OF MAY, 1863,	6
JACKSON'S ATTACK ON HOWARD, MAY 1,	18
BATTLE OF THE THIRD OF MAY,	45
SEDGWICK'S POSITION,	62
FROM THE POTOMAC TO HARRISBURG,	109
DIAGRAMS OF POSITIONS IN THE BATTLE OF GETTYSBURG:	
I.,	125
II.,	127
III.,	133
IV.,	136
GETTYSBURG: FINAL ATTACK OF THE FIRST DAY AND BATTLE OF THE SECOND DAY,	160
DIAGRAM OF THE ATTACK ON SICKLES AND SYKES,	165

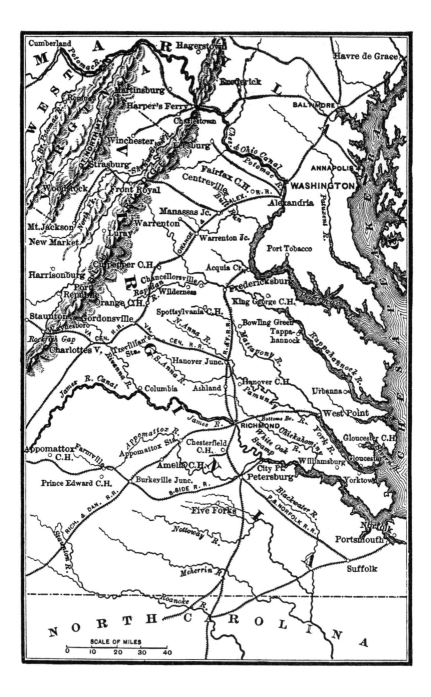

CHANCELLORSVILLE.

CHAPTER I.

THE OPENING OF 1863.—HOOKER'S PLANS.

AFTER the great disaster of Fredericksburg, General Burnside, the Commander of the Union Army, was superseded by Major-General Joseph Hooker, a graduate of West Point, who having formerly held a high position on the staff of General Gideon J. Pillow in the war with Mexico, was supposed to be well acquainted with military operations on a large scale. He had subsequently left the army, and had been engaged in civil pursuits for several years. He was a man of fine presence, of great personal magnetism, and had the reputation of being one of our most efficient and successful corps commanders.

When the campaign of Chancellorsville commenced, the Army of the Potomac was posted on the left bank of the Rappahannock, opposite Fredericksburg, among the Stafford hills, in a position which was considered almost impregnable. It rested upon the Potomac River, and as all its supplies came by water, they were not subject to delay or interruption of any kind; nor were they endangered by the movements of the enemy.

At the period referred to, General Hooker had under him a force of about 124,500 men of all arms, 11,500 of which were cavalry.

On the opposite side of the river, the Army of Northern Virginia, under General Robert E. Lee, numbered, according to their official reports, about sixty-two thousand men, three thousand of which were cavalry;[1] but the difference was amply compensated by the wide river in front of the enemy, and the fact that every available point and ford was well fortified and guarded. General Thomas J. Jackson, commonly called Stonewall Jackson, held the line below Hamilton's crossing to Port Royal. Two out of four divisions of Longstreet's corps were absent. The fourth, under Major-General Lafayette McLaws, was posted from Hamilton's crossing to Banks' Ford. Still farther up and beyond the front of either army, the crossing-places were watched by the rebel cavalry under Major-General J. E. B. Stuart, supported by the Third Division of Longstreet's corps, that of Anderson.

Both armies had spent the winter in much needed rest, after the toilsome and exhausting marches and bloody battles which terminated Lee's first invasion of Maryland. The discipline of our army was excellent, and it would have been hard to find a finer body of men, or better fighting

---

[1] Napoleon says 100,000 men on the rolls are only equivalent to about 80,000 muskets in action. It is doubtful if Hooker had over 113,000 men for actual combat. Lieut.-Colonel W. T. Forbes, Assistant Adjutant General, who has had access to the records, after a careful estimate, places the number as follows. First Corps, 16,000; Second Corps, 16,000; Third Corps, 18,000; Fifth Corps, 15,000; Sixth Corps, 22,000; Eleventh Corps, 15,000; Twelfth Corps, 11,000; total infantry and artillery, 113,000; Pleasonton's cavalry, 1,500; total effective force, 114,500. He estimates Lee's army at 62,000, which the Confederate authorities, Hotchkiss and Allan, place as follows: Anderson's and McLaws divisions of Longstreet's Corps, 17,000; Jackson's Corps, 33,500; Stuart's Cavalry, 2,700: Artillery, 5,000; add 4,000 on engineer, hospital duty, etc. This estimate is exclusive of Stoneman's force.

material than that assembled on this occasion, in readiness to open the spring campaign. Hooker was justly popular with his troops. They had confidence in his ability as a general, and he had gained their good will by anticipating their wants, and by generously granting furloughs to those who were pining from home-sickness ; trusting that old associations and the honor of the men would induce them to rejoin their colors when their leaves of absence had expired. In this way he almost stopped the desertion which had been so prevalent under Burnside. Only one portion of the army was dissatisfied ; the position recently occupied by General Franz Sigel, the favorite commander of the Eleventh Corps, had been given to General O. O. Howard. The numerous Germans in that corps were discontented at the change. They cared little for Howard's reputation as the Havelock of the army ; an appellation he had gained from his zeal as a Congregationalist. They felt, when their countryman Sigel was deprived of his command, that it was a blow to their nationality, and therefore lost some of the enthusiasm which always accompanies the personal influence of a popular leader.

The rainy season was nearly over, the time had come for action, and it was essential to strike a decisive blow before the term of service of the nine months and two years' men had drawn to a close. Hooker's plan of campaign was simple, efficacious, and should have been successful. The rebels occupied a long line and could not be strong everywhere. He resolved to make a pretence of crossing with three corps, under Major-General Sedgwick, below Fredericksburg, while the remaining four corps under Major-General Slocum made a detour and crossed twenty-seven miles above at Kelly's Ford. The latter were then to march down the river against the left flank of the rebel army and re-open Banks' Ford; thus re-uniting the two wings of the army and giving a secure line of retreat in case of disaster. When this was accomplished it was proposed to give battle in the open country near the ford, the position there being a commanding one and taking the whole line of rebel works on the heights of Fredericksburg in reverse. Owing to his great preponderance of force, Hooker had little reason to doubt that the result would be favorable to our arms. To carry out this plan and make it a complete surprise to the enemy it became necessary to leave Gibbons' division of Couch's corps behind, for as his encampment at Falmouth was in full view of the Confederate forces on the opposite side, to withdraw it would have been to notify them that some unusual movement was going on. So far the idea was simply to crush the opposing army, but Hooker's plan went farther and involved the capture of Lee's entire force. To accomplish this he directed Stoneman to start two weeks in advance of the main body with ten thousand cavalry, cross at the upper fords of the Rappahannock, and sweep down upon Lee's communications with Richmond, breaking up railroads and canals, cutting telegraph wires, and intercepting supplies of all kinds. As the rebel commissariat found great difficulty in keeping more than four days' rations on hand at a time, Stoneman's raid would almost necessarily force Lee to fall back on his depots and give up Fredericksburg. One column under Averell was to attack Culpeper and Gordonsville, the other under Buford to move to Louisa Court House, and thence to the Fredericksburg Railroad. Both columns were to unite behind the Pamunkey, and in case our army was successful Stoneman was directed to plant his force behind some river in an advantageous position on Lee's line of retreat, where he could detain the rebel army until Hooker could again assail it and compel it to surrender. A brave programme! Let us see how it was carried out.

It was an essential part of Hooker's project that the cavalry should begin operations two weeks before the infantry. If they did their work thoroughly, Lee would be out of provisions, and his retreat would give us all the moral effect of a victory. The rebel cavalry at this time being reduced to about 3,000 men, it was not supposed that Stoneman would encounter any serious resistance. He accordingly started on April 13th to carry out his instructions, but another rain storm, which made the river unfordable, and very bad roads, detained him until the 28th. It has been suggested that he might have crossed higher up, but cavalry officers who were there, tell me that every ravine had become an impassable river. Hooker became impatient and refused to wait any longer; so when the water subsided, all—infantry, artillery, and cavalry—were sent over together. The result was that the battle was ended before Stoneman got fairly to work, and his operations had little or no effect in obstructing Lee's movements.

To confuse the enemy as much as possible, demonstrations had been made at both ends of the line. On April 21st a small infantry force was sent to threaten Kelly's Ford. On the same day, I went with part of my division down the river to Port Conway, opposite Port Royal, twenty miles below Fredericksburg, made a pretence of crossing in pontoons, and built fires in every direction at night, to give the impression of a large force. On the 24th General Wadsworth went on an expedition to the same place, and two regiments under Colonel Morrow, Twenty-fourth Michigan, crossed over in boats, and returned. These movements caused Jackson to strengthen his force in that quarter. On the 27th, the storm having abated, Meade's corps (the Fifth), Howard's

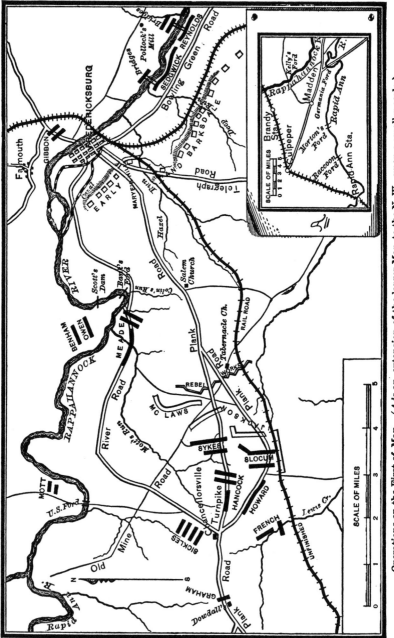

Operations on the First of May (A is an extension of the larger Map to the N. W., upon a smaller scale.)

corps (the Eleventh), and Slocum's corps (the Twelfth), the whole being under command of General Slocum, left camp for Kelly's Ford, each accompanied by three batteries. A detachment was thrown over, in boats, on the evening of the 28th, which dispersed the picket guard; and by the next morning the entire force was across the river and on their way to the Rapidan, the Fifth Corps taking the direction of Elley's Ford and the Eleventh and Twelfth Corps that of Germania Ford. Stoneman's cavalry crossed at the same time with the others, and moved to Culpeper, where he halted for a time to reorganize his force, and get rid of surplus horses, baggage, etc., which were sent to the rear. The next day Averell kept on to Rapidan Station with 4,000 sabres, to engage W. H. F. Lee's rebel brigade, so that it could not interfere with the operations of the main body, which moved southeast across Morton's Ford and Racoon Ford to Louisa Court House, where the work of destruction was to begin. Stoneman's further movements will be related hereafter. One small brigade of three regiments with two batteries was placed under the command of General Pleasonton and directed to report to General Slocum, to precede the infantry on the different roads.

Stuart, who commanded two brigades of rebel cavalry, under Fitz Hugh Lee and W. H. F. Lee, and whose duty it was to watch these upper fords, received news of the crossing at 9 P.M., on the 28th.

The turning column reached Chancellorsville with but little opposition, as both Lee and Stuart thought it was making for Gordonsville and the Virginia Central Railroad. In consequence of this miscalculation, Stuart planted himself at Brandy Station. When he found that he was out of position and that it was too late to prevent the crossing at Germania Ford, he made a circuit with Fitz Hugh Lee's brigade to get between Slocum and Lee, and sent W. H. F. Lee's brigade to impede Stoneman's operations. The passage of Germania Ford turned Elley's Ford and United States Ford, and Mahone's and Posey's brigades, who were on guard there, retreated on Chancellorsville, where Anderson had come up with Wright's brigade too late to prevent the crossing.

By 6 P.M. on the 30th, Hooker found himself in command of four corps at Chancellorsville, with another—that of Sickles—near at hand. Anderson fell back to Tabernacle Church as our troops advanced, and began to fortify a line there. Stuart sent Fitz Hugh Lee's brigade, which was very much exhausted, to Todd's Tavern for the night, while he started with a small escort, to explain the situation to General Lee at Fredericksburg. On the road, not far from Spottsylvania, he came unexpectedly upon one of Pleasonton's regiments, the Sixth New York Cavalry, numbering about 200 men, which was returning from a reconnoissance it had made in that direction. He avoided the encounter and sent back to Todd's Tavern, at first for a regiment, but subsequently for the entire brigade. When these reinforcements came up a furious cavalry contest took place, with charges and counter-charges, and hand to hand combats. It was not without an element of romance, in that lonely spot, far from either army, under the resplendent light of the full moon; recalling, in the words of a Southern chronicler, some scene of knightly glory. Our troops were surrounded, but cut their way out with the loss of their gallant commander, Lieutenant-Colonel McVicar, who led them to the charge.

Meanwhile the other portion of the contemplated movement had also been going forward. On the 28th, the Sixth Corps, under Sedgwick, and the First Corps, under Reynolds, were moved down near the river, three or four miles below Fredericksburg, and bivouacked there in a pouring rain. As it was possible that the two corps might be attacked when they reached the other side, the Third Corps, under Sickles, was posted in the rear as a reserve.

The next day two bridges were laid at Franklin's old crossing for the Sixth Corps, and two more a mile below for the First Corps. Men in rifle-pits on the other side impeded the placing of the pontoons for a while, but detachments sent over in boats stormed their intrenchments, and drove them out. Brooks' division of the Sixth Corps and Wadsworth's division of the First Corps then crossed and threw up *tête-de-ponts*. The enemy made no other opposition than a vigorous shelling by their guns on the heights, which did but little damage. A considerable number of these missiles were aimed at my division and at that of General J. C. Robinson, which were held in reserve on the north side of the river; but as our men were pretty well sheltered, there were but few casualties.

It soon became evident that the enemy would not attack the bridge heads, they being well guarded by artillery on the north bank, so Sickles' corps was detached on the 30th and ordered to Chancellorsville.

Sedgwick used the remainder of his men to great advantage by marching them back and forth among the hills in such a way as to lead Lee to suppose that a very large force confronted him. As, however, Sedgwick did not advance, and more accurate reports were furnished by Stuart in relation to what had taken place up the river, Lee saw, on the night of the 30th, that the movement in front of Fredericksburg was a feint, and his real antagonist was at Chancellorsville. He had previously ordered Jackson's corps up from Moss Creek and now advanced with the main body of his army to meet Hooker, leaving Early's division of Jackson's corps and

Barksdale's brigade of McLaws' division of Longstreet's corps to hold the heights of Fredericksburg against Sedgwick. Jackson, who was always prompt, started at midnight, and at 8 A.M. the next day stood by the side of Anderson at Tabernacle Church. McLaws' division had already arrived, having preceded him by a few hours.

The error in the movements thus far made is plain. It is a maxim in war that a single hour's delay, when an enemy is strengthening his position or when reinforcements are coming up, will frequently cost the lives of a thousand men. In the present instance it was simply suicidal for Hooker to delay action until Anderson had fortified his lines and Lee had come forward with the main body to join him. Hooker should have pressed on immediately to seize the objective. Banks' Ford was almost within his grasp, and only a portion of Anderson's division barred the way. The possession of that ford would have brought Sedgwick twelve miles nearer to him, and would have forced Lee to fight at a great disadvantage both as to position and numbers. Hooker knew, from a captured despatch which Pleasonton placed in his hands, that Lee was still in Fredericksburg on the 30th, uncertain how to act; for he did not know the strength of Sedgwick's column, and feared that the main attack might come from that direction. The four corps at Chancellorsville amounted to about forty-six thousand men ; and 18,000 more were close at hand under Sickles. The troops had made but a short march and were comparatively fresh. Four miles further on lay the great prize for which Hooker was contending. He had only to put out his hand to reach it, but he delayed action all that long night and until eleven o'clock the next morning. When he did make the effort the line he was about to occupy was well fortified and held by all but one division and one brigade of Lee's army.

CHAPTER II.

FRIDAY, THE FIRST OF MAY.

THERE are two excellent roads leading from Chancellorsville to Fredericksburg—one a plank road, which keeps up near the sources of the streams along the dividing line between Mott Run on the north and Lewis Creek and Massaponax Creek on the South, and the other called the old turnpike, which was more direct but more broken, as it passed over several ravines. There was still a third road, a very poor one, which ran near the river and came out at Banks' Ford.

On May 1st, at 11 A.M., Hooker moved out to attack Lee in four columns.

Slocum's corps, followed by that of Howard, took the plank road on the right.

Sykes' division of Meade's corps, followed by Hancock's division of Couch's corps, went by the turnpike in the centre.

The remainder of Meade's corps—Griffin's division, followed by that of Humphreys—took the river road.

Lastly, French's division of Couch's corps was under orders to turn off and march to Todd's Tavern.

Each column was preceded by a detachment of Pleasonton's cavalry, which, in fact, had been close to Anderson's pickets all the morning.

Before these troops started, Sickles' corps arrived, after a short march, from Hartwood Church, and were posted in rear of the Chancellorsville House as a reserve, with one brigade thrown out to Dowdall's Tavern, otherwise known as Melzi Chancellor's house. Another brigade was left at the Ford to guard the passage against Fitz Hugh Lee's cavalry.

Hooker, who was a very sanguine man, expected to be able to form line of battle by 2 P.M., with his right resting near Tabernacle Church, and his left covering Banks' Ford. It did not seem to occur to him that the enemy might be there before him and prevent the formation, or that he would have any difficulty in moving and deploying his troops; but he soon found himself hampered in every direction by dense and almost impenetrable thickets, which had a tendency to break up every organization that tried to pass through them into mere crowds of men without order or alignment. Under these circumstances concert of action became exceedingly difficult, and when attempts were made to communicate orders off of the roads, aids wandered hopelessly through the woods, struggling in the thick undergrowth, without being able to find any one. It was worse than fighting in a dense fog.[1] The enemy, of course, were also impeded in their movements, but they had the advantage of being better acquainted with the country, and in case they were beaten they had a line at Tabernacle Church already intrenched to fall back upon. The ravines also, which crossed the upper roads at right angles, offered excellent defensive positions for them.

McLaws, who had advanced on the turnpike, managed to

---

[1] One brigade of Griffin's division was out all night trying to find its way through the thickets, and did not reach the main army until 4 A.M. Wilcox's brigade, which came the next day from Banks' Ford to reinforce the enemy, had a similar experience.

form line of battle with his division on each side of the pike, against Sykes, who had now come forward to sustain his cavalry detachment, which, in spite of their gallantry—for they rode up and fired in the faces of the enemy—were driven in by the Eleventh Virginia Infantry of Mahone's brigade. Jackson on his arrival, had stopped the fortifying which Anderson had commenced, and according to his invariable custom to find and fight his enemy as soon as possible, had moved forward; so that the two armies encountered each other about two and a half miles from Chancellorsville. Sykes indeed, met the advance of McLaws' division only a mile out, and drove it back steadily a mile farther, when it was reinforced by Anderson's division, and Ramseur's brigade of Rodes' division. Anderson gave Sykes a lively fight and succeeded in getting in on his flanks; for, owing to the divergence of the roads, neither Slocum on the right nor Meade's two divisions on the left were abreast with him. He tried to connect with Slocum by throwing out a regiment deployed as skirmishers, but did not succeed. As the enemy were gaining the advantage he fell back behind Hancock, who came to the front and took his place. Slocum now formed on the right, with his left resting on the plank road, and his right on high ground which commanded the country around. Altogether the general line was a good one; for there were large open spaces where the artillery could move and manœuvre, and the army were almost out of the thickets. The reserves could have struggled through those in the rear, and have filled the gaps, so that there is no reason to suppose our forces could not have continued to advance, or at all events have held the position, which, from its elevation and the other advantages I have stated, was an important one, especially as the column on the river road was in sight of Banks' Ford, which it could have seized and held, or have struck the right flank of the enemy with great effect. The troops had come out to obtain possession of Banks' Ford, and all the surplus artillery was waiting there. To retreat without making any adequate effort to carry out his plans made the General appear timid, and had a bad effect on the morale of the army. It would have been time enough to fall back in case of defeat ; and if such a result was anticipated, the engineers with their 4,000 men, aided by Sickles' corps, could easily have laid out a strong line in the rear for the troops to fall back upon. General Warren, Chief Engineer on Hooker's staff, thought the commanding ridge with the open space in front, upon which Hancock was posted, a very advantageous position for the army to occupy, and urged Couch not to abandon it until he (Warren) had conferred with Hooker. After the order came to retire, Couch sent to obtain permission to remain, but it was peremptorily refused. Hooker soon afterward changed his mind and countermanded his first order, but it was then too late ; our troops had left the ridge and the enemy were in possession of it. There was too much vacillation at headquarters. Slocum, who was pressing the enemy back, was very much vexed when he received the order, but obeyed it, and retreated without being molested. It is true, Wright's brigade had formed on his right, but the advance of the Eleventh corps would have taken that in flank, so that the prospect was generally good at this time for an advance. The column on the river road also retired without interference. As Couch had waited to hear from Hooker, Hancock's right flank became somewhat exposed by the delay, but he fell back without serious loss. French also, who had started for Todd's Tavern, returned. He encountered the enemy, but was ordered in and did not engage them.

That portion of the country around Chancellorsville within

the Union lines on the morning of May 2d, may, with some exceptions, be described as a plain, covered by dense thickets, with open spaces in the vicinity of the houses, varied by the high ground at Talley's on the west and by the hills of Fairview and Hazel Grove on the south, and terminating in a deep ravine near the river. Our general line was separated from that of the enemy by small streams, which principally ran through ravines, forming obstacles useful for defensive purposes. This was the case on the east and south, but on the west, where Howard's line terminated, there was nothing but the usual thickets to impede the enemy's approach.

As the narrative proceeds, the position of the Confederate army, who held the broken ground on the other side of these ravines, will be more particularly described.

After all, a defensive battle in such a country is not a bad thing, for where there are axes and timber it is easy to fortify and hard to force the line ; always provided that free communications are kept open to the central reserve and from one part of the line to another. It must be confessed that the concealment of the thickets is also favorable to the initiative, as it enables the attacking party to mass his troops against the weak parts without being observed. Hooker probably thought if Lee assailed a superior force in an intrenched position he would certainly be beaten ; and if he did not attack he would soon be forced to fall back on his depots near Richmond for food and ammunition. In either case the prestige would remain with the Union general.

The rebels followed up our army closely, and it is quite possible that a sudden attack, when it was heaped up around Chancellorsville, might have been disastrous to us. Gradually, under the skilful guidance of Captain Payne of the

Engineers, who had made himself well acquainted with the country, the different corps took the positions they had occupied on the previous night, and order came out of chaos. The line, as thus established, covered all the roads which passed through Chancellorsville. The left, held by Meade's corps, rested on the Rappahannock, near Scott's Dam; the line was then continued in a southerly direction by Couch's corps, facing east, French's division being extended to a point near to and east of Chancellorsville, with Hancock's division of the same corps holding an outpost still farther to the east. Next came the Twelfth Corps under Slocum, facing south, and then, at some distance to the west, in echelon to the rear along the Plank Road, Howard's corps was posted. The Third Corps under Sickles was kept in reserve, back of the mansion. The next morning two brigades and two batteries of Birney's division were interposed between Slocum and Howard, with a strong line of skirmishers thrown out in front. The Eighth Pennsylvania Cavalry picketed the roads and kept the enemy in sight. The thickets which surrounded this position were almost impenetrable, so that an advance against the enemy's lines became exceedingly difficult and manœuvring nearly impracticable, nor was this the only defect. Batteries could be established on the high ground to the east, which commanded the front facing in that direction, while our own artillery had but little scope; and last, but most important of all, the right of Howard's corps was "in the air," that is, it rested on no obstacle.

Hooker was sensible that this flank was weak, and sent Graham's brigade of Sickles' corps with a battery to strengthen it; but Howard took umbrage at this, as a reflection on the bravery of his troops or his own want of skill, and told Graham that he did not need his services; that he felt so secure in his position that he would send his compliments to the whole rebel army if they lay in front of him, and invite them to attack him. As Hooker had just acquiesced in the appointment of Howard to be Commander of the Eleventh Corps, he disliked to show a want of confidence in him at the very beginning of his career, and therefore yielded to his wishes and ordered the reinforcements to return and report to Sickles again.

Chancellorsville being a great centre of communication with the plank road and turnpike leading east and west, and less important roads to the south, and southeast, Hooker desired above all things to retain it; for if it should once fall into the hands of the enemy, our army would be unable to move in any direction except to the rear.·

General Lee formed his line with Wickham's and Owens' regiments of cavalry on his right, opposite Meade's corps, supported by Perry's brigade of Anderson's division; Jackson's line stretched from the Plank Road around toward the Furnace.

Before night set in, Wright and Stuart attacked an outlying post of Slocum's corps and drove it in on the main body. They then brought up some artillery and opened fire against Slocum's position on the crest of the hill. Failing to make any impression they soon retired and all was quiet once more.

The enemy soon posted batteries on the high ground a mile east of Chancellorsville, and opened on Hancock's front with considerable effect. They also enfiladed Geary's division of Slocum's corps, and became very annoying, but Knap's battery of the Twelfth Corps replied effectively and kept their fire down to a great extent.

As the Union army was hidden by the thick undergrowth, Lee spent the rest of the day in making a series of feigned attacks to ascertain where our troops were posted.

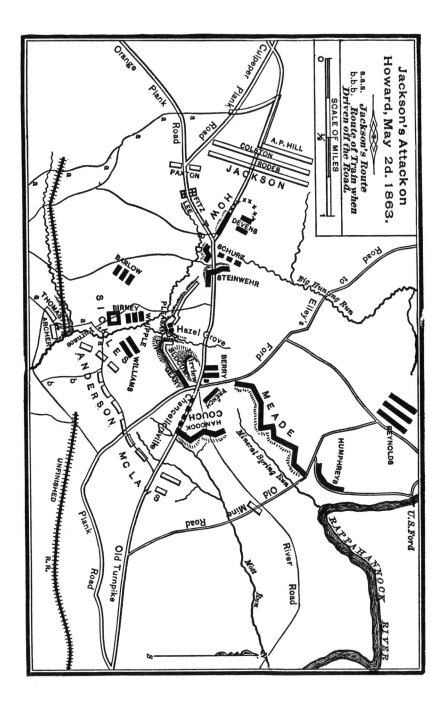

Jackson's Attack on Howard, May 2d. 1863.

a.a.a. *Jackson's Route*
b.b.b. *Route of Train when Driven off the Road.*

SCALE OF MILES

When night set in, the sound of the axe was heard in every direction, for both armies thought it prudent to strengthen their front as much as possible.

The prospect for Lee as darkness closed over the scene was far from encouraging. He had examined the position of the Union army carefully, and had satisfied himself that as regards its centre and left it was unassailable. Let any man with a musket on his shoulder, encumbered with a cartridge-box, haversack, canteen, etc., attempt to climb over a body of felled timber to get at an enemy who is coolly shooting at him from behind a log breastwork, and he will realize the difficulty of forcing a way through such obstacles. Our artillery, too, swept every avenue of approach, so that the line might be considered as almost impregnable. Before giving up the attack, however, Stuart was directed to cautiously reconnoitre on the right, where Howard was posted, and see if there was not a vulnerable point there.

CHAPTER III.

THE DISASTROUS SECOND OF MAY.

At dawn of day General Lee and General Jackson were sitting by the side of the plank road, on some empty cracker boxes, discussing the situation, when Stuart came up and reported the result of his reconnoissance. He said the right flank of Howard's corps was defenceless and easily assailable. Jackson at once asked permission to take his own corps—about 26,000 muskets—make a detour through the woods to conceal his march from observation, and fall unexpectedly upon the weak point referred to by Stuart. It was a startling proposition and contrary to all the principles of strategy, for when Jackson was gone Lee would be left with but a few men to withstand the shock of Hooker's entire army, and might be driven back to Fredericksburg or crushed. If the Eleventh Corps had prepared for Jackson's approach by a line properly fortified, with redoubts on the flanks, the men protected in front by felled timber and sheltered by breastworks, with the artillery at the angles, crossing its fire in front, Jackson's corps would have been powerless to advance, and could have been held as in a vise, while Lee, one-half of his force being absent, would have found himself helpless against the combined attack of our other corps which could have assailed him in front and on each flank.

There was, therefore, great risk in attempting such a

manœuvre, for nothing short of utter blindness on the part of the Union commanders could make it successful.

Still, something had to be done, for inaction would result in a retreat, and in the present instance, if the worst came to the worst, Jackson could fall back on Gordonsville, and Lee toward the Virginia Central Railroad, where they could reunite their columns by rail, before Hooker could march across the country and prevent the junction. Jackson received the required permission, and started off at once by a secluded road, keeping Fitz Hugh Lee's brigade of cavalry between his column and the Union army to shield his march from observation.

At 2 A.M. Hooker sent orders for the First Corps, under Reynolds, to which I belonged, to take up its bridges and join him by way of United States Ford, and by 9 A.M. we were on our way.

The first sound of battle came from some guns posted on the eminence from which Hancock had retreated the day before. A battery there opened fire on the army trains which had been parked in the open plain in front of the Chancellorsville House, and drove them pell mell to the rear.

At dawn Hooker rode around, accompanied by Sickles, to inspect his lines. He approved the position generally, but upon Sickles' recommendation he threw in a division of the Third Corps between the Eleventh and Twelfth, as he thought the interval too great there.

As soon as Jackson was *en route*, Lee began to demonstrate against our centre and left, to make Hooker believe the main attack was to be there, and to prevent him from observing the turning column in its progress toward the right. A vigorous cannonade began against Meade, and a musketry fire was opened on Couch and Slocum ; the heavi-

est attack being on Hancock's position, which was in advance of the main line.

In spite of every precaution, Jackson's column as it moved
southward was seen to pass over a bare hill about a mile
and a half from Birney's front, and its numbers were pretty
accurately estimated. General Birney at once reported
this important fact at General Hooker's headquarters. It is
always pleasant to think your adversary is beaten, and
Hooker thought at first Jackson might be retreating on Gordonsville. It was evident enough that he was either doing
that or making a circuit to attack Howard. To provide for
the latter contingency the following order was issued:

HEADQUARTERS ARMY OF THE POTOMAC,
CHANCELLORSVILLE, Va., May 2, 1863, 9.30 A.M.
MAJOR-GENERAL SLOCUM AND MAJOR-GENERAL HOWARD:

I am directed by the Major-General Commanding to say that the
disposition you have made of your corps has been with a view to a front
attack by the enemy. If he should throw himself upon your flank,
he wishes you to examine the ground and determine upon the positions
you will take in that event, in order that you may be prepared for him
in whatever direction he advances. He suggests that you have heavy
reserves well in hand to meet this contingency. The right of your line
does not appear to be strong enough. No artificial defences worth
naming have been thrown up, and there appears to be a scarcity of
troops at that point, and not, in the General's opinion, as favorably
posted as might be.

We have good reason to suppose that the enemy is moving to our
right. Please advance your pickets for purposes of observation as far
as may be safe, in order to obtain timely information of their approval,

(Signed)   JAMES H. VAN ALLEN,
Brigadier-General and Aide-de-camp.

For what subsequently occurred Hooker was doubtless
highly censurable, but it was not unreasonable for him to
suppose, after giving these orders to a corps commander,

that they would be carried out, and that minor combats far out on the roads would precede and give ample notice of Jackson's approach in time to reinforce that part of the line.

When the enemy were observed, Sickles went out with Clark's battery and an infantry support to shell their train. This had the effect of driving them off of that road on to another which led in the same direction, but was less exposed, as it went through the woods. A second reconnoissance was sent to see if the movement continued. Sickles then obtained Hooker's consent to start out with two divisions to attack Jackson's corps in flank and cut it off from the main body.

Sickles started on this mission at 1 P.M. with Birney's division, preceded by Randolph's battery. As Jackson might turn on him with his whole force, Whipple's division of his own corps reinforced his left, and Barlow's brigade of the Eleventh Corps his right. He was greatly delayed by the swamps and the necessity of building bridges, but finally crossed Lewis Creek and reached the road upon which Jackson was marching. He soon after, by the efforts of Berdan's sharpshooters, surrounded and captured the Twenty-third Georgia regiment, which had been left to watch the approaches from our lines. Information obtained from prisoners showed that Jackson could not be retreating, and that his object was to strike a blow somewhere.

Birney's advance, and the capture of the Twenty-third Georgia were met by corresponding movements on the part of the enemy. A rebel battery was established on the high ground at the Welford House, which checked Birney's progress until it was silenced by Livingston's battery, which was brought forward for that purpose. Pleasonton's cavalry was now sent to the Foundry as an additional reinforcement. Sickles' intention was to cut Jackson off entirely from Mc-

Laws' and Anderson's divisions, and then to attack the latter
in flank, a plan which promised good results. In the meantime Pleasonton's cavalry was sent forward to follow up
Jackson's movement. Sickles requested permission to attack McLaws, but Hooker again became irresolute; so that
this large Union force was detained at the Furnace without a
definite object, and the works it had occupied were vacant.
While Sickles was not allowed to strike the flank, Slocum's
two divisions under Geary and Williams were sent to push
back the fortified front of the enemy in the woods; a much
more difficult operation. Geary attacked on the plank road,
but made no serious impression, and returned. Williams
struck farther to the south, but was checked by part of Anderson's division. A combined attack against Lee's front
and left flank, undertaken with spirit earlier in the day,
would in all probability have driven him off toward Fredericksburg and have widened the distance between his force
and that of Jackson; but now the latter was close at hand
and it was too late to attempt it. As the time came for the
turning column to make its appearance on Howard's right, a
fierce attack was again made against Hancock with infantry
and artillery, to distract Hooker's attention from the real
point at issue.

Pleasonton, after dismounting one regiment and sending
it into the woods to reconnoitre, finding his cavalry were of
no use in such a country, and that Jackson was getting farther and farther away, rode leisurely back, at Sickles' suggestion, to Hazel Grove, which was an open space of considerable elevation to the right of the Twelfth Corps. As he
drew near, the roar of battle burst upon his ears from the
right of the line and a scene of horror and confusion presented
itself, presaging the rout of the entire army if some immediate measures were not taken to stem the tide of disaster-

CHAPTER IV.

THE ROUT OF THE ELEVENTH CORPS.

NOTWITHSTANDING Hooker's order of 9.30 A.M., calling Howard's attention to the weakness of his right flank, and the
probability that Jackson was marching to attack it, no precautions were taken against the impending danger. The simple establishing of a front of two regiments toward the west
when half his command would hardly have been sufficient,
unless protected by works of some kind, was perfectly idle
as a barrier against the torrent about to overwhelm the
Eleventh Corps. So far as I can ascertain, only two companies were thrown out on picket, and they were unsupported
by grand guards, so that they did not detain the enemy a
moment, and the rebels and our pickets all came in together.
Great stress has been laid upon the fact that Howard did
have a reserve force—Barlow's brigade of 2,500 men—facing
west, which Hooker withdrew to reinforce Sickles ; but it is
not shown that Howard made any remonstrance or attached
any great importance to its removal. Even if it had remained, as there were no strong intrenchments in front of it,
it is not probable that it would have been able to resist
Jackson's entire corps for any length of time. There was no
reason other than Howard's utter want of appreciation of the
gravity of the situation to prevent him from forming a strong
line of defence to protect his right flank. If made with

felled timber in front and redoubts on the flanks, Jackson could not have overleaped it, or even attacked it without heavy loss. If he stopped to do so, Sickles' corps and Williams' division of the Twelfth Corps, with the reserve forces under Berry and French, would soon have confronted him. If he had attempted to keep on farther down to attack the United States Ford, he would have met the First Corps there, and would have permanently severed all connection between himself and Lee, besides endangering his line of retreat. The apathy and indifference Howard manifested in relation to Jackson's approach can only be explained in the supposition that he really believed that Jackson had fled to Gordonsville, and that the demonstrations on his front and right proceeded merely from Stuart's cavalry; and yet why any one should suppose that Lee would part with half his army, and send it away to Gordonsville where there was no enemy and nothing to be done, is more than I can imagine. Jackson was celebrated for making these turning movements; besides, it was easy, by questioning prisoners, to verify the fact that he had no surplus trains with him. Nothing, in short, but ammunition wagons, and ambulances for the wounded; a sure indication that his movement meant fight and not retreat.

From 10 A.M., when Hooker's order was received, to 6 P.M., when the assault came, there was ample time for Howard to form an impregnable line. His division commanders did not share his indifference. General Schurz pointed out to him that his flank was in the air, but he seemed perfectly satisfied with his line as it was, and not at all desirous of changing it in any particular. Schurz, of his own volition, without the knowledge of his chief, posted three regiments in close column of division, and formed them in the same direction as the two regiments and two guns which were expected to keep Jackson back, but the shock, when it came, was so sudden that these columns did not have time to deploy. Devens, having two reserve regiments, also faced them that way, of his own accord, behind the other two, but having no encouragement to form line in that direction it is probable both generals hesitated to do so.

Jackson having debouched from the country road into the plank road, was separated from Lee by nearly six miles of pathless forest. He kept on until he reached the turnpike, and then halted his command in order that he might reconnoitre and form line of battle. He went up on a high hill and personally examined the position of the Eleventh Corps. Finding that it was still open to attack, and that no preparations had been made to receive him, he formed Rodes' and Colston's divisions two hundred yards apart, perpendicular to the plank road, with the road in the centre, and with Hill's division both on the plank road and turnpike as a support to the other two. Fitz Lee's brigade of cavalry was left on the plank road to menace Howard from that direction.

It will be seen by a glance at the map that his lines overlapped that of the Eleventh Corps for a long distance, both in front and rear. The first notice our troops had of his approach did not come from our pickets—for their retreat and his attack were almost simultaneous—but from the deer, rabbits, and other wild animals of the forest, driven from their coverts by his advance. It is always convenient to have a scape-goat in case of disaster, and the German element in the Eleventh Corps have been fiercely censured and their name became a byword for giving way on this occasion. It is full time justice should be done by calling attention to the position of that corps. I assert that when a force is not deployed, but is struck suddenly and violently on its flank, resistance is *impracticable*. Not Napoleon's Old

Guard, not the best and bravest troops that ever existed, could hold together in such a case, for the first men assailed are—to use a homely but expressive word—driven into a *huddle;* and a huddle cannot fight, for it has no front and no organization. Under such circumstances, the men have but a choice of two evils, either to stay where they are and be slaughtered, without the power of defending themselves, or to run; and the only sensible thing for them to do is to run and rally on some other organization. The attempt to change front and meet this attack *on such short notice* would have been hopeless enough, drawn up as Howard's men were, even if they had been all in line with arms in their hands; but it is a beautiful commentary on the vigilance displayed, that in many cases the muskets were stacked and the men lounging about, some playing cards, others cooking their supper, intermingled with the pack-mules and beef cattle they were unloading. It will be remembered that in the order previously quoted, Howard was directed *"to advance his pickets for the purpose of observation,"* in order *that he might have ample time for preparation.* The object of this injunction is plain enough. It was to make sufficient resistance to Jackson's advance to detain it, and not only give time to the Eleventh Corps to form, but enable Hooker to send his reserves to that part of the line. The pickets, therefore, should have been far out and strongly backed with a large force which would take advantage of every accident of ground to delay the rebel column as long as possible. Howard seemed to have no curiosity himself, as he sent out no parties; but Sickles and Pleasonton had their spies and detachments on the watch, and these came in constantly with the information, which was duly transmitted to Howard, that Jackson was actually coming. Schurz also became uneasy and sent out parties to reconnoitre. General Noble, at that time Colonel of the Seventeenth Connecticut Infantry, two companies of whose regiment were on the picket line there, writes as follows: "The disaster resulted from Howard's and Devens' utter disregard and inattention under warnings that came in from the front and flank all through the day. Horseman after horseman rode into my post and was sent to headquarters with the information that the enemy were heavily marching along our front and proceeding to our right; and last of all an officer reported the rebels massing for attack. Howard scouted the report and insulted the informants, charging them with telling a story that was the offspring of their imaginations or their fears."

If this be true, there has been but one similar case in our annals, and that was the massacre of the garrison of Fort Sims, by the savages, in 1813, near Mobile, Alabama; soon after a negro had been severely flogged by the commanding officer for reporting that he had seen Indians lurking around the post.

Adjutant Wilkenson, of the same regiment, confirms General Noble's statement and says, "Why a stronger force was not sent out as skirmishers and the left of our line changed to front the foe is more than I am able to understand."

General Schimmelpfennig, commanding a brigade of Schurz's division, says he sent out a reconnoissance and reported the hostile movements fully two hours before the enemy charged.

The Germans were bitterly denounced for this catastrophe, I think very unjustly, for in the first place less than one-half of the Eleventh Corps were Germans, and in the second place the troops that did form line and temporarily stop Jackson's advance were Germans; principally Colonel Adolph Buschbeck's brigade of Steinwehr's division, aided by a few regiments of Schurz's division, who gave a

volley or two.   Buschbeck held a weak intrenched line perpendicular to the plank road for three-quarters of an hour,
with artillery on the right, losing one-third of his force.   The
enemy then folded around his flanks and took him in reverse, when further resistance became hopeless and his men
retreated in good order to the rear of Sickles' line at Hazel
Grove where they supported the artillery and offered to lead
a bayonet charge, if the official reports are to be believed.
Warren says he took charge of some batteries of the Eleventh
Corps and formed them in line across the Plank Road without any infantry support whatever.

In reference to this surprise, Couch remarks that no troops
could have stood under such circumstances, and I fully
agree with him.

An officer of the Eleventh Corps who was present informed
General Wainwright, formerly Colonel of the Seventy-sixth
New York, that he was playing cards in the ditch, and the
first notice he had of the enemy was seeing them looking
down on him from the parapet above.

As for Devens, who was nearest the enemy, it is quite
probable that any attempt by him to change front to the
west previous to the attack would have been looked upon by
Howard as a reflection on his own generalship and would
have been met with disfavor, if not with a positive repri-
mand.   The only semblance of precaution taken, therefore,
was the throwing out two regiments to face Jackson's advance.   Devens could not disgarnish his main line without
Howard's permission, and it is not fair, therefore, to hold
him responsible for the disaster.   As it was, he was severely
wounded in attempting to rally his men.   The only pickets
thrown out appear to have been *two companies of the Seventeenth Connecticut Infantry.*

Just as Jackson was about to attack, a furious assault was

made at the other end of the line, where Meade was posted. This was repulsed but it served to distract Hooker's attention from the real point of danger on the right.

It would seem from all accounts that nothing could vanquish Howard's incredulity. He appeared to take so little interest in Jackson's approach that when Captain George E. Farmer, one of Pleasonton's staff, reported to him that he had found a rebel battery posted directly on the flank of the Eleventh Corps, he was, to use his own language, "*courteously received, but Howard did not seem to believe there was any force of the enemy in his immediate front.*" Sickles and Pleasonton were doing all they could to ascertain Jackson's position, for at this time a small detachment of the Third Corps were making a reconnoissance on the Orange Court House Plank Road, and Rodes states that our cavalry was met there and skirmished with Stuart's advance. Farmer said *he saw no Union pickets*, but noticed on his return that Howard's men were away from their arms, which were stacked, and that they were playing cards, etc., utterly unsuspicious of danger and unprepared for a contest. Notwithstanding the reports of Jackson's movement from spies and scouts, Howard ordered no change in his lines.

An attempt has been made to hold Colonel Farmer responsible for this surprise, on the ground that he should have charged the battery and brought in some prisoners, who would give full information ; but there had been warnings enough, and prisoners enough, and as Colonel Farmer had but forty men, he would have had to dismount half of them to make the assault, and with part of his force holding the horses, he could only have used about twenty men in the attack, which is rather too few to capture guns supported by an army. Besides, Farmer was sent out by General Pleasonton with specific instructions, and was not obliged to recognize the authority of other officers who desired him to make a Don Quixote of himself to no purpose.

If the two wings of the rebel army had been kept apart, the small force left under Lee could easily have been crushed, or driven off toward Richmond. The commander of the Eleventh Corps, however, far from making any new works, did not man those he had, but left his own lines and went with Barlow's brigade to see what Sickles was doing.

The subsequent investigation of this sad business by the Congressional Committee on the Conduct of the War was very much of a farce, and necessarily unreliable; for so long as both Hooker and Howard were left in high command, it was absurd to suppose their subordinates would testify against them. Any officer that did so would have soon found his military career brought to a close.

Howard was in one or two instances mildly censured for not keeping a better lookout, but as a general thing the whole blame was thrown on the Germans. Hooker himself attributed the trouble to the fact that Howard did not follow up Jackson's movements, and allowed his men to stray from their arms.

A great French military writer has said, "It is permissible for an officer to be defeated; but never to be surprised."

It is, of course, only fair to hear what Howard himself has to say in relation to this matter.

He writes in his official report of the battle as follows:

Now as to the cause of the disaster to my corps.

First.—Though constantly threatened, and apprised of the moving of the enemy, yet the woods were so dense that he was able to mass a large force, whose exact whereabouts neither patrols, reconnoissances, nor scouts ascertained.

He succeeded in forming a column opposite to and outflanking my right.

Second.—By the panic produced by the enemy's reverse fire, regiments and artillery were thrown suddenly upon those in position.

Third.—The absence of General Barlow's brigade, which I had previously located in reserve, and in *echelon* with Colonel Von Gilsa's, so as to cover his right flank.

The first proposition implies that Howard did not know Jackson intended to attack his right, and therefore did not prepare for him in that direction, but as his front was well fortified, and his flank unprotected, it was plainly his duty to strengthen the weak part of his line. To suppose that Jackson would run a great risk, and spend an entire day in making this long circuit for the purpose of assailing his enemy in front, is hardly reasonable; for he could have swung his line around against it at once, had he desired to do so.

The fierce rush of the rebels, who came in almost simultaneously with the pickets, first struck General Von Gilsa's two small regiments and the two guns in the road, the only force that actually fronted them in line.

Von Gilsa galloped at once to Howard's Headquarters at Dowdall's Tavern to ask for immediate reinforcements. He was told, "he must hold his post with the men he had, and trust to God ; " information which was received by the irate German with objurgations that were not at all of an orthodox character.

Devens' division, thus taken in flank, was driven back upon Schurz's division, and that being unable to form, was heaped up after some resistance on Steinwehr's division, in the utmost confusion and disorder. Steinwehr had only Buschbeck's brigade with him ; the other — that of Barlow — having been sent out to reinforce Sickles ; but he formed line promptly, behind a weak intrenchment, which had been thrown across the road, and with the aid of his artillery kept

Jackson at bay for three-quarters of an hour. Howard exerted himself bravely then, and did all he could to rally the fugitives; but Rodes' division, which attacked him, was soon reinforced by that of Colston, and the two together folded around his flanks, took his line in reverse, and finally carried the position with a rush; and then Buschbeck's brigade retired in good order through the flying crowd, who were streaming in wild disorder to the rear past Hooker's headquarters.

And now, with the right of our line all gone, with a yawning gap where Sickles' corps and Williams' division had previously been posted, with Lee thundering against our centre and left, and Jackson taking all our defences in reverse, his first line being close on Chancellorsville itself, it seemed as if the total rout of the army was inevitable.

Just before this attack Hooker had decided to interpose more force between the wings of the rebel army, in order to permanently dissever Jackson from the main body. If Sickles had been allowed to attack the left flank of the enemy opposite the Furnace, as he requested permission to do earlier in the afternoon, this co-operative movement could hardly have failed to produce great results; afterward it was too late to attempt it. As already stated, Williams' division struck Anderson in front on Birney's left, and Geary attacked McLaws' across the Plank Road to the right of Hancock. Geary found the enemy strongly posted, and as he made no progress, returned to his works. When the rout of the Eleventh Corps took place, Williams also hastened back, but was fired on by Jackson's troops, who now occupied the intrenchments he had left. Sickles thinks if this had not occurred several regiments of the enemy would have been cut off from the main body.

CHAPTER V.

JACKSON'S ADVANCE IS CHECKED.

THE constantly increasing uproar, and the wild rush of fugitives past the Chancellorsville House, told Hooker what had occurred, and roused him to convulsive life. His staff charged on the flying crowd, but failed to stop them, and it became necessary to form a line of fresh troops speedily, as Jackson was sweeping everything before him. It was not easy to find an adequate force for this emergency. The whole line was now actively engaged, Slocum being attacked on the south, and Couch and Meade on the east. Fortunately, Berry's division was held in reserve, and was available. They were true and tried men, and went forward at once to the rescue. Berry was directed to form across the Plank Road, drive the rebels back, and retake the lost intrenchments ; an order easy to give, but very difficult to execute. The most he could do, under the circumstances, was to form his line in the valley opposite Fairview, and hold his position there, the enemy already having possession of the higher ground beyond.

Before Berry went out, Warren had stopped several of the Eleventh Corps batteries, and had formed them across the Plank Road, behind the position of the infantry. Winslow's Battery D, of the First New York, and Dimick's Battery H, of the First United States, were already there, with Hooker in person, having anticipated the movement. These guns were very destructive, and were the principal agent in checking the enemy. As soon as they formed in line, Warren gave orders to Colonel Best, Chief of Artillery to the Twelfth Corps, to post more batteries on the eminence called Fairview, to the rear and left of the others.

Few persons appreciate the steadiness and courage required, when all around is flight and confusion, for a force to advance steadily to the post of danger in front and meet the exulting enemy. Such men are heroes, and far more worthy of honor than those who fight in the full blaze of successful warfare.

The thickets being unfavorable to cavalry, Sickles had sent Pleasonton back to Hazel Grove with two mounted regiments, the Eighth and Seventeenth Pennsylvania and Martin's battery, while the Sixth New York was scouting the woods on his right, dismounted. Upon reaching the open space which he had left when he went to the front, Pleasonton found the place full of the debris of the combat—men, horses, caissons, ambulances—all hurrying furiously to the rear. To clear the way he charged on the flying mass, at Sickles' suggestion, who had ridden in advance of his troops, which were still behind at the Furnace. Sickles ordered Pleasonton to take command of the artillery, and the latter took charge of twenty-two guns, consisting of his own and the Third Corps batteries. The latter had already been rallied and formed in line by Captain J. F. Huntington, of the Ohio battery. As senior officer present he assumed command of the Third Corps artillery. Unfortunately there was no time to load or aim, for the rebels were close at hand, and their triumphant yells were heard as they took possession of the works which Buschbeck had so gallantly defended. This advantageous position, which was on an eminence overlooking Chancellorsville and the Plank Road, and which was really the key of the battle-field, was about to be lost. There was but one way to delay Jackson, some force must be sacrificed, and Pleasonton ordered Major Peter Keenan, commanding the Eighth Pennsylvania Cavalry, to charge the ten thousand men in front with his four hundred. Keenan saw in a moment that if he threw his little force into that seething mass of infantry, horses and men would go down on all sides, and few would be left to tell the tale. A sad smile lit up his noble countenance as he said, "*General, I will do it.*" Thus, at thirty-four years of age, he laid down his life, literally impaled on the bayonets of the enemy, saving the army from capture and his country from the unutterable degradation of slave-holding rule in the Northern States. The service rendered on that occasion is worthy to be recorded in history with the sacrifices of Arnold Winckelried in Switzerland, and the Chevalier d'Assas in France.[1]

A large part of his command were lost, but the short interval thus gained was of priceless value. Pleasonton was enabled to clear a space in front of him, and twenty-two guns, loaded with double canister, were brought to bear upon the enemy. They came bursting over the parapet they had just taken with loud and continuous yells, and formed line of battle within three hundred yards. All his guns fired into their masses at once. The discharge seemed fairly to blow them back over the works from which they had just emerged. Their artillery, under Colonel Crutchfield, which had been brought up, was almost annihilated by the fire of the battery on the Plank Road. This gave time to reload the guns.

---

[1] Major J. E. Carpenter, one of the officers who headed this charge, asserts that Keenan made it without orders, his only instructions being to report to General Howard to assist in rallying the Eleventh Corps. Pleasonton's testimony, however, is positive on the subject, and is supported by that of his aide, Colonel Clifford Thompson. Perhaps Carpenter did not hear all the conversation that passed between Pleasonton and Keenan.

The enemy rallied and opened a furious musketry fire from the woods against Pleasonton and Berry. Both stood firm, and then came two charges in succession which reached almost to the muzzles of Pleasonton's guns, which were only supported by two small regiments of cavalry—the Sixth New York, and a new and untried regiment, the Seventeenth Pennsylvania. The whole did not amount to over 1,000 men. Archer's brigade, on Jackson's left, which had not been stayed by Keenan's charge, gained the woods and the Plank Road, and opened a severe enfilading fire. Huntington changed front with his own battery and repelled the assault. The One Hundred and Tenth Pennsylvania regiment, of Whipple's division, arrived in time to strengthen the cavalry support, and many of the Eleventh Corps men fell into line also. The last charge of the enemy was baffled by the opportune arrival of Birney's and Whipple's divisions, and Barlow's brigade.

By this time, too (about 9 P.M.), Hays' brigade of French's corps had been posted on the right, in rear and oblique to Berry's second line. The latter had greatly strengthened his position with log breastworks, etc. Captain Best, of the Fourth United States Artillery, in the meantime had exerted himself to collect forty or fifty guns belonging to the Twelfth, Third, and some he had stopped from the Eleventh Corps, and had arranged them at Fairview, to fire over the heads of Berry's troops into the thicket where the enemy were posted and along the Plank Road.

Hooker was so disheartened at the unexpected success of the enemy, that when the first shock came he sent word to Sickles to save his command if he could. There is little doubt that at one time he thought of retreating and leaving the Third Corps to its fate; for when the enemy charged there was an awful gap in our lines; Birney's, Whipple's, and Williams' divisions and Barlow's brigade were all absent. Fortunately Jackson was unable to press his advantage. The ardor of the charge, the darkness, the thickets and the abattis in which his forces became entangled, caused Rodes' and Colston's divisions to be all intermingled, creating such disorder and confusion that military organization was suspended, and orders could neither be communicated nor obeyed. Jackson therefore halted his men in the edge of the woods, about a mile and a half from Chancellorsville, posted two brigades on the two roads that came in from the south, and sent for Hill's division, which was in rear and which had not been engaged, to take the front, while the other two divisions fell back to the open space at Dowdall's Tavern to reform their lines. Pending this movement he rode out on the Plank Road with part of his staff and a few orderlies to reconnoitre, cautioning his pickets not to fire at him on his return. When he came back new men had been posted, and his approach was mistaken for the advance of Pleasonton's cavalry. His own troops fired into him with fatal effect. Nearly all his escort were killed or wounded and he received three balls, which shattered both arms. His horse ran toward the Union lines, and although he succeeded in turning him back, he was dashed against the trees and nearly unhorsed. He reached the Confederate lines about the time our artillery again opened up the Plank Road with a fire which swept everything from its front. Several of his attendants were killed and others wounded. The rebels found the utmost difficulty in keeping their men in line under this tremendous fire. Sentries had to be posted, and great precautions taken to prevent the troops from giving way. General Pender recognized Jackson as he was carried past, and complained of the demoralizing effect of this cannonade, but Jackson replied sharply and sternly, " You

must hold your ground, General Pender." He was re-
moved to the Wilderness Tavern, and as General Lee was in
some fear that Averell's cavalry, then at Elley's Ford, might
make a dash and capture him, he was sent on to Guiney's
Station, on the Fredericksburg and Richmond Railroad,
where he died on the 10th of May. Whether the rebels
killed him, or whether some of his wounds came from our
own troops, the First Massachusetts or Seventy-third New
York, who were firing heavily in that direction, is a matter
of some doubt. While leaning over him and expressing his
sympathy, A. P. Hill was also wounded by the fire from a
section of Dimick's battery, posted in advance in the Plank
Road,[1] and the command of his corps was assigned at his request to the cavalry general, J. E. B. Stuart.

When our artillery fire ceased, Hill's troops took position
in front of the others.

---

[1] Young Dimick was the son of a distinguished general of the regular army.
Though wounded on this occasion he refused to leave the field. The next day he
again sought the post of danger and was mortally wounded while holding the
Plank Road.

CHAPTER VI.

SICKLES FIGHTS HIS WAY BACK.—ARRIVAL OF THE FIRST CORPS.

SICKLES, with his ten thousand men heaped up at Hazel Grove, was still cut off from the main body and could only communicate with Hooker's headquarters by means of by-paths and at great risk. The last orders he received, at 5 P.M., had been to attack Jackson's right flank and check his advance. He determined to do this and force his way back, and with the co-operation of Williams' and Berry's divisions, retake the Plank Road with the bayonet. Ward's brigade was posted in the front line and Hayman's and Graham's brigades a hundred yards in rear. A special column, under Colonel Egan of the Fortieth New York, was formed on the extreme left. The muskets were uncapped and at midnight the command moved silently against the enemy, and in spite of a terrific outburst of musketry and artillery from the open space at Dowdall's, the Plank Road and the works which Buschbeck had defended were regained. Berry at once moved forward his line to hold them. Many guns and caissons taken from Howard's corps, and Whipple's ammunition train of pack mules were also recovered. The confusion into which the enemy were thrown by this assault against their right, enabled Berry to easily repulse the attack on him, and he continued to hold the position. The result of this brilliant movement was the reoccupation of a great part

of the works Howard had lost, and the capture of two guns
and three caissons from the enemy. It is said that in this
conflict some of Sickles' men, in consequence of the thickets
and confusion, finding themselves surrounded, surrendered
as they supposed to the enemy, but to their delight found
themselves in Berry's division, among their old comrades.

Soon after this fight was over Mott's brigade of the Third
Corps, which had been on duty at the Ford, rejoined the
main body.

Both sides now rested on their arms and prepared to renew the struggle at daylight. Hooker, in view of a possible
defeat, directed his engineer officers to lay out a new and
stronger line, to cover his bridges, to which he could retreat
in case of necessity.

At sunset the First Corps went into bivouac on the south
side of United States Ford, about four miles and a half from
Chancellorsville. The men were glad enough to rest after
their tedious march on a hot day, loaded down with eight
days' rations. General Reynolds left me temporarily in
charge of the corps, while he rode on to confer with Hooker.
We heard afar off the roar of the battle caused by Jackson's
attack, and saw the evening sky reddened with the fires of
combat, but knowing Hooker had a large force, we felt no
anxiety as to the result, and took it for granted that we would
not be wanted until the next day. I was preparing a piece
of india-rubber cloth as a couch when I saw one of Reynolds'
aids, Captain Wadsworth, coming down the road at full
speed. He brought the startling news that the Eleventh
Corps had fled, and if we did not go forward at once, the
army would be hopelessly defeated. We were soon on the
road, somewhat oppressed by the news, but not dismayed.
We marched through the thickening twilight of the woods
amid a silence at first only broken by the plaintive song of

the whip-poor-will, until the full moon rose in all its splendor. As we proceeded we came upon crowds of the Eleventh Corps fugitives still hastening to the rear. They seemed wholly disheartened. We halted for a time, in order that our position in line of battle might be selected, and then moved on. As we approached the field a midnight battle commenced, and the shells seemed to burst in sparkles in the trees above our heads, but not near enough to reach us. It was Sickles fighting his way home again. When we came nearer and filed to the right to take position on the Elley's Ford road, the men struck up John Brown's song, and gave the chorus with a will. Their cheerful demeanor and proud bearing renewed the confidence of the army, who felt that the arrival of Reynolds' corps, with its historic record, was no ordinary reinforcement.

We were now on the extreme right of the other forces, on the Elley's Ford road, with the right flank thrown back behind Hunting Creek.

Hooker was very much discouraged by the rout of the Eleventh Corps. An occurrence of this kind always has a tendency to demoralize an army and render it less trustworthy; for the real strength of an armed force is much more in *opinion* than it is in *numbers*. A small body of men, if made to believe the enemy are giving way, will do and dare anything; but when they think the struggle is hopeless, they will not resist even a weak attack, for each thinks he is to be sacrificed to save the rest. Hence Hooker did not feel the same reliance on his men as he did before the disaster. He determined, nevertheless, to continue the battle, but contract his lines by bringing them nearer to Chancellorsville. The real key of the battle-field now was the eminence at Hazel Grove. So long as we held it the enemy could not advance without presenting his right flank to our batteries.

If he obtained possession of it he could plant guns which would enfilade Slocum's line and fire directly into our forces below. Birney's division at this time was posted in advance of Best's guns on the left, Berry was on the right, with Williams' division of the Twelfth Corps behind Birney, and Whipple's division in rear of Berry.

The position of Hazel Grove commanded Chancellorsville, where all the roads meet, and which it was vital to Hooker to hold. For if he lost that, he could not advance in any direction, and only his line of retreat to the Ford would remain open to him. Pleasonton spent the night in fortifying this hill, and placed forty guns in position there; but it was of no avail, for it was outside of the new line Sickles was directed to occupy at daylight, and Hooker was not aware of its importance. A request was sent to the latter to obtain his consent to hold it, but he was asleep, and the staff-officer in charge, who had had no experience whatever in military matters, positively refused to awaken him until daylight, and then it was too late, for that was the time set for the troops to fall back to the new line.

At 9 P.M. Hooker sent an order to Sedgwick, who was supposed to be at Falmouth and to have 26,000 men, to throw bridges over, cross, drive away Early's 9,000, who held the heights of Fredericksburg, and then to come forward on the Plank Road, and be ready at daylight on the 3d to take Lee's force in reverse, while Hooker attacked it in front.

This order was given under the impression that Sedgwick had not crossed with his main body, but only with Howe's division, whereas he was at the bridge heads, three miles below Fredericksburg, on the south side of the river. Hooker probably forgot that he had ordered a demonstration to be made against the Bowling Green road on the 1st, and that Sedgwick went over to make it.

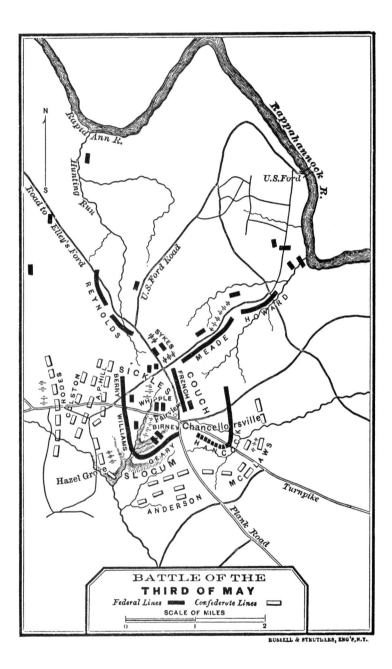

BATTLE OF THE
THIRD OF MAY

Federal Lines ▰▰▰   Confederate Lines ▭

SCALE OF MILES

0   1   2

RUSSELL & STRUTHERS, ENG'S, N.Y.

CHAPTER VII.

THE BATTLE OF THE THIRD OF MAY.

THE Eleventh Corps were now sent to the extreme left of the line to reorganize. There they were sheltered behind the strong works thrown up by Humphreys' division, and were not so liable to be attacked.

The new line laid out by Hooker's order was on a low ridge perpendicular to the Plank Road, and opposite and at right angles to the right of Slocum's front. It was strongly supported by the artillery of the Third, Twelfth, and part of the Eleventh Corps, massed under Captain Best on the heights at Fairview, in the rear and to the left. Sickles was ordered to fall back to it at dawn of day, Birney to lead the way, and Whipple (Graham's brigade) to bring up the rear. The Plank Road ran through the centre of the position, Birney being on the left and Berry on the right, with Whipple's division on a short line in rear, as a reserve. French's division of Couch's corps was posted on Berry's right, the other division (that of Hancock) remained between Mott Run and Chancellorsville.

When the movement began, Birney's division, on the left of Whipple's, occupied the high ground at Hazel Grove, facing the Plank Road, Graham's brigade being on the extreme left. This was a very aggressive position, since it took every column that advanced against Sickles' new line directly in flank, and therefore it was indispensable for the rebel commander to capture Hazel Grove before he advanced against the main body of the Third Corps, which held the Plank Road. This hill was not quite so high as that at Fairview, but our artillery on it had great range, and the post should have been maintained at all hazards. The cavalry who had so ably defended it fell back, in obedience to orders, to the Chancellorsville House, to support the batteries in that vicinity, and I think one regiment was sent to report to Sedgwick. Whipple commenced the movement by sending off his artillery and that of Birney. Graham's brigade was the rear guard. Its retreat was covered by the fire of Huntington's battery on the right. The moment the enemy saw that Graham was retiring, Archer's brigade of A. P. Hill's division charged, attained the top of the hill, and succeeded in capturing four guns. Elated by his success, Archer pressed forward against Huntington's battery, but was rudely repulsed; for Sickles opened on him also with a battery from Fairview. He managed to hold the four guns until Doles' brigade of Rodes' division came to his aid. The two took the hill, for Whipple had no instructions to defend it. He retired in perfect order to the new position assigned him. Huntington's battery, supported by two regiments sent out by Sickles, covered the retreat, but suffered considerable loss in doing so, as one regiment was withdrawn and the other gave way. Ward's brigade was then sent to the right and Hayman's brigade held in reserve.

Stuart, who was now in command of Jackson's corps, saw at a glance the immense importance of this capture, and did not delay a moment in crowning the hill with thirty pieces of artillery, which soon began to play with fatal effect upon our troops below; upon Chancellorsville; and upon the crest occupied by Slocum, which it enfiladed, and as McLaws' batteries also enfiladed Slocum's line from the opposite side, it seems almost miraculous that he was able to hold it at all.

Simultaneously with the attack against Hazel Grove came a fierce onslaught on that part of Sickles' line to the left of the road, accompanied by fierce yells and cries of "*Remember Jackson !*" a watch-word which it was supposed would excite the rebels to strenuous efforts to avenge the fatal wound of their great leader. It was handsomely met and driven back by Mott's brigade, which had come up from the Ford, and now held the front on that part of the line. A brilliant counter-charge by the Fifth and Seventh New Jersey captured many prisoners and colors.

Sickles' men fought with great determination, but being assailed by infantry in front and battered almost in flank by the artillery posted at Hazel Grove, the line was manifestly untenable. After an obstinate contest the men fell back to the second line, which was but partially fortified, and soon after to the third line, which was more strongly intrenched, and which they held to the close of the fight.

McGowan's, Lane's, and Heth's brigades of A. P. Hill's division charged resolutely over this line also; but they suffered heavily from Best's guns at Fairview, and were driven back by Colonel Franklin's and Colonel Bowman's brigades of Whipple's division, which made an effective counter-charge. Whipple's other brigade, that of Graham, had been sent to relieve one of Slocum's brigades on the left of the line, which was out of ammunition. It held its position there for two hours.

While this attack was taking place on the left of the road, Pender's and Thomas' brigades, also of Hill's division, charged over the works on the right; but when the others retreated they were left without support and were compelled to retire also. They reformed, however; tried it again, and once more succeeded in holding temporary possession of part of the line, but were soon driven out again.

French's division of Couch's corps was now brought up, and Carroll's brigade struck the rebels on the left, and doubled them back on the centre, capturing a great many prisoners and confusing and rendering abortive Hill's attack in front. Hill sent for his reserves to come up, and three rebel brigades were thrown against Carroll, who was supported by the remainder of French's division and a brigade from Humphreys' division of Meade's corps, and French's flank movement was checked. Then another front attack was organized by the enemy, under cover of their artillery at Hazel Grove, and Nichols', Iverson's, and O'Neil's brigades charged over everything, even up to Best's batteries at Fairview, which they captured; but our men rallied, and drove them headlong down the hill, back to the first line Sickles had occupied at daylight. It was a combat of giants; a tremendous struggle between patriotism on the one hand and vengeance on the other.

French now tried to follow up this advantage by again pressing against the Confederate left, but it was reinforced by still another brigade, and he could make no progress.

The struggle increased in violence. The rebels were determined to break through the lines, and our men were equally determined not to give way. Well might De Trobriand style it "a mad and desperate battle." Mahone said afterward: "The Federals fought like devils at Chancellorsville." Again Rodes' and Hill's divisions renewed the attempt and were temporarily successful, and again was the bleeding remnant of their forces flung back in disorder. Doles' and Ramseur's brigades of Rodes' division, managed to pass up the ravine to the right of Slocum's works and gain his right and rear, but were unsupported there, and Doles was driven out by a concentrated artillery and musketry fire. Ramseur, who now found himself directly on Sickles' left flank, succeeded in holding on until the old Stonewall brigade under Paxton came to his aid, and then they carried Fairview again, only to be driven out as the others had been.

The battle had now lasted several hours, and the troops engaged, as well as the artillery, were almost out of ammunition. There should have been some staff officer specially charged with this subject, but there seemed to be no one who could give orders in relation to it.

The last line of our works was finally taken by the enemy, who having succeeded in driving off the Third Maryland of the Twelfth Corps, on Berry's left, entered near the road and enfiladed the line to the right and left. Sickles sent Ward's brigade to take the place of the Third Maryland, but it did not reach the position assigned it in time, the enemy being already in possession. In attempting to remedy this disaster, Berry was killed, and his successor, General Mott, was wounded. The command then devolved upon General Revere, who, probably considering further contest hopeless, led his men out of action without authority—an offence for which he was afterward tried and dismissed the service.[1]

As the cannon cartridges gave out, the enemy brought up numerous batteries, under Colonel Carter, in close proximity to Fairview, and soon overcame all resistance in that direction, driving the troops and guns from the plain.

Anderson now made a junction with Stuart, and their combined efforts drove the Third Corps and Williams' division of the Twelfth Corps back, leaving only Geary and Hancock to maintain the struggle. Geary was without support, but he still fought on. He faced two regiments west at right angles to his original line, and by the aid of his artillery held on for an hour longer ; his right brigade facing south, west, and north.

---

[1] Generals Meade, Sedgwick, and others thought he was unjustly condemned. President Lincoln subsequently remitted the sentence and restored him to his rank.

The Third Corps left their last position at Chancellors-ville slowly and sullenly. Hayman's brigade, not far from the Chancellorsville House, finding the enemy a good deal disorganized, and coming forward in a languid and ineffi-cient manner, turned—by Sickles' direction—and charged, capturing several hundred prisoners and several colors, and relieving Graham, who was now holding on with the bayonet, from a most perilous flank attack, enabling him to with-draw in good order. Sickles himself was soon after injured by a spent shot or piece of shell, which struck his waist-belt. His corps and French's division had lost 5,000 out of 22,000.

Our front gradually melted away and passed to the new line in rear through Humphreys' division of the Fifth Corps, which was posted about half a mile north of the Chancellors-ville House in the edge of the thicket, to cover the retreat. At last only indomitable Hancock remained, fighting Mc-Laws with his front line, and keeping back Stuart and Ander-son with his rear line.

The enemy, Jackson's Corps, showed little disposition to follow up their success. The fact is, these veterans were about fought out, and became almost inert. They did not, at the last, even press Hancock, who was still strong in ar-tillery, and he withdrew his main body in good order, losing however, the Twenty-seventh Connecticut regiment, which was posted at the apex of his line on the south, and was not brought back in time, in consequence of the failure of a sub-ordinate officer to carry out his orders.

Before Hancock left, his line was taken in reverse, and he was obliged to throw back part of his force to the left to re-sist Anderson, who was trying to force the passage of Mott Run. The line in that direction was firmly held by Colonel Miles of the Sixty-first New York, who was shot through the body while encouraging his men to defend the position.

Stuart's command had lost 7,500 in his attack, and it could hardly have resisted a fresh force if it had been thrown in. General William Hays, of the Second Corps, who was taken prisoner, says they were worn out, and Rodes admits in his report that Jackson's veterans clung to their intrenchments, and that Ramseur and others who passed them, urged them to go forward in vain.

Before the close of the action Hooker was importuned for reinforcements, but without avail. Perhaps he intended to send them, for about this time he rushed out and made a passionate appeal to Geary's men to charge and retake the works they had lost; promising to aid them by throwing in a heavy force on the enemy's left flank. At this appeal the exhausted troops put their caps on their bayonets, waved them aloft, and with loud cheers charged on the rebels and drove them out once more; but sixty guns opened upon them at close range with terrible effect; the promised reinforcements did not come; they were surrounded with ever increasing enemies, and forced to give up everything and retreat. Stuart and Anderson then formed their lines on the south of and parallel to the Plank Road, facing north, and began to fortify the position.

Had they been disposed to follow up the retreat closely they would have been unable to do so, for now a new and terrible barrier intervened; the woods on each side of the Plank Road had been set on fire by the artillery and the wounded and dying were burning in the flames without a possibility of rescuing them. Let us draw a veil over this scene, for it is pitiful to dwell upon it.

There was no further change in Stuart's line until the close of the battle; but Anderson's division was soon after detached against Sedgwick.

The new line thus taken up by the Union Army was a

semi-ellipse, with the left resting on the Rappahannock and the right on the Rapidan. Its centre was at Bullock's House, about three-fourths of a mile north of Chancellorsville. The approaches were well guarded with artillery, and the line partially intrenched. The enemy did not assail it. They made a reconnoissance in the afternoon, but Weed's artillery at the apex of the line was too strongly posted to be forced, and Lee soon found other employment for his troops, for Sedgwick was approaching to attack his rear.

In the history of lost empires we almost invariably find that the cause of their final overthrow on the battle-field may be traced to the violation of one military principle, which is that *the attempt to overpower a central force by converging columns, is almost always fatal to the assailants,* for a force in the centre, by virtue of its position, has nearly double the strength of one on the circumference. Yet this is the first mistake made by every tyro in generalship. A strong blow can be given by a sledge-hammer, but if we divide it into twenty small hammers, the blows will necessarily be scattering and uncertain. Let us suppose an army holds the junction of six roads. It seems theoretically plausible that different detachments encircling it, by all attacking at the same time, must confuse and overpower it ; but in practice the idea is rarely realized, for no two routes are precisely alike, the columns never move simultaneously, and therefore never arrive at the same time. Some of this is due to the character of the commanders. One man is full of dash, and goes forward at once ; another is timid, or at least over-cautious, and advances slowly ; a third stops to recall some outlying detachments, or to make elaborate preparations. The result is, the outer army has lost its strength and is always beaten in detail. One portion is sure to be defeated before the others arrive. We shall have occasion to refer to this principle again in reference to the battle of Gettysburg. The history of our own war shows that an attack against the front and rear of a force is not necessarily fatal. Baird's division at Chickamauga defended itself successfully against an assault of this kind, and Hancock faced his division both ways at Chancellorsville and repelled every attempt to force his position. But Hooker thought otherwise. He felt certain that if Sedgwick assailed Lee in rear, while he advanced in front, the Confederate army was doomed. When the time came, however, to carry out this programme, if we may use a homely simile borrowed from General De Peyster, Hooker did not hold up his end of the log, and the whole weight fell upon Sedgwick.

About this time a pillar of the Chancellorsville House was struck by a cannon-ball, and Hooker, who was leaning against it at the moment, was prostrated and severely injured. He revived in a few minutes, mounted his horse and rode to the rear, but it was some time before he turned over the command to Couch, who was second in rank. After this stroke he suffered a great deal from paroxysms of pain, and was manifestly unfit to give orders, although he soon resumed the command.

The historian almost refuses to chronicle the startling fact that 37,000 men were kept out of the fight, most of whom had not fired a shot, and all of whom were eager to go in. The whole of the First Corps and three-fourths of the Fifth Corps had not been engaged. These, with 5,000 of the Eleventh Corps, who desired to retrieve the disaster of the previous day and were ready to advance, made a new army, which had it been used against Stuart's tired men would necessarily have driven them off the field; for there were but 26,000 of them when the fight commenced. To

make the matter worse, a large part of this force—the First
and Fifth Corps—stood with arms in their hands, as specta-
tors, almost directly on the left flank of the enemy; so that
their mere advance would have swept everything before it.
Hancock, too, says that his men were fresh enough to go
forward again.

Couch succeeded to the command after Hooker was
wounded, and made dispositions for the final stand around
the Chancellorsville House, where the battle lasted some
time longer, and where a battery of the Fifth Corps was
sacrificed to cover the retreat of the troops. He did not,
however, take the responsibility of renewing the contest
with fresh troops, perhaps deterred by the fact that Anderson's and McLaws' divisions had now effected a junction
with Stuart's corps; so that the chances were somewhat
less favorable than they would have been had Sickles and
French been reinforced before the junction took place. He
says, at the close of the action, that fifty guns posted to the
right and front of the Chancellorsville House would have
swept the enemy away.

I think Hooker was beset with the idea of keeping back a
large portion of his force to be used in case of emergency.
It appears from a statement made by General Alexander S.
Webb, who had made a daring personal reconnoissance of the
enemy's movement, that he was present when Meade—acting
on his (Webb's) representations, and speaking for himself
and Reynolds—asked Hooker's permission to let the First
and Fifth Corps take part in the battle. It is fair, however,
to state that Hooker, having been injured and in great pain,
was hardly accountable for his want of decision at this time.
Indeed, General Tremaine, who was a colonel on Sickles' staff,
says that Hooker did intend to use his reserve force as soon as
the enemy were utterly exhausted. President Lincoln seems

to have had a presentiment of what would occur, for his parting words to Hooker and Couch were, to use all the troops and not keep any back.

I have stated that both Meade and Reynolds wished to put their corps in at the vital point, but were not allowed to do so. General Tremaine also states that, subsequently, when Hooker was suffering a paroxysm of pain, he was the bearer of a communication to him requesting reinforcements, which Hooker directed to be handed to General Meade, who was present, for his action. Meade would not take the responsibility thus offered him at so late a period in the action, though strongly urged to do so both by Tremaine and Colonel Dahlgren, without the express order of General Hooker, or the sanction of General Couch, who was his superior officer, and who was absent. Perhaps he was afraid that Hooker might resume the command at any moment and leave him to shoulder the responsibility of any disaster that might occur, without giving him the credit in case of success. Still he should have put the men in, for the success of the cause was above all personal considerations. A single division thrown in at this time would have retrieved the fortunes of the day. The delay of finding Couch would have been fatal; for immediate action was demanded.

Reynolds, indeed, considered himself obliged to wait for orders, but was so desirous to go in that he directed me to send Colonel Stone's brigade forward to make a reconnoissance, in the hope the enemy would attack it and thus bring on a fresh contest; for he intended to reinforce Stone with his whole corps. Stone went close enough to the rebels to overhear their conversation. He made a very successful reconnoissance and brought back a number of prisoners, but as no hint was given him of the object of the movement, he did not bring on a fight. Had he received the slightest intimation that such was Reynolds' wish, he would not have hesitated a moment, for his reputation for dash and gallantry was inferior to none in the army.

Sedgwick being on the south side of the river, three miles below the town, was farther off than Hooker supposed, and did not meet the expectations of the latter by brushing aside Early's 9,000 men from the fortified heights, and coming on in time to thunder on Lee's rear at daylight, and join hands with the main body at Chancellorsville.

The Sixth Corps started soon after midnight to carry out the order. General John Newton's division led the way, with General Shaler's brigade in advance. They were somewhat delayed by a false alarm in rear, and by the enemy's pickets in front, but made their way steadily toward Fredericksburg. When they reached Hazel Run they found a considerable body of the enemy on the Bowling Green Road at the bridge in readiness to dispute the passage. Colonel Hamblin, who was in charge of Newton's skirmish line, left a few of his men to open an energetic fire in front, while he assembled the others and made a charge which took the bridge and secured the right of way. The command reached Fredericksburg about 3 A.M. As the atmosphere was very hazy, Newton found himself almost on the enemy before he knew it ; near enough in fact to overhear their conversation. He fell back quietly to the town and occupied the streets which were not swept by the fire from the works above. He then waited for daylight to enable him to reconnoitre the position in his front, previous to making an attack ; and that was the hour Hooker had set for Sedgwick to join him in attacking Lee at Chancellorsville.

As soon as it was light Gibbon laid bridges, crossed over, and reported to Sedgwick with his division.

At dawn Newton deployed Wheaton's brigade and made a demonstration to develop the enemy's line. As the fortified heights commanded the Plank Road by which Sedgwick was to advance, it became necessary to attack immediately. The plan of assault which was devised by General Newton, and approved by General Sedgwick, was to attenuate the rebel force by attacking it on a wide front, so that it could not be strong anywhere, and to use the bayonet alone. Accordingly, Gibbon was directed to advance on the right to turn their flank there if possible, while Newton was to demonstrate against the centre and Howe to act against the left. Newton deployed Wheaton's brigade, opened fire along his front and kept the enemy employed there, but Gibbon was unable to advance on the right, because a canal and a raceway lay between him and the rebels, and they had taken up the flooring of the bridges over the latter. Howe did not succeed any better on the left, as in attempting to turn the first line of works he encountered the fire of a second line in rear and in *echelon* to the first, which took him directly in flank. A concentrated artillery fire was brought to bear on Gibbon, Early sent Hays' brigade from Marye's Hill to meet him, and Wilcox's brigade came up from Banks' Ford for the same purpose, so that he was obliged to fall back.

It was now 10 A.M. and there was no time to be lost. General Warren, who was in camp to represent Hooker, urged an immediate assault. This advice was followed. Newton formed two columns of assault and one deployed line in the centre, and Howe three deployed lines on the left.

Colonel Johns, of the Seventh Massachusetts, who was a graduate of West Point, led one of these columns directly against Marye's Hill, with two regiments of Eustis' brigade, supported by the other two regiments, deployed, while another column, consisting of two regiments under Colonel Spear, of the Sixty-first Pennsylvania, supported by two regiments (the Eighty-second Pennsylvania and Sixty-seventh New York) in column, under Colonel Shaler, was directed to act farther to the right, and the Light Division, under Colonel Burnham of the Fifth Massachusetts, attached to Newton's command, was ordered to deploy on the left against the intrenchments at the base of the hill. Spear's column, advancing through a narrow gorge, was broken and enfiladed by the artillery—indeed almost literally swept away—and Spear himself was killed. Johns had an equally difficult task, for he was compelled to advance up a broken stony gulch swept by two rebel howitzers. The head of his column was twice broken, but he rallied it each time. He was then badly wounded, and there was a brief pause, but Colonel Walsh, of the Thirty-sixth New York, rallied the men again, and they kept straight on over the works. Burnham with his Light Brigade captured the intrenchments below, which had been so fatal to our troops in the previous battle of Fredericksburg, and went into the works above with the others.[1] The fortified heights on the right of Hazel Run, held by Barksdale's brigade, being now occupied by our troops, those to the left were necessarily taken in reverse, and therefore Sedgwick thought it useless to attack them in front. Howe, nevertheless, carried them gallantly, but with considerable loss of life.

The coveted heights, which Burnside had been unable to take with his whole army, were in our possession, together with about a thousand prisoners ; but the loss of the Sixth Corps was severe, for nearly a thousand men were killed, wounded,

---

[1] When Spear's column was broken, the Eighty-second Pennsylvania, under Colonel Bassett, came forward in support, but was crushed with the same fire. Colonel Shaler's remaining regiment, the Sixty-seventh New York, followed by the remnant of Bassett's regiment, forced their way over the crest to the right of Colonel Johns' column.

and missing in less than five minutes. The attack was over so soon that Early did not get back Hays' brigade, which had been detached to oppose Gibbon, in time to assist in the defence. Newton says if there had been a hundred more men on Marye's Hill we could not have taken it.

The rebel force was now divided, and thrown off toward Richmond in eccentric directions.

All that remained for Sedgwick to do was to keep straight on the Plank Road toward Chancellorsville. Had he done so at once he would have anticipated the enemy in taking possession of the strong position of Salem Church, and perhaps have captured Wilcox's and Hays' brigades. But it was not intended by Providence that we should win this battle, which had been commenced by a boasting proclamation of what was to be accomplished ; and obstacles were constantly occurring of the most unexpected character. After directing Gibbon to hold the town and cover the bridges there, Sedgwick, instead of pushing on, halted to reform his men, and sent back for Brooks' division, which was still at its old position three miles below Fredericksburg, to come up and take the advance. It was full 3 P.M. before the final start was made. This delay gave Hays time to rejoin Early by making a detour around the head of Sedgwick's column, and Wilcox took advantage of it to select a strong position at Guest's House, open fire with his artillery, and detain Sedgwick still longer. Wilcox then retreated toward the river road, but finding he was not pursued, and that Sedgwick was advancing with great caution, he turned back and occupied for a short time the Toll Gate, half a mile from Salem Church, where McLaws' division was formed with one of Anderson's brigades on his left. When Sedgwick advanced Wilcox fell back and joined the main body at the church.

The other brigades of Anderson's were sent to hold the junction of the Mine road and the River road.

When the pursuit ceased, Early reassembled his command near Cox's house and made immediate arrangements to retake the Fredericksburg heights, and demonstrate against Sedgwick's rear.

McLaws formed his line about 2 P.M. in the strip of woods which runs along the low ridge at Salem Church ; two brigades being posted on each side of the road about three hundred yards back. Wilcox's brigade, when driven in, was directed to take post in the church and an adjacent schoolhouse, which were used as citadels. This was a strong position, for the rebels were sheltered by the woods, while our troops were forced to advance over an open country, cut up by ravines parallel to McLaws' front, which broke up their organization to some extent, and destroyed the *elan* of the attack. After a brief artillery contest, which soon ended, as the enemy were out of ammunition, Brooks' division went forward about 4 P.M., and made a gallant charge, in which Bartlett's brigade, aided by Williston's battery, captured the buildings and drove in part of Wilcox's line. The New Jersey brigade charged at the same time on his right, and Russell's brigade on his left. Wilcox placed himself at the head of his reserve regiments, and aided by Semmes' brigade, made a fierce counter-charge. The combat for the schoolhouse raged with great fury, each party breaking the other's line and being broken in turn. Finally, after much desperate fighting, Bartlett was obliged to yield the portion of the crest he had held which was a key to the position ; for as he was not strongly and promptly reinforced, as he should have been, his withdrawal from the church and school-house made a gap which forced the other portions of the line to retreat to avoid being taken in flank. Brooks was therefore driven back to the shelter of the guns at the Toll House. There Newton's division came up and formed on his right and part of Howe's division on his left.[1]

Bartlett's attack should have been deferred until Newton's entire division was near enough to support it. In that case it would undoubtedly have succeeded.

Sedgwick's left now rested on a point nearly a mile from Salem Church, while his right under Wheaton was somewhat advanced.

Up to this time the fight had been between Brooks' division and McLaws' mixed command. It was now decided that a second attempt should be made by Newton's division, but Newton states that the design was abandoned because Howe's division, which was to support him, had gone into camp without orders, and was not immediately available. Before new arrangements could be made darkness came on, and both armies bivouacked on the ground they occupied. Brooks' division in the assault just made had lost 1,500 men, and Sedgwick no longer felt confident of forcing his way alone through the obstacles that beset him. Nevertheless, trusting to the speedy and hearty co-operation of Hooker, he stood ready to renew the attempt on the morrow, although he foresaw the enemy would fortify their line during the night and make it truly formidable.

When Wilcox left Banks' Ford to aid in the defence of Salem Church, General H. W. Benham of the United States Engineer Corps, who commanded an engineer brigade there, threw over a bridge at Scott's Dam, about a mile below Banks' Ford, to communicate with Sedgwick, enable him to

---

[1] The Second Brigade of Newton's division was thrown in to cover the retreat: its steadiness, and a gallant charge made under very discouraging circumstances by the Second Rhode Island regiment, under Colonel Horatio Rogers, full on the left flank of the enemy, checked the advance of McLaws. The severe and well-directed fire of the Union artillery soon forced him back to the ridge.

retreat in case of disaster, and connect his headquarters with those of Hooker by telegraph.

Hooker disapproved the laying of the bridges, which he thought superfluous, as Sedgwick's orders were to keep on to Chancellorsville. Warren took advantage of this new and short route to return to the main army, in order to give Hooker information as to Sedgwick's position. He promised to send back full instructions for the guidance of the latter.

As soon as the bridge was laid, General J. T. Owens with his brigade of the Second Corps, which had been guarding the ford, crossed over and reported to Sedgwick.

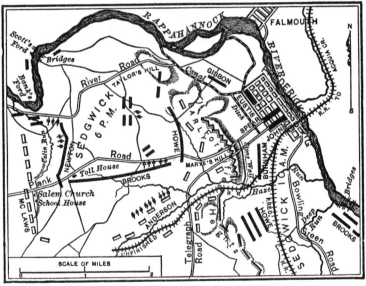

Sedgwick's Position.

Warren found Hooker in a deep sleep, and still suffering from the concussion that took place in the morning. He gathered from the little he did say, that Sedgwick must rely upon himself, and not upon the main body for deliverance, and he so informed Sedgwick.

CHAPTER VIII.

MAY FOURTH.—ATTACK ON SEDGWICK'S FORCE.

As HOOKER seemed disposed to be inactive, Lee thought he might venture to still further augment the force in front of Sedgwick, with a view to either capture the Sixth Corps or force it to recross the river. He therefore directed Anderson to reinforce McLaws with the remainder of his division, leaving only what was left of Jackson's old corps to confront Hooker. Anderson had gone over to the right, opposite the Eleventh and Twelfth Corps, and had opened with a battery upon the wagon trains which were parked in that vicinity, creating quite a stampede, until his guns were driven away by the Twelfth Corps. In this skirmish, General Whipple, commanding the Third division of Sickles' corps, was killed. In the meantime, Early had retaken the heights of Fredericksburg, which were merely held by a picket guard of Gibbons' division, so that, when Anderson arrived and took post on the right of McLaws, parallel to the Plank Road, Sedgwick found himself environed on three sides by the enemy; only the road to Banks' Ford remained open, and even that was endangered by bands of rebels, who roamed about in rear of our forces. At one time it is said they could have captured him and his headquarters. Fortunately the tents which constituted the latter were of so unpretending a character, that they gave no indication of being tenanted by the commanding general.

Hooker had resumed the command, although manifestly incapable of directing affairs; for the concussion must have affected his brain. At all events, although he had about thirty-seven thousand fresh men, ready and desirous of entering into the combat, and probably only had about seventeen thousand worn out men in front of him, he failed to do anything to relieve Sedgwick's force, which was now becoming seriously compromised. A feeble and ineffectual reconnoissance was indeed attempted, and as that was promptly resisted, Hooker gave up the idea of any advance, and left Sedgwick to get out of the difficulty the best way he could. At 11 A.M. Sedgwick wrote, stating the obstacles which beset him, and requesting the active assistance of the main army. He was directed, in reply, not to attack, unless the main body at Chancellorsville did the same. All remained quiet until 4 P.M. The Sixth Corps were then formed on three sides of a square inclosing Banks' Ford, with the flanks resting on the river. Howe's division faced east toward Fredericksburg, against Early, who confronted him in that direction, and his left stretched out to Taylor's Hill on the Rappahannock. Newton's division, together with Russell's brigade of Brooks' division, faced McLaws on the west, and Brooks' other two brigades—those of Bartlett and Torbert—were opposed to Anderson on the south. The entire line was very long and thin.

Early and McLaws had been skirmishing on their fronts all day, but it was 6 P.M. before everything was in readiness for the final advance. An attempt had, however, been made by Early to turn Howe's left and cut Sedgwick off from the river; but it was promptly met and the enemy were repulsed with a loss of two hundred prisoners and a battle-flag.

Sedgwick felt his position to be a precarious one. His

line was six miles long, and he had but about twenty thousand men with which to hold it against twenty-five thousand of the enemy. He thought, too, that reinforcements had come up from Richmond and that the enemy's force far exceeded his own. It was evident he could not recross the river in broad daylight without sacrificing a great part of his corps, and he determined to hold on until night. Benham took the precaution to throw over a second bridge, and this prudent measure, in Sedgwick's opinion, saved his command. Lee, after personally reconnoitring the position, gave orders to break in the centre of the Sixth Corps so as to defeat the two wings, throw them off in eccentric directions, and scatter the whole force. When this was attempted, Sedgwick detached Wheaton's brigade from Newton's right, and sent it to reinforce that part of the line. At 6 P.M. three guns were fired as a signal from Alexander's battery and the Confederate forces pressed forward to the attack. Newton's front was not assailed, and the right of Brooks' division easily repulsed the enemy who advanced in that direction, with the fire of the artillery and the skirmish line alone.

The main effort of the evening was made by Early's division, which advanced in columns of battalions, to turn Howe's left, and cut that flank off from the river. Howe's artillery, under charge of Major J. Watts de Peyster, a mere youth, was admirably posted and did great execution on these heavy columns. De Peyster himself rode out and established a battery, a considerable distance in advance of the main line, and the enemy pressed forward eagerly to capture it ; after doing so they were suddenly confronted by several regiments in ambush, which rose up and delivered a fire which threw Hays' and Hokes' brigades into great confusion, and caused them to make a precipitate retreat. An attack against Howe's right was also repulsed. In the ardor of pursuit,

Howe swung that flank around and captured the Eighth
Louisiana Regiment, but in doing so, he exposed his rear to
Gordon, who came down a ravine behind him, so that he was
compelled to fall back and take up a new line. Howe had
carefully selected a reserve position and made dispositions to
hold it. Fresh assaults on his left finally forced General
Neil to retreat to it with his brigade. The enemy followed
him up promptly, but were driven back in disorder by
Grant's Vermont brigade, two regiments of Newton's division and Butler's regular battery of the Second United States
Artillery. Newton thinks this last attack on Howe was
local and accidental, for as the other divisions were not assailed, a concentrated attack on Howe would have destroyed
him.

Darkness at last put an end to the strife. Newton, being
an engineer officer by profession, had previously been sent
by Sedgwick to select a new line to cover the bridges, and
the army was ordered to fall back there. It did so without confusion, the roads having been carefully picketed.
Brooks took position on Newton's left, after which Howe's
division, whose right flank for a time had been "in the air,"
withdrew also an hour later than the others, and prolonged
the line to the left. Howe complained that he was deserted
by Sedgwick, but the latter appears to have sent Wheaton's
brigade and other reinforcements to aid his retreat. The
movement to the rear was favored by the darkness and a
thick fog, which settled over the valleys, but did not extend
to the high ground. As Benham and Sedgwick, who were
classmates at West Point, walked on the slope of the hill
where the men were lying—the crest above being held
by thirty-four guns on the opposite side of the river—Benham cautioned Sedgwick not to recross under any circumstances without his entire command, nor without Hooker's

express sanction, advice which Sedgwick was wise enough to follow.

The enemy did not assail the new position or attempt to interfere with the crossing which soon after took place. When it was nearly concluded, an order came from Hooker countermanding it, but it was then too late to return.

Howe thinks Sedgwick should not have crossed, as the last attack on the left, which was the vital point, had been repulsed. This may be so, in the light of after-consideration, but it was very doubtful at the time, and as Sedgwick had lost a fraction under five thousand men in these operations, and was acting under the false information that additional forces had come up from Richmond, he felt that he had fully borne his share of the burden, and that it was better to place his corps beyond the risk of capture, than to run the chances of renewing the battle. It would, undoubtedly, have been of immense advantage to the cause if he could have continued to hold Taylor's Hill, which dominated the country round, and was the key of the battle-field; for in that case Hooker might have withdrawn from Lee's front and joined Sedgwick, which would have been attaining the object for which our main army left Falmouth, and made the turning movement. He would thus have gained a strategic if not a tactical victory; his shortcomings would have been forgotten, and he would have been regarded as one of the greatest strategists of the age. Hooker, however, had left so many things undone, that it is by no means certain he would have carried out this policy, although he expressed his intention to do so. Sedgwick's movement, in my opinion, added another example to the evil effects of converging columns against a central force.

There is little more to add in relation to Hooker's operations. On the night of the 4th, he called a council of war, and after stating the situation to them, absented himself, in order that they might have full liberty to discuss the subject. Reynolds was exhausted, and went to sleep, saying that his vote would be the same as that of Meade. Meade voted to remain, because he thought it would be impossible to cross in presence of the enemy. Sickles and Couch voted to retreat. Howard voted to remain, without reference to the situation of the army, because in his opinion his corps had behaved badly, and he wished to retrieve its reputation. Slocum was not present. The final result was that Hooker determined to cross, although the majority of votes were against it. The votes of Meade and Howard, however, were qualified in such a way as to give the impression they were in favor of a retreat.

Owing to a sudden rise in the river the bridges became too short, and there was some doubt as to the practicability of passing over them, but by taking down one, and piecing the others with it, the difficulty was overcome and the army retired, without being followed up, under cover of thirty-two guns posted on the heights on the opposite bank. Meade's corps acted as rear guard.

Hooker left his killed and wounded behind, and had lost 14 guns and 20,000 stand of arms.

It only remains to give a brief statement of the operations of Stoneman's cavalry. These were of no avail as regards the battle of Chancellorsville, for our army was defeated and in full retreat before Lee's main line of communication with Richmond was struck, and then all the damage was repaired in three or four days. There seems to have been a lack of information as to where to strike ; for the principal depot of the rebel army was at Guiney's station on the Fredericksburg and Richmond Railroad. The supplies there were but slightly guarded, and could easily have been captured. Had this been done, Lee would have been seriously embarrassed, notwithstanding his victory, and forced to fall back to obtain subsistence.

Stoneman, upon setting out on the expedition, left one division of 4,000 men under Averell to do the fighting, and dispose of any force that might attempt to interfere with the movements of the main body. Averell accordingly followed W. H. F. Lee's two regiments to Rapidan Station, and remained there skirmishing on the 1st of May. His antagonist then burned the bridge, and fell back on Gordonsville. As Averell was about to ford the river and follow, he received orders from Hooker to return; he came back to Elley's Ford on the 2d, which he reached at half past ten at night. As his return was useless and unnecessary, he has been severely censured, but it was not of his own volition. Soon after Fitz Hugh Lee made a dash at his camp, but was repulsed. On the 3d Averell made a reconnoissance on Hooker's right, with a view to attack the enemy there, but finding the country impracticable for cavalry, returned to Elley's Ford. Hooker, who was not in the best of humor at the time, became dissatisfied with his operations, relieved him from command, and appointed Pleasonton to take his place.

In the meantime, the main body under Stoneman pressed forward, and reached Louisa Court House early on the morning of the 2d. Parties were at once ordered out to destroy the Virginia Central Railroad above and below that point. One of W. H. F. Lee's regiments drove back a detachment of Union cavalry which was moving on Gordonsville, but reinforcements went forward and Lee was driven back in his turn.

In the evening Stoneman made his headquarters at Thompson's Cross Roads, and from there despatched regiments in different directions to burn and destroy.

One party under Colonel Wyndham, First New Jersey, was engaged all day on the 3d in injuring the canal at Columbia, and in attempts to blow up the aqueduct over the Rivanna.

Colonel Kilpatrick moved with his regiment, the Second New York, across the country, passing within two miles and a half of Richmond, and creating great consternation there. He struck and destroyed a portion of the Fredericksburg Railroad—Lee's main line of supply—on the 4th, at Hungary Station, ten miles from Richmond, and burned Meadow Bridge, over the Chickahominy at the railroad crossing. He then turned north again, crossed the Pamunkey, and ended his long ride at Gloucester Point, which was garrisoned by our troops.

Another regiment—the Twelfth Illinois, under Colonel Davis—went to Ashland and moved up and down the railroad, doing a good deal of damage. It captured a train full of Confederate wounded and paroled them. After a brief encounter with an infantry and artillery force at Tunstall's station, it also turned north, and made its way over the Pamunkey and Mattapony rivers to Gloucester Point.

Two regiments, the First Maine and First Maryland, under General Gregg, started down the South Anna River, burning bridges over common roads and railroads. After destroying Hanover Junction, it returned to headquarters.

One or two other small parties were sent on flying excursions to assist in the work of demolition.

On the 5th, Stoneman started to return, and the entire command with the exception of that portion which was at Gloucester Point, recrossed at Kelly's Ford on the 8th.

The losses in each army were heavy. An extract is here given from the official reports, but it is said the Confederate statement is far from being accurate.

LOSSES AT CHANCELLORSVILLE.

UNION.

	Killed and Wounded.	Missing.	Total.
First Corps (Reynolds)	192	100	292
Second Corps (Couch)	1,525	500	2,025
Third Corps (Sickles)...............	3,439	600	4,059
Fifth Corps (Meade)................	399	300	699
Sixth Corps (Sedgwick)	3,601	1,000	4,601
Eleventh Corps (Howard)..........	508	2,000	2,508
Twelfth Corps (Slocum)	2,383	500	2,883
Cavalry, etc......................	150		150
Total	12,197	5,000	17,197

CONFEDERATE.

	Killed and Wounded.	Missing.	Total.
Early's Division...................	851	500	1,351
A. P. Hill's Division	2,583	500 ?	3,083
Colston's Division	1,868	450 ?	2,318
Rodes' Division	2,178	713	2,891
Anderson's Division	1,180	210	1,390
McLaws' Division	1,379	380	1,759
Artillery and Cavalry.............	227		227
Total	10,266	2,753	13,019

The following extract from Harpers' "History of the Great Rebellion" states the causes of Hooker's defeat in a very able manner, but I do not agree with the author in his estimate of the great danger Lee ran from the converging columns of Sedgwick and Hooker. It is true Lee tried the same system, and succeeded, by sending Jackson around to attack Hooker's right, but the success was due solely to the utter lack of all preparation on the part of Howard to meet the emergency, and to Hooker's failure to make use of the ample means at his disposal to prevent the junction of Stuart and Anderson.

Mr. Alden, the author of the work in question, says :

There was not, in fact, any moment between Thursday afternoon and Tuesday morning when success was not wholly within the grasp of the Union army. The movement by which Chancellorsville was reached, and the Confederate position rendered worthless, was brilliantly conceived and admirably executed. The initial error, by which alone all else was rendered possible, was that halt [1] at Chancellorsville. Had the march been continued for an hour longer, or even been resumed early in the following morning, the army would have got clear of the Wilderness without meeting any great opposing force, and then it would have been in a position where its great superiority of numbers would have told.   The rout of Howard's corps was possible only from the grossest neglect of all military precautions. Jackson, after a toilsome march of ten hours, halted for three hours in open ground, not two miles from the Union lines. A single picket, sent for a mile up a broad road would have discovered the whole movement in ample time for Howard to have strengthened his position, or to have withdrawn from it without loss. The blame of this surprise can not, however, fairly be laid upon Hooker. He had a right to presume that whoever was in command there would have so picketed his lines as to prevent the possibility of being surprised in broad daylight. But even as it was, the disaster to the Eleventh Corps should have had no serious effect upon the general result. That was fully remedied when the pursuit was checked. On Sunday morning Hooker was in a better position than he had been on the evening before. He had lost 3,000 men and had been strengthened by 17,000, and now had 78,000 to oppose to 47,000. The Confederate army was divided, and could reunite only by winning a battle or by a day's march. The only thing which could have lost the battle of that day was the abandonment of the position at Hazel Grove, for from this alone was it possible to enfilade Slocum's line. But surely it is within the limits of military forethought that a general who has occupied a position for two days and three nights should have discovered the very key to that position, when it lay with-

---

[1] Recall of columns.

in a mile of his own headquarters. The disabling of Hooker could not, indeed, have been foreseen; but such an accident might happen to any commander upon any field, and there should have been somewhere some man with authority to have, within the space of three hours, brought into action some of the more than 30,000 men within sound, and almost within sight, of the battle then raging. How the hours from Sunday noon till Monday night were wasted has been shown. Hooker, indeed, reiterates that he could not assail the Confederate lines through the dense forests. But Lee broke through those very woods on Sunday, and was minded to attempt it again on Wednesday, when he found that the enemy had disappeared. The golden opportunity was lost, never to be recovered, and the Confederate Army of Northern Virginia gained a new lease of life.

It may not be out of place, as indicating the kind of service in which we were engaged, to quote the following letter, written after the retreat:

I am so cut, scratched, and bruised that I can hardly hold a pen in my hand. My limbs are covered with swellings from the bites of insects and torn from forcing my way through briers and thorny bushes; my eyes close involuntarily from lack of sleep and excessive fatigue. My legs are cramped from so much riding, and I have not yet succeeded in getting rid of the chill caused by sleeping on the wet ground in the cold rain. My clothes, up to last night, had not been taken off for a week. As I lay down every night with my boots and spurs on, my feet are very much swollen. I ought to be in bed at this moment instead of attempting to write.

The others must have suffered in the same way. Warren especially, as a medium of communication between Hooker and Sedgwick, made almost superhuman exertions to do without sleep and perform the important duties assigned him.

Each army now felt the need of rest and recuperation, and no military movements of importance took place for several weeks. Soon after the battle of Chancellorsville, Longstreet's two divisions, which had been operating in front of Suffolk, rejoined Lee at Fredericksburg. That portion of Stoneman's cavalry which had taken refuge in Gloucester Point also succeeded, by great boldness and skilful manœuvring on the part of Colonel Kilpatrick, in outwitting the enemy and getting to Urbanna, after crossing Dragon River, rebuilding a bridge there, and repulsing the rebel forces who tried to prevent them from reaching the Rappahannock. The command, when it arrived at Urbanna, passed over on the ferry-boat, under cover of a gunboat sent there for that purpose, and rejoined the Army of the Potomac at Falmouth, on the 3d of June, bringing in about 200 prisoners, 40 wagons, and 1,000 contrabands, as slaves were usually styled at that time.

CHAPTER IX.

PREPARATIONS TO RENEW THE CONFLICT.

THE close of the battle of Chancellorsville found the Union army still strong in numbers, defeated, but not disheartened, and ready, as soon as reinforcements and supplies arrived, and a brief period of rest and recuperation ensued, to take the field again. To resist the effects of this defeat and recruit our armies required, however, great determination and serious effort on the part of the Administration; for a large and powerful party still clogged and impeded its efforts, and were allowed full liberty to chill the patriotism of the masses, and oppose, with tongue and pen and every species of indirection, all efficient action which looked to national defence. This opposition was so strong and active that the President almost preferred the risk of losing another battle to the commotion which would be excited by attempts to enforce the draft; for hitherto we had relied entirely on voluntary enlistments to increase our strength in the field. Men are chilled by disaster and do not readily enlist after a defeat; yet the terms of service of thirty thousand of the two years and nine months men were expiring, and something had to be done. Our army, however, at the end of May was still formidable in numbers, and too strongly posted to be effectually assailed; especially as it had full and free communication with Washington and the

North, and could be assisted in case of need by the loyal militia of the free States.

The rebels had obtained a triumph, rather than a substantial victory, at Chancellorsville. It was gained, too, at a ruinous expense of life, and when the battle was over they found themselves too weak to follow up our retreating forces. While the whole South was exulting, their great commander, General Lee, was profoundly depressed. The resources of the Davis Government in men and means were limited, and it was evident that without a foreign alliance, prolonged defensive warfare by an army so far from its base, would ultimately exhaust the seceding States, without accomplishing their independence. It became necessary, therefore, for General Lee to choose one of two plans of campaign : either to fall back on the centre of his supplies at Richmond, and stand a siege there, or to invade the North. By retiring on Richmond he would save the great labor of transporting food and war material to the frontier, and would remove the Northern army still further from its sources of supply and its principal depots. One circumstance, however, would probably in any event, have impelled him to take the bolder course. The situation in Vicksburg was becoming alarming. It was evident the town must fall and with its surrender the Federal fleet would soon regain possession of the Mississippi. The fall of Vicksburg, supplemented by the retreat of Lee's army on Richmond, would dishearten the Southern people, and stimulate the North to renewed efforts. It was essential, therefore, to counterbalance the impending disaster in the West by some brilliant exploit in the East.

There was perhaps another reason for this great forward movement, founded on the relation of the Confederacy to the principal European powers. England still made a pretence of neutrality, but the aristocracy and ruling classes sided with the South, and a large association of their most influential men was established at Manchester to aid the slaveholding oligarchy. The rebels were fighting us with English guns and war material, furnished by blockade runners; while English Shenandoahs and Alabamas, manned by British seamen, under the Confederate flag, burned our merchant vessels and swept our commercial marine from the ocean. The French Government was equally hostile to us, and there was hardly a kingdom in Europe which did not sympathize with the South, allied as they were by their feudal customs to the deplorable system of Southern slavery. Russia alone favored our cause, and stood ready, if need be, to assist us with her fleet; probably more from antagonism to England and France, than from any other motive. The agents of the Confederate Government stated in their official despatches that if General Lee could establish his army firmly on Northern soil England would at once acknowledge the independence of the South; in which case ample loans could not only be obtained on Southern securities, but a foreign alliance might be formed, and perhaps a fleet furnished to re-open the Southern ports.

While thus elated by hopes of foreign intervention, the Confederate spies and sympathizers who thronged the North greatly encouraged the Davis Government by their glowing accounts of the disaffection there, in consequence of the heavy taxation, rendered necessary by the war, and by the unpopularity of the draft, which would soon have to be enforced as a defensive measure. They overrated the influence of the *Copperhead* or anti-war party, and prophesied that a rebel invasion would be followed by outbreaks in the principal cities, which would paralyze every effort to re-inforce the Federal forces in the field.

These reasons would have been quite sufficient of them·
selves to induce Lee to make the movement, but he himself
gives an additional one. He hoped by this advance to draw
Hooker out, where he could strike him a decisive blow, and
thus ensure the permanent triumph of the Confederacy. He
was weary of all this marching, campaigning, and blood-
shed, and was strongly desirous of settling the whole matter
at once. Having been reinforced after the battle of Chancellorsville by Longstreet's two divisions and a large body
of conscripts, he determined to advance. On May 31st, his
force, according to rebel statements, amounted to 88,754,
of which 68,352 were ready for duty. Recruits, too, were
constantly coming in from the draft, which was rigidly enforced in the Southern States.

Hooker having learned from his spies that there was much
talk of an invasion, wrote to the President on May 28th, that
the enemy was undoubtedly about to make a movement of
some kind. On June 3d, McLaws' and Hood's divisions
of Longstreet's corps started for the general rendezvous at
Culpeper. A change in the encampment on the opposite
side of the river was noted by the vigilant Union commander,
who at once ordered Sedgwick to lay two bridges at the old
crossing place, three miles below Fredericksburg, pass over
with a division, and press the enemy to ascertain if their
main body was still there. Fresh indications occurred on
the 4th, for Ewell's corps followed that of Longstreet. The
bridges being completed on the 5th, Howe's division of the
Sixth Corps was thrown over and Hill's corps came out of
their intrenchments to meet it. Some skirmishing ensued,
and Sedgwick reported, as his opinion, that the greater portion of the enemy's force still held their old positions.
Hooker, however, was determined to be prepared for all con·

tingencies, and therefore, on the same day, detached the Fifth Corps to be in readiness to meet the enemy should they attempt to force a passage anywhere between United States Ford and Banks' Ford. Resolved to obtain certain information at all hazards, on the 7th of June he ordered Pleasonton to make a forced reconnoissance with all the available cavalry of the army, in the direction of Culpeper, to ascertain whether the Confederate forces were really concentrating there, with a view to an invasion of the North.

Should this prove to be the case, Hooker desired to cross the river, to envelop and destroy Hill's corps, and then follow up the main body as they proceeded northward, thus intercepting their communications with Richmond. The authorities at Washington, however, did not look with much equanimity upon the possibility of finding Lee's army interposed between them and the Army of the Potomac, so they refused to sanction the plan and it was abandoned.

Nevertheless, in my opinion it was about the best method that could have been devised to check the invasion, provided Hooker did not lose his water-base ; for Lee always showed himself very sensitive whenever his communications with Richmond was threatened. If that was severed no more *ammunition* or military supplies would reach him. The amount of cartridges on hand was necessarily limited. It would soon be expended in constant skirmishes and engagements, and then he would be helpless and at the mercy of his antagonist. Consequently, the moment he heard that a portion of the Sixth Corps had crossed and confronted Hill, he directed Ewell and Longstreet to halt at Locust Grove, near Chancellorsville, and be in readiness to return to Fredericksburg to assist Hill in case there was any danger of his being overpowered. Finding Sedgwick's advance was a mere recon-

noissance, the two rebel corps resumed their march to Cul-
pepper.

Hooker deemed it essential to success, that all troops con-
nected with the theatre of invasion should be placed under
his command, so that they could act in unison. In his opinion most of their strength was wasted in discordant expeditions, which were useless as regards the general result. He
referred more particularly to General Dix's command at Old
Point Comfort, General Heintzelman's command in Washington, and General Schenck's troops posted at Baltimore, along
the Baltimore and Ohio Railroad and in the Valley of the
Shenandoah. This request was reasonable and should have
been granted. Hooker's demands, however, were not considered favorably. There was no very good feeling between General Halleck, who was commander of the army,
and himself; and as he felt that his efforts were neither
seconded nor approved at headquarters, he soon after re-
signed the command.

The main body of the Union cavalry at this time was at
Warrenton and Catlett's Station. Hooker, having been dissatisfied with the result of the cavalry operations during the
Chancellorsville campaign, had displaced Stoneman in favor
of Major-General Alfred Pleasonton.

CHAPTER X.

BATTLE OF BRANDY STATION (FLEETWOOD).

THE 8th of June was a day of preparation on both sides.
Pleasonton was engaged in collecting his troops and getting
everything in readiness to beat up the enemy's quarters the
next morning, and Stuart was preparing to cross for the purpose of either making a raid on the railroad, as Pleasonton states, or to take up a position to guard the right flank
of the invading force as it passed by our army. Major Mc-
Clellan, Stuart's adjutant-general, asserts the latter. Pleasonton's information was founded on captured despatches,
and on interviews held by some of our officers with the Confederates under a flag of truce.

The four batteries of Jones's cavalry brigade moved
down near the river opposite Beverly Ford on the 7th, to
cover the proposed crossing. They were imperfectly supported by the remainder of Stuart's force. Jones's brigade
was posted on the road to Beverly Ford, that of Fitz Lee [1]
on the other side of Hazel River; that of Robertson along
the Rappahannock below the railroad; that of W. H. F.
Lee on the road to Melford Ford, and that of Hampton in
reserve, near Fleetwood Hill—all too far off to be readily
available. In fact, the batteries were entirely unsuspicious
of danger, although they were a quarter of a mile from the

---

[1] A familiar abbreviation for Fitz Hugh Lee, adopted in the rebel reports.

nearest support and there was only a thin line of pickets between their guns and the river.

In the meantime Pleasonton's three divisions, "stiffened"—to use one of Hooker's expressions—by two brigades of infantry, stole down to the fords and lay there during the night, quietly, and without fires, ready at the first dawn of day to spring upon their too-confident adversaries and give them a rude awakening.

Pleasonton in person remained with Buford's division—the First—which was lying near Beverly Ford with Ames's infantry brigade.

The other two divisions, the Second, under Colonel Duffie, and the Third, under General Gregg—supported by Russell's infantry brigade, were in bivouac opposite Kelly's Ford.

As each commander is apt to overstate the enemy's force and underrate his own, it is not always easy to get at the facts. Pleasonton claims that the rebels had about twelve thousand cavalry and twelve guns. Major McClellan, of Stuart's staff, puts the number at nine thousand three hundred and thirty-five men, on paper, and twenty guns; but states there were nearly three thousand absentees.

General Gregg estimates the Union cavalry at about nine thousand men and six batteries, but—as will be seen hereafter—a third of this force was detached toward Stevensburg, and their operations had little or no effect on the general result. The batteries do not seem to have been brought forward in time to be of much service.

At daybreak Pleasonton's troops began to cross; Buford's division and Ames's infantry at Beverly Ford; the other two divisions, under Gregg and Duffie, with Russell's infantry at Kelly's Ford, six miles below. Each division was accompanied by two light batteries.

Pleasonton's plan was founded on the erroneous supposition that the enemy were at Culpeper. He used the infantry to keep the lines of retreat open, and directed the cavalry to rendezvous at Brandy Station. They were to arrive there at the same time, and attack together. Duffie's column was to make a circuit by way of Stevensburg. Unfortunately, Stuart was not at Culpeper, but at Brandy Station; that is, he occupied the point where they were to rendezvous, and the plan therefore appertained practically to the same vicious system of converging columns against a central force. What happened may be briefly stated as follows : The First Division, under Buford, came upon the enemy between Brandy Station and Beverly Ford. A battle ensued at St. James's Church, and as their whole force confronted him, and they had twenty pieces of artillery, he was unable to break their line. After fighting some hours he was obliged to turn back with a portion of his command to repel an attempt against his line of retreat. Gregg next appeared upon the scene, and succeeded in getting in Stuart's rear before the rebel general knew he was there. Buford having gone back toward Beverly Ford, as stated, Gregg in his turn, fought the whole of Stuart's force without the co-operation of either Buford or Duffie. It can hardly be said that Duffie's column took any part in the action, for he did not reach Brandy Station until late in the day. And then, as the rebel infantry were approaching, Pleasonton ordered a retreat.

For the future instruction of the reader it may be well to state that every cavalry charge, unless supported by artillery or infantry, is necessarily repulsed by a counter-charge ; for when the force of the attack is spent, the men who make it are always more or less scattered, and therefore unable to contend against the impetus of a fresh line of troops, who come against them at full speed and strike in mass.

Stuart's headquarters were twice taken by Gregg's division, and a company desk captured with very important despatches, but the enemy had the most men, and most artillery near the point attacked, and therefore always regained, by a counter-charge, the ground that had been lost.

Stuart claims to have repulsed the last attack of Pleasonton against Fleetwood Hill, and to have taken three guns, besides driving our cavalry back across the river.

Pleasonton claims to have fully accomplished the object of his reconnoissance, to have gained valuable information which enabled Hooker to thwart Lee's plans; and to have so crippled the rebel cavalry that its efficiency was very much impaired for the remainder of the campaign; so that Lee was forced to take the indirect route of the valley, instead of the direct one along the eastern base of the Blue Ridge, behind his cavalry as a screen; his original intention having been to enter Maryland at Poolesville and Monocacy.

GETTYSBURG.

GETTYSBURG.

CHAPTER I.

THE INVASION OF THE NORTH.

An invasion of the North being considered as both practicable and necessary, it only remained to select the most available route.

There was no object in passing east of Hooker's army, and it would have been wholly impracticable to do so, as the wide rivers to be crossed were controlled by our gunboats.

To attempt to cross the Rappahannock to the west, and in the immediate vicinity of Fredericksburg, would have been hazardous, because when an army is crossing, the portion which is over is liable to be crushed before it can be reinforced.

It would seem that Lee's first intention was to move along the eastern base of the Blue Ridge directly toward Washington.[1] The appearance of his army on Hooker's flank would be a kind of taunt and threat, calculated to draw the latter out of his shell, and induce him to make an attack. In such a case, as the rebels were in the highest spirits, in consequence of their recent victory at Chancellorsville, their commander had little doubt of the result. This plan was feasible

---

[1] See map facing page 1.

enough, provided his cavalry could beat back that of Pleasonton and act as a screen to conceal his movements. This
they were not in a condition to do after the battle of Brandy
Station, and Lee was thus forced to take the route down
the Shenandoah Valley, which had many advantages. The
mountain wall that intervened between the two armies, was
a sure defence against our forces, for it was covered by dense
thickets, and the roads that lead through the gaps, and
the gaps themselves, were easy to fortify and hold against
a superior force. If Hooker had attempted to assail these
positions, one corps could have held him in check, while the
other two captured Washington.

The movement also favored the subsistence of the troops,
for the valley being a rich agricultural region, Lee was enabled to dispense with much of his transportation and feed
his army off of the country.

There was one serious obstacle, however, to his further
progress in that direction, and that was the presence of a
gallant soldier, Milroy, with a very considerable Union garrison intrenched at Winchester.

It was essential to Lee's advance that the valley should be
cleared of Union troops, otherwise they would sally forth
after he passed and capture his convoys.

With this object in view, on the 10th Ewell's corps passed
through Gaines's Cross Roads, and halted near Flint Hill on
their way to Chester Gap and Front Royal.

The possibility of an invasion had been discussed for some
days in Washington, and Halleck had come to the conclusion
that it was better to withdraw the stores and ammunition
from Winchester, and retain the post there merely as a lookout, to give warning of the enemy's approach. Accordingly,
on the 11th, Milroy received orders from his department
commander, General Schenck, to send his armament and

supplies back to Harper's Ferry. Milroy remonstrated, saying that he could hold the place against any force that would probably attack him, and that it would be cruel to sacrifice the Union men who looked to him for protection.

In reply to this Schenck telegraphed him that he might remain, but must be in readiness to retreat whenever circumstances made it necessary.

Milroy, in answer to another inquiry, reported that he could move in six hours.

On the 12th he sent out two scouting parties, and learned there was a considerable force at Cedarsville, which he thought might form part of Stuart's raid, information of which had been communicated to him.

He could not believe it possible that an entire rebel corps was near him, for he supposed Lee's army was still at Fredericksburg. His superiors had not informed him, as they should have done by telegraph, that a large part of it had moved to Culpeper. He thought if Lee left Hooker's front at Fredericksburg, the Army of the Potomac would follow and he would receive full information and instructions. He telegraphed General Schenck late that night for specific orders, whether to hold his post or to retreat on Harper's Ferry, stating there appeared to be a considerable force in front of him. As the enemy soon after cut the wires, he never received any answer. He sent a messenger the same night to notify Colonel McReynolds, at Berryville, that there was a large body of the enemy on the Front Royal road, and directed him to send out scouts to Millwood, and keep himself advised of its approach, in order that he might prepare to fall back on Winchester the moment he was attacked by superior numbers.

On the 13th Ewell marched with two divisions directly on Winchester, while he sent the third—that of Rodes—to take

Berryville. Thanks to the timely warning McReynolds had received, his brigade got off in time, his rear being covered by Alexander's battery, the Sixth Maryland Infantry, and part of the First New York (Lincoln) Cavalry. These detained the enemy two hours, and then caught up with the main body. Jenkins' cavalry came upon the retreating force at Opequan Creek, where he made a fierce attack, which was promptly repulsed by the rear guard, aided by the artillery with canister. After this there was no further molestation, and McReynolds' command reached Winchester at 10 P.M —a march of thirty miles.

Soon after the affair at the Opequan, Major Morris, with 200 men, was attacked at Bunker Hill, an outlying post of Winchester. He occupied a fortified church, but moved out to meet the enemy, under the impression it was only a small raiding party. When he found two thousand men in line of battle he retreated, fighting, to the church again. There, as the doors were barricaded, and the walls loopholed, the rebels could make no impression, and were obliged to fall back to a respectful distance. In the night Morris managed to steal away, and soon rejoined the main body at Winchester.

The arrival of these reinforcements seriously embarrassed Milroy; and it will be seen hereafter that it would have been much better for all concerned if they had retreated to Harper's Ferry at once. They acted, however, strictly in obedience to orders.

Rodes's division, after the taking of Berryville, kept on toward Martinsburg, and bivouacked at a place called Summit Point.

On the morning of the 13th Milroy had sent out a detachment under General Elliot on the Strasburg road, and another under Colonel Ely on the Front Royal road, to reconnoitre. Elliott found no enemy, and returned. An attempt was made to cut him off from the town, but it was repulsed. His troops were then massed on the south side behind Mill Creek and a mill-race which ran parallel to it, and were protected by stone fences. Colonel Ely had a brisk artillery skirmish with Ewell's advance, and then fell back to Winchester, taking post at the junction of the Front Royal and Strasburg roads. The enemy did not attempt to cross the creek that night, but at 5 P.M. they advanced and captured a picket-post which commanded the Strasburg road, but were soon driven out.

From a prisoner captured in this skirmish Milroy learned the highly important intelligence that he was confronted by Ewell's corps and that Longstreet was rapidly approaching.

The most natural course under the circumstances would have been for him to retreat at once, but McReynolds's brigade had just arrived, exhausted by their forced march, and could go no further, without some hours' rest. To move without them would be to sacrifice a large part of his force. He still cherished the hope that Hooker's army would follow Lee up closely and come to his relief.

Ewell at night directed Early's division to attack the works on the north and west of the town at daylight the next morning, while Johnson's division demonstrated against the east and southeast.

Early on Sunday, the 14th, Milroy sent out a detachment to see if the enemy had established themselves on the Pughtown or Romney roads. The party returned about 2 P.M. and reported the roads clear, but soon after the rebels came in great force from that direction, so that Milroy's hopes of escaping by the route leading to the northwest were dissipated. Immediately west of Winchester, and parallel with Applebie Ridge, on which the main forts were situated, there is another ridge called Flint Ridge, where rifle pits had been commenced to command the Pughtown and Romney roads. These were held by one regiment, and part of another under Colonel Keifer of the One Hundred and Tenth Ohio, together with Battery "L" of the Fifth United States Artillery. Early's division made a sudden attack there, preliminary to which he opened fire with four batteries. He charged into these rifle-pits and took them, but the garrison retreated successfully, under cover of the fire, from the main works above, which were held by Elliot's and McReynolds's brigades. This was followed by an artillery duel, which was kept up until 8 P.M. without any special results.

Johnson's division at daybreak attacked the eastern side of the town, held by Colonel Ely's brigade, but was gallantly met and repulsed by the Eighth Pennsylvania and Eighty-seventh Pennsylvania. These two regiments, by Milroy's order, made a bold charge against the enemy as they were retiring, but the latter were so suddenly and strongly reinforced that the two regiments were glad to get back to their shelter in the fortified suburbs. They were followed up however, and after severe fighting Johnson gained possession of part of the town. This apparent success proved of no avail, for the forts above shelled him out. He therefore retired and made no further attempt in that direction.

Darkness ended the struggle for the day. Johnson then left one brigade to prevent Milroy from escaping toward the east and went off with the remainder of his division to form across the Martinsburg pike, about three miles north of Winchester, to intercept Milroy's retreat in that direction.

While these events were going on in the Valley, Imboden's cavalry was engaged in breaking up the Baltimore and Ohio Railroad near Romney, to prevent Milroy from receiving any reinforcements from the west.

The latter now found himself in a perilous situation. His cannon ammunition was nearly exhausted, and he had but one day's rations for his men. He resolved to give up all further attempts to defend the place, to abandon his wagon train and artillery, and to force his way through the hostile lines that night; taking with him only the horses and small arms. This involved his leaving also his sick and wounded, but it was unavoidable. He ordered all the guns spiked, and the ammunition thrown into the cisterns.

At 1 A.M. on the 15th, he moved silently out through a ravine and was not molested until he struck the Martinsburg road, about four miles from the town. There Elliot, who was in the advance with his brigade, met a rebel skirmish line, and soon ascertained that their main body were formed, partly on high ground in a woods east of the road, and partly in an open field east of and adjoining the woods. The enemy were in effect sheltered by a stone fence which bordered a railroad cut, with their reserve and artillery principally posted on elevated ground in rear.

The only thing to be done was to break through their lines as soon as possible. It was now about 3.30 A.M. Elliot, whose record of long, careful, and brilliant service in the regular army is an exemplary one, formed line of battle with his three regiments and fought the six regiments that held the road for about an hour with varied success, encountering a severe artillery fire and driving back their right in disorder by a gallant charge of the One Hundred and Tenth Ohio and One Hundred and Twenty-second Ohio; but unfortunately their left held firm, in spite of repeated attacks made by Colonel Shawl with two regiments, reinforced by two more and by part of Colonel Ely's brigade. Their force in front, too, was sustained by heavy reserves both of infantry and artillery.

A signal-gun fired at Winchester showed that the enemy there were aware of the flight and were in full pursuit. The main road being blocked, Milroy determined to try another, and directed the troops to fall back a short distance and turn to the right. Part of them did so, but the greater number, through some misunderstanding, filed to the left, and took the road to Bath. It was no longer possible to reunite the two columns and as Milroy's horse was shot under him about this time, he could use no personal exertions to remedy the disorder. A portion of the command who were not pursued reached Harper's Ferry by way of Smithfield late in the afternoon. Those who moved out on the Bath road also made good their escape, crossed the Potomac at Hancock, and rallied at Bloody Run. The greater part of Colonel Ely's brigade, and Colonel McReynolds's brigade, however, were captured. Milroy claims to have brought off 5,000 men of the garrison, and that the 2,000 paroled by Early, consisted principally of the sick and wounded. Early says he sent 108 officers and 3,250 enlisted men as prisoners to Richmond. Johnson, who intercepted the retreat, says he captured 2,300 prisoners, 175 horses, and 11 battle flags.

While two-thirds of Ewell's corps were attacking Winchester, the other division under Rodes, preceded by Jenkins's brigade of cavalry, pursued McReynolds's wagon train to Martinsburg, arriving there late in the afternoon of the 14th. The town was held as an outlying post of Harper's Ferry by a small detachment of all arms under Colonel Tyler, a subordinate of General Tyler, who formed his men outside of the place and resisted Rodes' attack until night, when his infantry escaped to Shepherdstown, and his artillery and cavalry to Williamsport. In carrying out these movements, however, he lost five guns and five caissons. He passed the river and rejoined the main body at Harper's Ferry. The latter place is wholly indefensible against an enemy holding the hills around it. It is like fighting at the bottom of a well. General Tyler had therefore very wisely moved across the river to Maryland Heights, where he had a strong fortified post. From that commanding eminence he could very soon shell out any force that attempted to occupy the town.

The Shenandoah Valley was now clear of Union troops, and soon became the great highway of the invasion. However disastrous Milroy's defeat may be considered on account of the losses incurred, it was not without its compensation. The detention of Ewell's force there gave time to the general Government and the Governors of the loyal States to raise troops and organize resistance, and it awakened the entire North to the necessity of immediate action.

Hooker, having learned that Ewell had passed Sperryville, advanced his right to prevent any crossing in his immediate vicinity, and confine the enemy to the Valley route. He sent the Third Corps to hold the fords opposite Culpeper, and the Fifth Corps to guard those lower down.

On the 13th he gave up his position opposite Fredericksburg, and started north toward Washington, giving orders to Sedgwick to recross and follow on to Dumfries. That night the First Corps reached Bealeton, and the Eleventh Catlett's station. Reynolds was placed in command of the left wing of the army (the First, Third, and Eleventh Corps) and I relieved him in command of the First Corps. The right wing (that is the Second, Fifth, Twelfth and Sixth Corps) was accompanied by Hooker in person, who reached Dumfries on the 14th.

As soon as Hill saw Sedgwick disappear behind the Stafford hills, he broke up his camp and started for Culpeper.

Some changes in the meantime had occurred in the Army of the Potomac, and General Hancock was assigned to the Second Corps instead of General Couch, who had been sent to organize the department of the Susquehanna at Harrisburg, Pennsylvania.

The teamsters and fugitives from Winchester, making for Chambersburg in all haste, told the inhabitants of the towns through which they passed that the rebels were close behind them. This created the wildest excitement. As many cases had occurred in which negroes had been seized, and sent South to be sold as slaves, the whole colored population took to the woods and filled up the roads in all directions. The appearance of Jenkins' brigade, who crossed at Williamsport on the morning of the 15th and reached Chambersburg the same day, added to the alarm.

Jenkins was at the head of 2,000 cavalry, and soon became a terror to the farmers in that vicinity by his heavy exactions in the way of horses, cattle, grain, etc. It must be confessed he paid for what he took in Confederate scrip, but as this paper money was not worth ten cents a bushel, there was very little consolation in receiving it. His followers made it a legal tender at the stores for everything they wanted. Having had some horses stolen, he sternly called on the city authorities to pay him their full value. They did so without a murmur—*in Confederate money*. He pocketed it with a grim smile, evidently appreciating the joke. He boasted greatly of his humanity and his respect for private property, but if the local papers are to be believed, it must be chronicled to his everlasting disgrace that he seized a great many negroes, who were tied and sent South as slaves. Black children were torn from their mothers, placed in front of his troops, and borne off to Virginia to be sold for the benefit of his soldiers. There was nothing out of character in that, he thought, for it was one of the sacred rights for which the South was contending.

Prompt measures were taken by the Northern States to meet the emergency. Mr. Lincoln called on the Governors of West Virginia, Maryland, Pennsylvania, and New York to raise 120,000 men for temporary service. It was easy to get the men, but difficult to arm them, as nearly all serviceable muskets were already in possession of the Army of the Potomac. As early as the 9th two new departments had been created for Pennsylvania: that of the Monongahela, with headquarters at Pittsburg, was assigned to Major-General W. T. H. Brooks; and that of the Susquehanna, with headquarters at Carlisle, to Major-General Darius N. Couch.

On the 15th Ewell reached Williamsport with a force estimated at twelve thousand men and sixteen guns.

Before Couch could reach Carlisle it was already occupied by Jenkins's cavalry, and the terrified farmers of that section of country were fleeing in crowds across the Susquehanna, driving their horses and cattle before them.

CHAPTER II.

A SHOWER of telegrams came to Hooker, notifying him of these untoward events, and demanding protection; but he simply moved one step toward the enemy. On the 15th he had three corps—the First, Sixth, and Eleventh—grouped around Centreville, with the Third Corps at Manassas, and the Second, Fifth, and Twelfth Corps in reserve at Fairfax Court House. The left flank of the army was guarded by Pleasonton's cavalry, posted at Warrenton. Hooker was not to be drawn away from the defence at Washington by any clamorous appeal for his services elsewhere; his plan being to move parallel to Lee's line of advance and strike his communications with Richmond at the first favorable opportunity. He obtained some reinforcements at this time, Stannard's Second Vermont brigade being assigned to my division of the First Corps, and Stahl's cavalry division, about six thousand strong, being directed to report to General Pleasonton for duty.

As Harrisburg lay directly in the track of the invading army, Governor Curtin made strenuous efforts to collect a force there. He called upon all able-bodied citizens to enroll themselves, and complained that Philadelphia failed to respond. New York acted promptly, and on the 15th two brigades arrived in Philadelphia on their way to the front.

On the same day Longstreet, having been relieved by Hill, left Culpeper with his corps and marched directly across the country east of the Blue Ridge to occupy Ashby's and Snicker's Gaps. Stuart's cavalry were to guard his right flank, but did not leave until the next day. The object of Longstreet's movement was to tempt Hooker to abandon his strong position in front of Washington and march against the Gaps, in which case it was hoped some opportunity might occur by which the rebels could either crush the Army of the Potomac in the open country or possibly outmanœuvre it, so as to intervene between it and Washington; but Hooker remained stationary.

Rodes's division of Ewell's corps reached Williamsport and remained there during the 16th, 17th, and 18th, to support Jenkins, and receive, and transmit to the rear, the cattle, horses, negroes, and provisions, taken by him.

The commotion created by the approach of the invader was not all one-sided. General Dix, who commanded at Fortress Monroe, received orders to advance on Richmond, which was weakly defended at this time. As through their manifold offences in the way of starving our prisoners, etc., the rebel President and his cabinet were afraid of reprisals, there was great dismay at the weakness of the garrison there, and bitter denunciations of Lee for leaving so small a force behind. The Union troops for this counter-invasion were landed at Yorktown and sent on to the White House. General Getty, in command of one column of about seven thousand men, moved on the 13th as far as Hanover Junction to destroy the bridge over the North and South Anna, and as much of the railroad as possible, in order to make a break in Lee's communications. At the same time

General Keys, with another column of about five thousand men, moved from the White House to secure Bottom's Bridge on the Chickahominy, and thus leave a clear road for Getty's column to advance on the city. The Davis Government, however, called out the militia and concentrated enough men for defence by weakening the garrisons in South Carolina and elsewhere; but there is no doubt the fright at one time was so serious that it was in contemplation to recall Lee's forces; especially on the 15th of June, when it was learned that General Keys's column was at New Kent Court House within fifteen miles of the city.

On the 16th Stuart's cavalry left the Rappahannock—with the exception of the Fifteenth Virginia, which remained with Hill—and bivouacked at Salem with Fitz Lee's brigade at Piedmont. Their orders were to keep along the eastern base of the Blue Ridge, and guard the front of Longstreet's corps in the Gaps.

Our own cavalry were concentrated at Warrenton and Catlett's.

On the 17th Fitz Lee's brigade was sent forward from Piedmont to Aldie, via Middleburg, to anticipate our troops in holding the Gap there; it being considered important to occupy the Bull Run range of mountains as a screen for Lee's further operations. Fitz Lee's brigade was supported by that of Robertson which was moved to Rectortown, where it was also available as a reserve to W. H. F. Lee's brigade which had gone forward to occupy Thoroughfare Gap. No opposition was anticipated in the latter place, Pleasonton having moved to Centreville with his main body. Stuart made his headquarters at Middleburg on the 17th.

Fitz Lee halted near Dover to close up his command, and sent his pickets on to Aldie Gap. Pleasonton, who was scouting in the vicinity, had no orders to go through the pass, but felt prompted to do so by one of those presentiments which rarely deceive. He pushed on, therefore, with Gregg's division until about 2.30 P.M., when he came upon the rebel pickets, who fell back on the main body. The latter had made a march of forty miles to reach the Gap, and Fitz Lee chose a strong position on a hill directly west of Aldie, in which to fight a defensive battle. His line covered the road to Snicker's Gap, but could be turned by the road to Middleburg and Ashby's Gap.

A sanguinary contest ensued, which, including the pursuit, lasted until 9 P.M. The rebel front was strengthened by a ditch and a line of hay-stacks. After fighting for three hours the battle was finally decided by a gallant charge of the First Maine Cavalry, who, after our line had been broken and driven back, were led by Kilpatrick in person, against a regiment of mounted infantry on the Ashby's Gap road, capturing four guns. The Harris Light Cavalry had been in disfavor for having failed in an attack at Brandy Station, but now they redeemed themselves, made several brilliant charges, and greatly contributed to the success of the day.

The rebels claim to have taken 134 prisoners, and some flags in this affair, and state that they only fell back to Middleburg in obedience to Stuart's orders. Ascertaining that Colonel Duffie was advancing on that place with his regiment,[1] Stuart thought, by concentrating his entire force there, he could overwhelm him. This may account for the retreat, but it is very certain that the loss of the pass at Aldie was a serious blow to the rebel cause. This, supplemented by Colonel Duffie's operations, which will be described hereafter, gave Hooker possession of Loudon County, and threw the invading column far to the west. If the enemy had suc-

---

[1] Colonel Duffie had been relieved from the command of his division.

ceeded in posting forces in the gaps of the Bull Run range of mountains, and in occupying the wooded country between Thoroughfare Gap and Leesburg, they would not only have hidden all their own movements from view, but would have had command of the Potomac from Harper's Ferry to within thirty miles of Washington, so that they could have operated on either side of the river.

While Gregg's division were thus engaged, Colonel Duffie started under orders with his regiment from Centreville for Middleburg, by way of Thoroughfare Gap. The enemy (W. H. F. Lee's brigade) were already there, but he forced them out, and kept on to Middleburg, which was reached about 9.30 A.M. He found Stuart's rear guard or escort there, and drove them out. Stuart fell back to Rector's Cross Roads, and sent word to all his forces to concentrate against Duffie. Duffie barricaded the streets of the town and prepared to hold it until reinforcements could reach him from Aldie, not being aware that there was any impediment in that direction. At 7 P.M. the different rebel brigades advanced on him from the direction of Aldie, Union, and Upperville. By sheltering his men behind stone walls and barricades, he repelled several assaults, but at last was surrounded by overwhelming forces, and compelled to retreat by the road upon which he had advanced in the morning. He fell back until he crossed Little River, picketed the stream and halted there to get some rest. This gave time to the enemy to surround him, and by half past one the next morning all the roads in the neighborhood were full of cavalry ; an entire brigade being formed on that which led to Aldie. He tried to force his way through the latter, but was received with heavy volleys on both flanks, and with loud calls to surrender. He directed Captain Bliss and Captain Bixby, who were in advance, to charge through everything in front of them, and the way was cleared for the main body, which at last gained the junction of the Aldie road with that which leads to White Plains. He then retreated on the latter, with his men all intermixed with those of the enemy and fighting every step of the way. He finally disengaged his force from this *mêlée* and made his way through Hopewell Gap back to Centreville, losing two-thirds of his command.

In this affair at Middleburg, Stuart states that he was unable with his entire force to drive the First Rhode Island regiment from a position it had chosen, and speaks with admiration of the gallantry it displayed.

On the 18th, Stuart took post outside of that town with Robertson and W. H. F. Lee's brigade. Fitz Lee's brigade was on his left at Union, and Jones's brigade was ordered up as a reserve.

Pleasonton moved forward with all his available force and occupied Middleburg and Philemont on the road to Snicker's Gap; releasing some of Duffie's men who had been captured the day before. Gregg's division encountered the enemy a short distance beyond Middleburg and drove them five miles in the direction of Ashby's Gap. There was no regular line formation, but the Indian mode of fighting was adopted on both sides, by taking advantage of every stone, fence, bush, or hollow, to shelter the men. Before the action was over Kilpatrick's command came up and took a prominent part.

Buford's division, which had advanced beyond Philemont on the Snicker's Gap road, also became warmly engaged. They turned the left flank of the rebels and pressed on successfully, but the squadron left to guard the bridge over Goose Creek was overpowered by numbers and the bridge was burned. Part of Pleasonton's force made a reconnoissance toward Warrenton and engaged Hampton's brigade there.

On the 19th Pleasonton held the positions he had gained and sent back for an infantry support.

As there were indications that the whole of Stuart's cavalry would be thrown on Gregg's division at Upperville, Pleasonton went forward with his entire force and a brigade of infantry to support it. After a series of brilliant engagements he drove Stuart steadily back into Ashby's Gap, where he took refuge behind Longstreet's Corps, a portion of which came up. Pleasonton then returned to Upperville and next day to Aldie. The object of these movements—to gain possession of Loudon County—having been attained, Hooker was wary, and did not propose to be lured away from his strong position, to take part in cavalry battles at a distance without a definite object. He still found it difficult to realize that Lee would still further lengthen out his long line from Richmond, and endanger his communications, by invading Pennsylvania; and he therefore waited for further developments. Lee, however, impelled by public opinion behind him, which it was hardly safe to brave, still went forward, and directed Ewell to cross the Potomac with his main body and Longstreet to fall back behind the Shenandoah to act in conjunction with Hill, who had relieved Ewell at Winchester on the 17th, against any attempt to strike the rear of his long column. Like Achilles he felt that he was only vulnerable in his heel.

Several small skirmishes occurred about this time between detachments of General Schenck's command, which picketed the north bank of the Potomac, and bands of rebel partisans. The former were surprised and captured in two or three instances. In one of these expeditions a locomotive and twenty-three cars were disabled on the Baltimore and Ohio Railroad. Imboden, too, who occupied Cumberland on the 17th, in order to favor the general plan of invasion, tore up some miles of the track west of that town, with a view to prevent any reinforcements coming from that direction.

It would have been much better for the interests of the Southern Confederacy if Lee, instead of making a downright invasion had been content to remain in the Valley and threaten Hooker with two corps, while he used the third to procure unlimited supplies in Pennsylvania, and to sever all connection between the East and the West, by breaking up the railroads and cutting the telegraph wires. Such a result, however, would hardly have been sufficient to meet the expectations of the Southern people, who were bent upon nothing else than the entire subjugation of the North and the occupation of our principal cities.

Pleasonton's operations having cleared the way, Hooker moved forward promptly on the 18th to occupy the gaps. The Twelfth Corps were sent to Leesburg, the Fifth to Aldie, and the Second to Thoroughfare Gap. The other corps formed a second line in reserve. This covered Washington and gave Hooker an excellent base of operations.

In answer to his demand for reinforcements, Crawford's division of Pennsylvania Reserves, and Abercrombie's division were sent to him. As the latter was just going out of service, it was of no use. Hooker contended that his army constituted the proper defence of Washington, and that it was not necessary to keep a large force inactive there, who could be of much more service at the front. The authorities were timid, however, did not see the force of this reasoning, and therefore refused to place Schenck's and Heintzelman's commands under his orders.

The enemy made a feeble attempt about this time to

occupy Harper's Ferry, but were promptly shelled out by our batteries on Maryland Heights.

Lee having failed, on account of the discomfiture of his cavalry, in crossing the Potomac at Edwards's Ferry, was forced either to remain where he was or go forward. Impelled by public opinion he kept on his way up the Cumberland Valley. Hooker being very desirous of keeping the invasion west of the Blue Ridge, asked Heintzelman to co-operate with him by sending the 2,000 men which seemed to be of no service at Poolesville to the passes of South Mountain, which is an extension of the same range; but Heintzelman said those passes were outside of his jurisdiction, and the men were needed in Poolesville. Hooker replied somewhat angrily that he would try and do without the men. The two generals had quarrelled, and there was not the best feeling between them.

All of Ewell's corps were across the river on the 22d, and Jenkins's cavalry pushed on to Chambersburg. He was ordered to remain there until reinforced, but failed to do so, as Union troops were approaching from the direction of Carlisle.

Longstreet and Hill were left behind to prevent Hooker from striking the rear of this long column. Hooker still remained quiescent, engaged in trying to obtain 15,000 men as reinforcements. He was but partially successful, for as soon as the New York regiments reached Baltimore, Lockwood's brigade of Maryland troops, about three thousand, was ordered to join the Army of the Potomac, and was assigned to the Twelfth Corps.

The Army of the Potomac at this time was posted as follows: the Twelfth Corps at Leesburg, supported by the Eleventh on Goose Creek, between Leesburg and Aldie; the Fifth Corps near Aldie, and the Second at the next pass below, both supported by the Third Corps at Gum Springs. The First Corps was behind the Eleventh and Twelfth Corps, near Guilford, on the Loudon and Hampshire Railroad. Our cavalry, which had left Aldie, covered the approaches to Leesburg. On the 23d they had a sharp engagement at Dover, on the road from Aldie to Leesburg, with part of Stuart's force, who beat up their quarters, but they drove off their assailants without much difficulty.

Lee now, with a prudent regard to a possible defeat, requested the authorities at Richmond to have a reserve army under Beauregard assemble at Culpeper; a request which was looked upon by Davis as one quite impossible to carry out, owing to the scarcity of troops, and the necessity of reinforcing Johnson in the West and Beauregard in the South.

Two of Ewell's divisions, those of Rodes and Johnson, reached the frightened town of Chambersburg on the 23d. The other, under Early, took the road to York, *via* Gettysburg, and halted on that day at Waynesborough.

By this time twenty regiments of militia were on their way from New York to Baltimore and Harrisburg.

Longstreet crossed the Potomac at Williamsport, and Hill at Shepherdstown, on the 24th. Their columns united at Hagerstown the next day. Thus supported, Ewell's main body resumed its march to Carlisle, which it occupied on the 27th; gathering large supplies there and along the road by means of foraging parties sent out to depredate on the farmers. As soon as they reached the town, Jenkins's brigade left for Harrisburg.

Hooker having now satisfied himself that the Capital was safe from a *coup-de-main*, and that the main body of the rebels were still marching up the Cumberland Valley, determined to move in a parallel line on the east side of South

Mountain, where he could occupy the gaps at once, in case
the enemy turned east, toward Washington and Baltimore.
To carry out this design his army began to cross the Potomac at Edwards's Ferry on the 25th, and at night Reynolds's
corps was in front and Sickles's corps in rear of Middletown,
in readiness to hold either Crampton's or Turner's Gap.
Howard's corps was thrown forward to Boonsborough.

On the 26th Slocum's corps was sent to Harper's Ferry to
act in conjunction with the garrison there—supposed to be
10,000 strong—against the enemy's line of communication
with Richmond.   The Second, Fifth, and Sixth Corps were
advanced to Frederick, Md., as a support to the First, Third,
and Eleventh Corps.   Gregg's cavalry division remained behind to cover the crossing, which was all completed the next
day, after which they too marched to Frederick.

On the 25th, Early, leaving his division at Greenwood,
went to Chambersburg to consult Ewell, who gave him
definite orders to occupy York, break up the Central Railroad, burn the bridge over the Susquehanna at Wrightsville,
and afterward rejoin the main body at Carlisle.

It seems strange that Lee should suppose that the Union
army would continue inactive all this time, south of Washington, where it was only confronted by Stuart's cavalry,
and it is remarkable to find him so totally in the dark with
regard to Hooker's movements.   It has been extensively assumed by rebel writers that this ignorance was caused by
the injudicious raid made by Stuart, who thought it would
be a great benefit to the Confederate cause if he could ride
entirely around the Union lines and rejoin Lee's advance at
York.   He had made several of these circuits during his
military career, and had gained important advantages from
them in the way of breaking up communications, capturing
despatches, etc.   It is thought that he hoped by threaten-

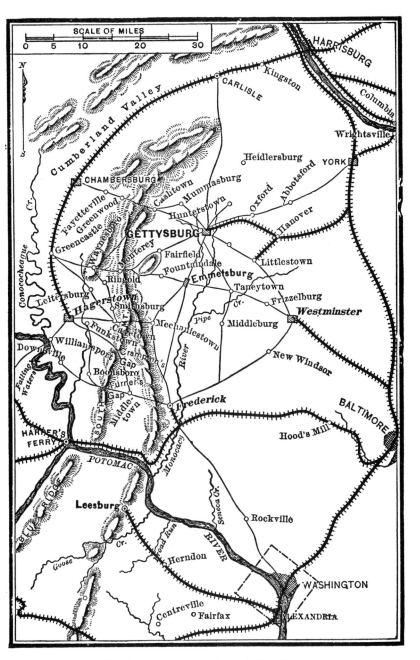

The Country from the Potomac to Harrisburg.

ing Hooker's rear to detain him and delay his crossing the river, and thus give time to Lee to capture Harrisburg, and perhaps Philadelphia. His raid on this occasion was undoubtedly a mistake. When he rejoined the main body, his men were exhausted, his horses broken down, and the battle of Gettysburg was nearly over. As cavalry are the eyes of an army, it has been said that Stuart's absence prevented Lee from ascertaining the movements and position of Hooker's army. Stuart has been loudly blamed by the rebel chroniclers for leaving the main body, but this is unjust; Lee not only knew of the movement, but approved it; for he directed Stuart to pass between Hooker and Washington, and move with part of his force to Carlisle and the other part to Gettysburg. Besides, Stuart left Robertson's and Jones' brigades behind, with orders to follow up the rear of the Union army until it crossed, and then to rejoin the main body. In the meantime they were to hold the gaps in the Blue Ridge, for fear Hooker might send a force to occupy them. These two brigades, with Imboden's brigade, and White's battalion, made quite a large cavalry force: Imboden, however, was also detached to break up the Baltimore and Ohio Railroad to prevent forces from the West from taking Lee in rear; all of which goes to show how sensitive the Confederate commander was in regard to any danger threatening his communications with Richmond.

At 1 A.M on the 25th, Stuart started on his expedition and advanced to Haymarket, where he unexpectedly came upon Hancock's corps, which had left Thoroughfare Gap, and was on its way to Gum Springs. He opened fire against them but was soon driven off. He then returned to Buckland and Gainesville; for to keep on, in presence of our troops, would have frustrated the object of his expedition by indicating its purpose.

This was the day in which Longstreet and Hill united their columns at Hagerstown. Some Union spies who counted the rebel forces as they passed through the town made their number to be 91,000 infantry, 280 guns and 1,100 cavalry. This statement, though much exaggerated, gained great credence at the time, and added to the excitement among the loyal people throughout the Northern States, while the copperhead element were proportionally active and jubilant.

On the 26th, General French assumed command of the garrison at Harper's Ferry, then posted at Maryland Heights.

On the same day the Richmond Government were much alarmed by the unexpected appearance of Colonel Spear's Eleventh Pennsylvania cavalry within eleven miles of the city. Spear had made quite a successful and very destructive raid on the railroads and other lines of communication. He made, too, a very important capture by bringing in General W. H. F. Lee, who was wounded at the battle of Brandy Station, and who was a son of General Robert E. Lee. The Davis Government had determined to hang one of our captains who was a prisoner in Libby, and the fact that a son of General Robert E. Lee was in our power prevented them from carrying out their intention for fear he might be hanged by way of retaliation.

Early's division of Ewell's corps, stopped at Gettysburg on its way to York. The other two divisions kept on toward Carlisle.

These movements at once caused Governor Curtin of Pennsylvania to call out 60,000 men for the defence of the State. They were styled the emergency militia. As there was little else than shot-guns for them, these hasty gatherings did not promise to be very effective.

The Governor still complained of a lack of zeal in Philadelphia. The people there, said "Isn't this awful!" but very few volunteered. They soon awoke from their apathy, however, and took prompt measures to defend the city.

On the 27th the commands of Longstreet and Hill reached Chambersburg, and Ewell's two divisions occupied Carlisle, while Jenkins pushed on to Kingston, within thirteen miles of Harrisburg. At the same time Early was engaged in wreaking destruction upon the Northern Central Railroad, and by night he entered York. About the only opposition he encountered came from a militia regiment at Gettysburg, but this was soon driven away.

There was wild commotion throughout the North, and people began to feel that the boast of the Georgia Senator Toombs, that he would call the roll of his slaves at the foot of Bunker Hill Monument, might soon be realized. The enemy seemed very near and the Army of the Potomac far away.

On the same day Stuart succeeded with great difficulty in crossing the Potomac in the vicinity of Drainsville. He found our troops were now all north of the river, so that one object of his expedition—to detain them on the south side—had failed.

On the 28th he resumed his march, and as he passed close to Washington and Baltimore, he created considerable excitement in those cities. At Rockville he came upon a large train full of supplies, on its way to Frederick, Maryland, and captured it with its slender escort, after which he kept on in a northerly direction through Brookeville and Cookesville, travelling all night.

On this day the Adjutant-General at Richmond telegraphed for troops to be sent there at once from the Carolinas and elsewhere, for he estimated the Union forces at the White House at thirty thousand men, and considered the capital to be in great danger. Neither Davis nor his cabinet had the slightest desire to have any successes Lee might obtain at the North supplemented by their own execution at the South, a result they felt was not wholly improbable, in the excited state of public feeling at that time, if the city should be taken.

Lee, ignorant that Hooker was following him up, continued his aggressive advance. Early took prompt measures to seize the bridge over the Susquehanna at Wrightsville. If successful, he intended to cross over and amuse himself by destroying all direct connection between Philadelphia and the West, by railroad and telegraph. This done, he proposed to march along the north side of the river, capture Harrisburg and rejoin Ewell at Carlisle. As Gordon's brigade approached the bridge, after driving away some militia, they found it in flames, the Union commander at Columbia, Colonel Frick, having given orders for its destruction. Early gained some compensation for his failure in this respect by levying a contribution on York of one-hundred thousand dollars in cash; two hundred barrels of flour; thirty thousand bushels of corn; one thousand pairs of shoes, etc.

The Union army still remained in Frederick, with the left wing (three corps) under Reynolds thrown out toward the enemy, the Eleventh Corps under Howard at Boonsborough, the First Corps under my command at Middletown, supported by the Third Corps under Birney, two or three miles in rear, with Buford's division of cavalry holding the passes of South Mountain, the remainder of the cavalry being at Frederick.

Hooker thought it useless to keep a garrison of 10,000 men in a passive attitude at Harper's Ferry. I think he was quite right, for the war could not be decided by the possession of military posts or even of cities, for hostilities would never cease until one army or the other was destroyed. He therefore applied to Washington for permission to add this force to that of Slocum, in order that the two might act directly against Lee's communications by following up his rear while preserving their own line of retreat. Slocum had been already ordered there, for this purpose, but Halleck would not consent that the garrison of Harper's Ferry should be withdrawn under any circumstances, and positively refused Hooker's request. Hooker then considering himself thwarted in all his plans by the authorities at Washington, offered his resignation. It was promptly accepted, and Major-General George G. Meade, then the commander of the Fifth Corps, was assigned to the command of the Army of the Potomac. He was a general of fine intellect, of great personal bravery, and had had a good deal of experience in the war in handling troops, but had never achieved any brilliant success, or met with any serious reverse.

Upon ascertaiuing that the enemy were at York and Carlisle, Hooker had determined to throw out his different corps in a fan shape toward the Susquehanna, and advance in that direction with three corps on the left to defend that flank, in case Longstreet and Hill should turn East, instead of keeping on toward the North. At the same time it was his intention to have Slocum follow up Lee's advance, by keeping in his rear, to capture his trains and couriers, and to cut off his retreat should he be defeated.

General Meade's first order was for all the troops to concentrate in Frederick, where he proposed to have a grand review; but at the urgent remonstrance of General Butterfield, who had been Hooker's Chief of Staff, and who

stated that this delay would give Lee time to cross the Susquehanna, and capture Harrisburg and Philadelphia,
Hooker's orders were allowed to stand, with some exceptions. Meade appears to have disapproved all movements
against Lee's line of retreat, for he ordered Slocum to rejoin the main army, and had the hardihood to break up the
post at Harper's Ferry, in spite of the fact that Hooker had
just been relieved from command for requesting permission
to do so. The bulk of the garrison, under Major-General
French, was directed to take post as a reserve at Frederick,
when our forces moved forward. The general idea of our
advance was to interpose between the enemy and Philadelphia if he went north, or between him and Baltimore and
Washington in case he turned back. The orders at night
were for Buford's division of cavalry to take post on the left
flank, in the direction of Fairfield; Gregg's division on the
right flank at Westminster; and Kilpatrick's division in advance of the centre, at Littlestown, the different corps to
be posted between New Windsor and Emmetsburg.

Ewell's corps, as stated, were at Carlisle and York, Lee
and Longstreet's at Chambersburg, and Hill's corps at
Fayetteville.

Lee was startled to learn from a countryman who came
in on the 28th that Hooker was at Frederick, and not south
of the Potomac, as he had supposed. He saw at once that
his communications with Richmond, about which he was so
solicitous, were greatly endangered, for the Union army
could be formed to interpose between him and Williamsport, and still keep a safe line of retreat open to Washington. This might not be so great a misfortune to the enemy as regards food and forage; for they could probably
live on the country for some time, by making predatory excursions in different directions, but when it came to obtain-

ing fresh supplies of ammunition, the matter would become very serious. An army only carries a limited amount of this into the field and must rely upon frequent convoys to keep up the supply, which is constantly decreasing from the partial engagements and skirmishes, so prevalent in a hostile country.

The wisdom of Hooker's policy in desiring to assail the rebel communications is demonstrated by the fact that Lee immediately turned back. The head of the serpent faced about as soon as its tail was trodden upon. He came to the conclusion to prevent an attack against his rear by threatening Baltimore with his whole force. This would necessarily cause the Union army to march farther east to confront him, and thus prevent it from operating in heavy force in the Cumberland Valley. Accordingly on the night of the 28th, Lee sent expresses to all his corps commanders to concentrate at Gettysburg. If he had known that Meade was about to withdraw all the troops acting against his line of retreat he would probably have gone on and taken Harrisburg.

As the new commander of the Union army was a favorite of General Halleck, no notice was taken of his disregard of instructions in detaching the garrison of Harper's Ferry. General Couch, who commanded the Department of the Susquehanna, was also placed under his orders, a favor which had been denied to Hooker. The troubles of the latter were not quite over, for on his appearing in Washington to explain his action, he was immediately put under arrest for visiting the Capital without his (Halleck's) permission; a piece of petty persecution which might have been spared under the circumstances. It was, however, a short and easy method of settling all complaints that were inconvenient to answer.

CHAPTER III.

STUART'S RAID—THE ENEMY IN FRONT OF HARRIS-
BURG—MEADE'S PLANS.

At dawn of day on the 29th, Stuart's command, after riding all night, reached the Baltimore and Ohio Railroad and commenced disabling it, so far as the limited time at their disposal would allow, by burning a bridge at Sykesville and tearing up a portion of the track at Hood's Mill. They remained at the latter place during the day to rest, but started again in the afternoon, and reached Westminster about 5 P.M. At this place they were gallantly attacked by the First Delaware Cavalry, which Stuart says was driven off after hard fighting and pursued some distance toward Balti-more, adding very much to the panic there. At night the head of his column halted at Union Mills, half way between Westminster and Littlestown. It may as well be stated here that Stuart found himself greatly embarrassed by at-tempting to hold on to the long train he had captured at Rockville. It lengthened out his column to such an extent that it became difficult to defend all parts of the line with-out scattering and weakening his command. As Kilpatrick's division was waiting to intercept him at Littlestown, this consideration became a matter of considerable importance. Gregg's division also moved in the morning to head him off at Westminster, but owing to the roads being very much blocked up by our infantry and trains marching in that direction, Gregg did not succeed in reaching his destination until some hours after Stuart had passed.

At night two brigades of Buford's division of cavalry covered the left flank of the Union army near Fairfield, with one brigade at Mechanicstown. The First and Eleventh Corps were at Emmetsburg, the Third and Twelfth at Middleburg, the Fifth Corps at Taneytown, the Second Corps at Uniontown, and the Sixth Corps at New Windsor.

The advance of the rebel cavalry under Jenkins were now within sight of Harrisburg, and skirmishing only four miles from the town. Jenkins's object was to make a thorough reconnoissance in order to ascertain the best positions to be taken for an attack. There was a perfect exodus from the city. All business was suspended, too, in Philadelphia, and the authorities there busied themselves in hastening the work on the fortifications in the suburbs of the city. They were active enough now, and large numbers were enrolled. Pleasonton, who was under general orders to guard the flank nearest the enemy, directed Buford on the 29th to occupy Gettysburg the next day, and hold it until the Army of the Potomac came to his relief. He realized the importance of the position to the future success of our arms.

Hill's corps was at Fayetteville on the 29th, but one division, that of Heth, was thrown forward on that day to Cashtown, within eight miles of Gettysburg. The object of the movement was to join Ewell at York, and co-operate with him in the destruction of the railroads on the other side of the Susquehanna, etc. This plan, as I have already stated, was suddenly changed on the evening of the 28th, when Lee found his communications endangered, and now all the advanced troops under his command turned back to concentrate at Gettysburg. Longstreet left Chambersburg and marched to Fayetteville, leaving Pickett's division behind to guard the trains. Early received the order to return in the afternoon of the 29th, recalled Gordon's brigade from Wrightsville, and made preparations to start the next morning. Rodes's and Johnson's divisions left Carlisle and marched on Gettysburg; the former by the direct route, and the latter by way of Greenwood, to convoy the trains full of stolen property.

A number of partisan skirmishes took place during the day, which were creditable to our troops, particularly that at McConnellsburg, to the west of Chambersburg.

The raid against Richmond ended by the return of Colonel Spear's regiment to the White House. Hooker had urged that General Dix assume command of all his available troops, march against Richmond, and plant himself firmly on Lee's line of communications, but his recommendations were slighted by Halleck. There was much disappointment in the North at this failure to make a serious attack on the rebel capital, for it was generally believed that it might have been captured by a *coup de main.*

On the 30th General Meade advanced his army still nearer the Susquehanna. At evening his extreme left, the First Corps, was at Marsh Creek, on the Emmetsburg road, while the extreme right, the Sixth Corps, was away off at Manchester. The intermediate corps were posted, the Eleventh at Emmetsburg; the Second at Uniontown; the Third at Taneytown; the Fifth at Union Mills, and the Twelfth at Frizzelburg. General French moved from Harper's Ferry with the bulk of the garrison and occupied Frederick. The First Corps was ordered to Gettysburg, but General Reynolds halted it at Marsh Creek, as the enemy were reported to be coming from the direction of Fairfield.

Meade now resolved to take up a defensive position on

Pipe Creek. He threw out his forces as before in a fan shape, but any corps encountering the enemy was expected to fight in retreat until it reached the new line, where all the corps were to assemble. This line as laid out was a long one, extending from Manchester to Middleburg, a distance of about twenty-five miles. Falling back to fight again, is hardly to be commended, as it chills the ardor of the men ; nor is it certain that Lee would have attacked the intrenchments at Pipe Creek. If he found them formidable he might have preferred to fight on the defensive with two corps, while the Third Corps took Harrisburg, and broke up the railroad lines to the west, or marched directly against Philadelphia ; or, as Pipe Creek did not interfere with his communications in any way he might have chosen to let it severely alone, and have kept on depredating in Pennsylvania, after capturing Harrisburg. This would have forced Meade sooner or later to attack him.

On the night of the 30th Ewell's corps had reached Heidlersburg, nine miles from Gettysburg, with the exception of Johnson's division, which was at Greenwood. Rodes's division had marched direct from Carlisle by way of Petersburg. Longstreet with two divisions was at Fayetteville ; the other division, that of Pickett, was left at Chambersburg to guard the trains. Hill's corps had reached Cashtown and Mummasburg, except Anderson's division, which was still back at the mountain pass on the Chambersburg road.

Stuart, ascertaining that Early was no longer at York, and not knowing that the army was concentrating on Gettysburg, turned toward Carlisle. He had bivouacked half way between Westminster and Littlestown, but having ascertained that Kilpatrick was waiting for him at the latter place, attempted to avoid the encounter by going through cross roads to Hanover. He found Farnsworth's brigade of cavalry there, however, and charged their rear, driving them back and capturing some prisoners and ambulances. The Fifth New York made a counter-charge under Major Hammond and drove him out again. He claims to have taken the town by the aid of Hampton's brigade, which arrived in time to reinforce him. Custer's brigade then came up from Abbotstown. The battle lasted until night, when Stuart gave up the contest and retreated, leaving Kilpatrick in possession.

Part of his cavalry also attacked the Fifth and Sixth Michigan regiments at Littlestown, but were repulsed. He then, having no time to spare, kept on his way toward York to find the army he had lost. He passed within seven miles of Ewell's column on its way to Gettysburg, and neither knew that the other was near. Had they effected a junction it would have saved the rebel cavalry a long, fruitless, and exhausting march, which kept them out of the battle on the first day. It was one of those accidental circumstances which seemed to favor us in this campaign, while almost every incident at Chancellorsville was against us.

Finding Ewell had left York, Stuart turned and marched on Carlisle, which he found occupied by our troops. He demanded the surrender of the place under a threat of bombardment. General W. F. Smith, one of the heroes of the Peninsula, was not to be affected by menaces; and Stuart, whose time was precious and who had no ammunition to spare, turned off in hopes of reaching Gettysburg in time to take part in the battle. He arrived there on the afternoon of the 2d, with horses and men worn out by their extraordinary exertions; on their way whole regiments slept in the saddle. This force when it reached the field found

Robertson's, Jones's, and Jenkins's brigades, and White's battalion ready to join it.

By evening Meade was fully apprised, by telegrams and Buford's scouts, that the enemy were concentrating on Gettysburg. He knew that Reynolds at Marsh Creek was only about six miles from Hill at Cashtown, but he sent no orders that night. He simply stated that the enemy were marching on Gettysburg, and he would issue orders when they developed their intentions. Thus the opposing forces were moving in directions that would necessarily bring them in contact, and a fight or a retreat was inevitable.

Reynolds had the true spirit of a soldier. He was a Pennsylvanian, and, inflamed at seeing the devastation of his native State, was most desirous of getting at the enemy as soon as possible. I speak from my own knowledge, for I was his second in command, and he told me at Poolesville soon after crossing the river, that it was necessary to attack the enemy at once, to prevent his plundering the whole State. As he had great confidence in his men, it was not difficult to divine what his decision would be. He determined to advance and hold Gettysburg. He directed the Eleventh Corps to come up as a support to the First, and he recommended, but did not order, the Third Corps to do the same.

Buford, with two of his cavalry brigades, reached the place that night, but not without considerable difficulty. He left Fountaindale Gap early in the morning and attempted to move directly to his destination, but he came upon Pettigrew's brigade of Hill's corps, and was obliged to fall back to the mountains again. Later in the day he succeeded, by going around by way of Emmetsburg. Before evening set in, he had thrown out his pickets almost to Cashtown and Hunterstown, posting Gamble's brigade across the Cham-

bersburg pike, and Devin's brigade across the Mummasburg road, his main body being about a mile west of the
town.

While these great movements were going on, some minor
affairs showed great gallantry on the part of partisan officers.
Captain Ulric Dahlgren made a raid upon the rebel communications, capturing some guns and prisoners, and gaining very important information which will be referred to
hereafter.

The two armies now about to contest on the perilous
ridges of Gettysburg the possession of the Northern States,
and the ultimate triumph of freedom or slavery, were in
numbers as follows, according to the estimate made by the
Count of Paris, who is an impartial observer, and who has
made a close study of the question:

The Army of the Potomac under General Meade, 82,000 men and 300
guns.

The Army of Northern Virginia under General Lee, 73,500 men and
190 guns.

Stuart had 11,100 cavalry and 16 guns.

Pleasonton had about the same number of cavalry, and 27 guns.

CHAPTER IV.

THE FIRST DAY OF THE BATTLE OF GETTYSBURG, WEDNESDAY, JULY 1, 1863.

On the morning of the 1st of July, General Buford, as stated, held the ridges to the west of Gettysburg, with his cavalry division, composed of Gamble's and Devens's brigades. His vedettes were thrown far out toward the enemy to give timely notice of any movement, for he was determined to prevent the rebels from entering the town if possible, and knew the First Corps would soon be up to support him. The enemy were not aware that there was any considerable force in the vicinity, and in the morning sent forward Heth's division of Hill's corps to occupy the place, anticipating no difficulty in doing so. Buford in the meantime had dismounted a large part of his force, had strengthened his line of skirmishers, and planted his batteries at the most commanding points.

General Reynolds, in consequence of the duties devolving upon him as commander of the Left Wing of the army, that is of the First, Third, and Eleventh Corps, had turned over the command of the First Corps to me. He now made immediate dispositions to go forward to assist Buford.

As my corps was largely engaged in the first day's operations, I must be excused for having a good deal to say in the first person in relation to them. Reynolds sent for me about six o'clock in the morning, read to me the various despatches he had received from Meade and Buford, and told me he should go forward at once with the nearest division—that of Wadsworth—to aid the cavalry. He then instructed me to draw in my pickets, assemble the artillery and the remainder of the corps, and join him as soon as possible. Having given these orders he rode off at the head of the column, and I never saw him again.

The position of the two armies on the morning of the 1st of July, was as follows: The First Corps at Marsh Creek; the Second and Third Corps at Taneytown; the latter being under orders to march to Emmetsburg, to relieve the Eleventh Corps, which was directed to join the First Corps at Gettysburg; the Twelfth Corps was at Two Taverns; the Fifth Corps at Hanover, and the Sixth Corps

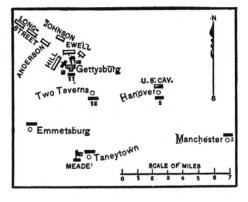

about thirty-five miles off to the right at Manchester. Kilpatrick's and Gregg's divisions of cavalry were also at Hanover. The Confederate army was advancing on Gettysburg from the west and north. The concentration of their troops and the dispersion of ours are indicated on the map.

It must be remembered that the enemy had but *three* corps, while the Union army had *seven*. Each of their corps represented a *third,* and each of ours a *seventh,* of our total force. The same ratio extended to divisions and brigades.

Heth's division, which started early in the morning to occupy the town, soon found itself confronted by Buford's skirmishers, and formed line of battle with Archer's and Davis's brigades in front, followed by those of Pettigrew and Brockenborough. At 9 A.M. the first gun was heard. Buford had three cannon-shots fired as a signal for his skirmish line to open on the enemy, and the battle of Gettysburg began.[1]

As the rebels had had several encounters with militia, who were easily dispersed, they did not expect to meet any serious resistance at this time, and advanced confidently and carelessly. Buford gave way slowly, taking advantage of every accident of ground to protract the struggle. After an hour's fighting he felt anxious, and went up into the steeple of the Theological Seminary from which a wide view could be obtained, to see if the First Corps was in sight. One division of it was close at hand, and soon Reynolds, who had preceded it, climbed up into the belfry to confer with him there, and examine the country around. Although there is no positive testimony to that effect, his attention was doubtless attracted to Cemetery Ridge in his rear, as it was one of the most prominent features of the landscape. An aide of General Howard—presumably Major Hall--soon after Reynolds descended from the belfry, came up to ask if he had any instructions with regard to the Eleventh Corps. Reynolds, in reply, directed that General Howard bring his corps forward at once and *form them on Cemetery Hill* as a reserve. General Howard has no recollection of having received any

---

[1] Lt.-Col. Kress, of General Wadsworth's staff, entered Gettysburg about this time and found General Buford surrounded by his staff in front of the tavern there. Buford turned to him and said. "What are you doing here, sir?" Kress replied that he came on to get some shoes for Wadsworth's division. Buford told him he had better return immediately to his command. Kress said, "Why, what is the matter, general?" At that moment the far off sound of a single gun was heard, and Buford replied, as he mounted his horse and galloped off, "*That's the matter.*"

such orders, but as he did get orders to come forward, and as his corps was to occupy *some place* in rear, as a support to the First Corps, nothing is more probable than that General Reynolds directed him to go there; for its military advantages were obvious enough to any experienced commander.   Lieutenant Rosengarten, of General Reynolds's staff, states positively that he was present and heard the order given for Howard to post his troops on Cemetery Ridge. The matter is of some moment, as the position in question ultimately gave us the victory, and Howard received the

thanks of Congress for selecting it. It is not to be supposed that either Howard or Rosengarten would misstate the matter. It is quite probable that Reynolds chose the hill simply as a position upon which his force 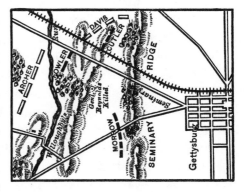 could rally if driven back, and Howard selected it as a suitable battle-field for the army. It has since been universally conceded that it was admirably adapted for that purpose.

It will be seen from the above map, that there are two roads coming into Gettysburg from the west, making a considerable angle with each other.   Each is intersected by ridges running north and south.   On that nearest to the town, and about three-fourths of a mile from the central square, there is a large brick building, which was used as a Lutheran Theological Seminary.   A small stream of water called Willoughby's Run winds between the next two ridges. The battle on the first day was principally fought on the heights on each side of this stream.

Buford being aware that Ewell's corps would soon be on its way from Heidlersburg to the field of battle was obliged to form line facing north with Devin's brigade, and leave Gamble's brigade to keep back the overpowering weight of Hill's corps advancing from the west.

While this fighting was going on, and Reynolds and Wadsworth were presssing to the front, I was engaged in withdrawing the pickets and assembling the other two divisions, together with the corps artillery. As soon as I saw that my orders were in process of execution, I galloped to the front, leaving the troops to follow, and caught up with Meredith's brigade of Wadsworth's division, commonly called "The Iron Brigade," just as it was going into action.

In the meantime the enemy approaching from the west were pressing with great force against Buford's slender skirmish line, and Reynolds went forward with Cutler's brigade to sustain it. He skilfully posted Hall's Second Maine battery in the road, and threw forward two regiments, the Fourteenth Brooklyn and Ninety-fifth New York, a short distance in advance on the left. At the same time he directed General Wadsworth to place the remaining three regiments of the brigade, the One Hundred and Forty-seventh New York, the Seventy-sixth New York, and the Fifty-sixth Pennsylvania on the right of the road. When this formation was completed the cavalry brigade under Gamble, which had been fighting there, withdrew and formed in column on the left of the infantry; but the other cavalry brigade under Devin, which was not facing in that direction, still held its position, awaiting the advance of Ewell's corps from the north.

As Davis's rebel brigade of Heth's division fronting Wadsworth were hidden behind an intervening ridge, Wadsworth did not see them at first, but formed his three regiments perpendicularly to the road, without a reconnoissance. The result was that Davis came over the hill almost directly on the right flank of this line, which being unable to defend itself, was forced back and directed by Wadsworth to take post in a piece of woods in rear on Seminary Ridge. The two regiments on the right accordingly withdrew, but the One Hundred and Forty-seventh New York, which was next to the road, did not receive the order, as their Colonel was shot down before he could deliver it. They were at once surrounded and very much cut up before they could be rescued from their perilous position.

The two regiments on the right, which were forced back, were veterans, conspicuous for gallantry in every battle in which the Army of the Potomac had been engaged since the Peninsula campaign. As Wadsworth withdrew them without notifying Hall's battery in the road, or the two regiments posted by Reynolds on the left, both became exposed to a disastrous flank attack on the right. Hall finding a cloud of skirmishers launched against his battery which was now without support, was compelled to retreat. The horses of the last gun were all shot or bayonetted. The non-military reader will see that while a battery can keep back masses of men it cannot contend with a line of skirmishers. To resist them would be very much like fighting mosquitoes with musket-balls. The two regiments posted by Reynolds, the Fourteenth Brooklyn and Ninety-fifth New York, finding their support gone on the right, while Archer's rebel brigade was advancing to envelop their left, fell back leisurely under Colonel Fowler of the Fourteenth Brooklyn, who assumed command of both as the ranking officer present.

I reached the field just as the attack on Cutler's brigade was going on, and at once sent my adjutant-general, Major Halstead, and young Meredith L. Jones, who was acting as aide on my staff, to General Reynolds to ask instructions. Under the impression that the enemy's columns were approaching on both roads, Reynolds said, "Tell Doubleday I will hold on to this road," referring to the Chambersburg road, "and he must hold on to that one;" meaning the road to Fairfield or Hagerstown. At the same time he sent Jones back at full speed to bring up a battery.

The rebels, however, did not advance on the Fairfield road until late in the afternoon. They must have been in force upon it some miles back, for the cavalry so reported, and this caused me during the entire day to give more attention than was necessary to my left, as I feared the enemy might separate my corps from the Third and Eleventh Corps at Emmetsburg. Such a movement would be equivalent to interposing between the First Corps and the main army.

There was a piece of woods between the two roads, with open ground on each side. It seemed to me this was the key of the position, for if this woods was strongly held, the enemy could not pass on either road without being taken in flank by the infantry, and in front by the cavalry. I therefore urged the men as they filed past me to hold it at all hazards. Full of enthusiasm and the memory of their past achievements they said to me proudly, "*If we can't hold it, where will you find the men who can?*"

As they went forward under command of Colonel Morrow[1] of the Twenty-fourth Michigan Volunteers, a brave and capable soldier, who, when a mere youth, was engaged in the Mexican War, I rode over to the left to see if the enemy's

---

[1] I sent orders to Morrow under the supposition that he was the ranking officer of the brigade. Colonel W. W. Robinson, Seventh Wisconsin, was entitled to the command, and exercised it during the remainder of the battle.

line extended beyond ours, and if there would be any attempt to flank our troops in that direction. I saw, however, only a few skirmishers, and returned to organize a reserve. I knew there was fighting going on between Cutler's brigade and the rebels in his front, but as General Reynolds was there in person, I only attended to my own part of the line; and halted the Sixth Wisconsin regiment as it was going into action, together with a hundred men of the Brigade Guard, taken from the One Hundred and Forty-ninth Pennsylvania, to station them in the open space between the Seminary and the woods, as a reserve, the whole being under the command of Lieut.-Colonel R. R. Dawes, of the Sixth Wisconsin.

It is proper to state that General Meredith, the permanent commander of the brigade, was wounded as he was coming up, some time after its arrival, by a shell which exploded in front of his horse.

Both parties were now trying to obtain possession of the woods. Archer's rebel brigade, preceded by a skirmish line, was crossing Willoughby's Run to enter them on one side as the Iron Brigade went in on the other. General Reynolds was on horseback in the edge of the woods, surrounded by his staff. He felt some anxiety as to the result, and turned his head frequently to see if our troops would be up in time. While looking back in this way, a rebel sharpshooter shot him through the back of the head, the bullet coming out near the eye. He fell dead in an instant, without a word. The country sustained great loss in his death. I lamented him as almost a life-long companion. We were at West Point together, and had served in the same regiment—the old Third Artillery—upon first entering service, along with our present Commander-in-Chief, General Sherman, and General George H. Thomas. When quite young we had fought in the same battles in Mexico. There was little time, however, to indulge in these recollections. The situation was very peculiar. The rebel left under Davis had driven in Cutler's brigade and our left under Morrow had charged into the woods, preceded by the Second Wisconsin under Colonel Fairchild, swept suddenly and unexpectedly around the right flank of Archer's brigade, and captured a large part of it, including Archer himself. The fact is, the enemy were careless and underrated us, thinking, it is said, that they had only militia to contend with. The Iron Brigade had a different head-gear from the rest of the army and were recognized at once by their old antagonists. Some of the latter were heard to exclaim " There are those d——d black-hatted fellows again ! 'Taint no militia. It's the Army of the Potomac."

Having captured Archer and his men, many of the Iron Brigade kept on beyond Willoughby's Run, and formed on the heights on the opposite side.

The command now devolved upon me, with its great responsibilities. The disaster on the right required immediate attention, for the enemy, with loud yells, were pursuing Cutler's brigade toward the town. I at once ordered my reserve under Lieutenant-Colonel Dawes to advance against their flank. If they faced Dawes, I reasoned that they would present their other flank to Cutler's men, so that I felt quite confident of the result. In war, however, unexpected changes are constantly occurring. Cutler's brigade had been withdrawn by order of General Wadsworth, without my knowledge, to the suburbs of Gettysburg. Fortunately, Fowler's two regiments came on to join Dawes, who went forward with great spirit, but who was altogether too weak to assail so large a force. As he approached, the rebels ceased to pursue Cutler, and rushed into the railroad cut to obtain the shelter of the grading. They made a fierce and obstinate resistance,

but, while Fowler confronted them above, about twenty
of Dawes' men were formed across the cut by his adjutant, E. P. Brooks, to fire through it.   The rebels could not
resist this; the greater number gave themselves up as
prisoners, and the others scattered over the country and
escaped.

This success relieved the One Hundred and Forty-seventh
New York, which, as I stated, was surrounded when Cutler
fell back, and it also enabled us to regain the gun which
Hall had been obliged to abandon.

The enemy having vanished from our immediate front,
I withdrew the Iron
Brigade from its ad-
vanced position be-
yond the creek, re-
formed the line on
the ridge where Gen-
eral Reynolds had
originally placed it,
and awaited a fresh
attack, or orders from
General Meade. The

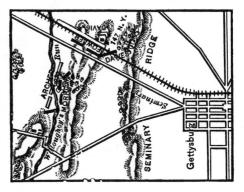

two regiments of Cutler's brigade were brought back from
the town, and, notwithstanding the check they had received,
they fought with great gallantry throughout the three days'
battle that ensued.

There was now a lull in the combat. I was waiting for
the remainder of the First Corps to come up, and Heth was
reorganizing his shattered front line, and preparing to
bring his two other brigades forward. The remnant of
Archer's brigade was placed on the right, and made to
face south against Buford's cavalry, which, it was feared,
might attack that flank. What was left of Davis's brigade

was sent to the extreme left of the line, and Pegram's artillery was brought forward and posted on the high ground
west of Willoughby's Run.

Thus prepared, and with Pender's strong division in
rear, ready to cover his retreat if defeated, or to follow
up his success if victorious, Heth advanced to renew the
attack.

As I had but four weak infantry brigades at this time
against eight large brigades which were about to assail my
line, I would have been justified in falling back, but I determined to hold on to the position until ordered to leave it. I
did not believe in the system, so prevalent at that time, of
avoiding the enemy. I quite agreed with Reynolds that it
was best to meet him as soon as possible, for the rebellion, if
reduced to a war of positions, would never end so long as the
main army of the Confederates was left in a condition to take
the field. A retreat, too, has a bad effect on the men. It
gives them the impression that their generals think them too
weak to contend with the enemy. I was not aware, at this
time, that Howard was on the ground, for he had given me
no indication of his presence, but I knew that General
Meade was at Taneytown; and as, on the previous evening,
he had informed General Reynolds that the enemy's army
were concentrating on Gettysburg, I thought it probable he
would ride to the front to see for himself what was going
on, and issue definite orders of some kind. As Gettysburg
covered the great roads from Chambersburg to York, Baltimore, and Washington, and as its possession by Lee would
materially shorten and strengthen his line of retreat, I was in
favor of making great sacrifices to hold it.

While we were thus temporarily successful, having captured or dispersed all the forces in our immediate front, a
very misleading despatch was sent to General Meade by Gen-

eral Howard. It seems that General Howard had reached Gettysburg in advance of his corps, just after the two regiments of Cutler's brigade, which had been outflanked, fell back to the town by General Wadsworth's order. Upon witnessing this retreat, which was somewhat disorderly, General Howard hastened to send a special messenger to General Meade with the baleful intelligence that the First Corps had fled from the field at the first contact with the enemy, thus magnifying a forced retreat of two regiments, acting under orders, into the flight of an entire corps, two-thirds of which had not yet reached the field. It is unnecessary to say that this astounding news created the greatest feeling against the corps, who were loudly cursed for their supposed lack of spirit and patriotism.

About 11 A.M. the remainder of the First Corps came up, together with Cooper's, Stewart's, Reynolds's, and Stevens's batteries. By this time the enemy's artillery had been posted on every commanding position to the west of us, several of their batteries firing down the Chambersburg pike. I was very desirous to hold this road, as it was in the centre of the enemy's line, who were advancing on each side of it, and Calef—exposed as his battery was—fired over the crest of ground where he was posted, and notwithstanding the storm of missiles that assailed him, held his own handsomely, and inflicted great damage on his adversaries. He was soon after relieved by Reynolds's Battery "L" of the First New York, which was sustained by Colonel Roy Stone's brigade of Pennsylvania troops, which I ordered there for that purpose. Stone formed his men on the left of the pike, behind a ridge running north and south, and partially sheltered them by a stone fence, some distance in advance, from which he had driven the rebel skirmish line, after an obstinate contest.

It was a hot place for troops ; for the whole position was alive with bursting shells, but the men went forward in fine spirits and, under the impression that the place was to be held at all hazards, they cried out, " *We have come to stay !* " The battle afterward became so severe that the greater portion did stay, laying down their lives there for the cause they loved so well.   Morrow's brigade remained in the woods where Reynolds was killed, and Biddle's brigade was posted on its left in the open ground along the crest of the same ridge, with Cooper's battery in the interval.   Cutler's brigade

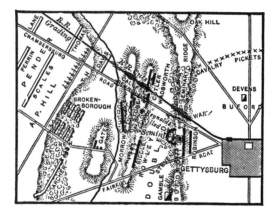

took up its former position on the right of the road.   Having disposed of Wadsworth's division and my own division, which was now under command of Brigadier-General Rowley, I directed General Robinson's division to remain in reserve at the Seminary, and to throw up a small semicircular rail intrenchment in the grove in front of the building.   Toward the close of the action this defence, weak and imperfect as it was, proved to be of great service.

The accompanying map shows the position of troops and batteries at this time.

It will be seen that Heth's division is formed on the western ridge which bounds Willoughby's Run and along a cross-road which intersects the Chambersburg road at right angles.

Pender's division, posted in rear as a support to Heth, was formed in the following order by brigades : Thomas, Lane, Scales, and McGowan (under Perrin) ; the first named on the rebel left and Perrin on the right.   To sustain Heth's advance and crush out all opposition, both Pegràm's and McIntosh's artillery were posted on the crest of the ridge west of the Run.

While this was going on, General Howard, who was await-ing the arrival of his corps, had climbed into the steeple of the seminary to obtain a view of the surrounding country. At 11.30 A.M he learned that General Reynolds was killed, and that the command of the three corps (the First, Eleventh, and Third) constituting the Left Wing of the army devolved upon him by virtue of his rank.   He saw that the First Corps was contending against large odds and sent back for the Eleventh Corps to come up at double-quick.   Upon assuming command of the Left Wing he turned over his own corps to Major-General Carl Schurz, who then gave up the command of his division to General Barlow.   Howard notified General Meade of Reynolds's death, but forgot to take back or modify the false state-ment he had made about the First Corps, now engaged be-fore his eyes, in a most desperate contest with a largely superior force ; so that General Meade was still left under the impression that the First Corps had fled from the field.

Howard also sent a request to Slocum, who was at Two Taverns, only about five miles from Gettysburg, to come forward, but Slocum declined, without orders from Meade. He probably thought if any one commander could assume the direction of other corps, he might antagonize the plans of the General-in-Chief.

Upon receiving the news of the death of General Reynolds

and the disorder which it was supposed had been created by that event, General Meade superseded Howard by sending his junior officer, General Hancock, to assume command of the field, with directions to notify him of the condition of affairs at the front. He also ordered General John Newton of the Sixth Corps to take command of the First Corps.

The head of the Eleventh Corps reached Gettysburg at 12.45 P.M., and the rear at 1.45 P.M. Schimmelpfennig's division led the way, followed by that of Barlow. The two were directed to prolong the line of the First Corps to the right along Seminary Ridge. The remaining division, that of Steinwehr, with the reserve artillery under Major Osborne, were ordered to occupy Cemetery Hill, in rear of Gettysburg, as a reserve to the entire line. Before this disposition could be carried out, however, Buford rode up to me with the information that his scouts reported the advance of Ewell's corps from Heidlersburg directly on my right flank. I sent a staff officer to communicate this intelligence to General Howard, with a message that I would endeavor to hold my ground against A. P. Hill's corps if he could, by means of the Eleventh Corps, keep Ewell from attacking my right. He accordingly directed the Eleventh Corps to change front to meet Ewell. As it did so, Devin's cavalry brigade fell back and took up a position to the right and rear of this line just south of the railroad bridge.

The concentration of Rodes's and Early's divisions—the one from Carlisle and the other from York—took place with great exactness; both arriving in sight of Gettysburg at the same time. The other division, that of Johnson, took a longer route from Carlisle by way of Greenwood, to escort the trains, and did not reach the battle-field until sunset. Anderson's division of Hill's corps was also back at the pass in the mountains on the Chambersburg road. It had halted to allow Johnson to pass, and then followed him to Gettysburg, reaching there about dusk.

The first indication I had that Ewell had arrived, and was taking part in the battle, came from a battery posted on an eminence called Oak Hill, almost directly in the prolongation of my line, and about a mile north of Colonel Stone's position. This opened fire about 1.30 P.M., and rendered new dispositions necessary; for Howard had not guarded my right flank as proposed, and indeed soon had more than he could do to maintain his line. When the guns referred to opened fire, Wadsworth, without waiting for orders, threw Cutler's brigade back into the woods on Seminary Ridge, north of the railroad grading; a movement I sanctioned as necessary. Morrow's brigade was concealed from the view of the enemy, in the woods where Reynolds fell, and Biddle's brigade, by my order, changed front to the north. It could do so with impunity, as it was behind a ridge which concealed its left flank from Hill's corps, and was further protected in that direction by two companies of the Twentieth New York State Militia, who occupied a house and barn in advance, sent there by the colonel of that regiment, Theodore B. Gates, whose skill and energy were of great service to me during the battle.

It would of course have been impossible to hold the line if Hill attacked on the west and Ewell assailed me at the same time on the north; but I occupied the central position, and their converging columns did not strike together until the grand final advance at the close of the day, and therefore I was able to resist several of their isolated attacks before the last crash came.

Stone's brigade in the centre had a difficult angle to defend, but was partially sheltered by a ridge on the west. His position was in truth the key-point of the first day's battle. It overlooked the field, and its possession by the enemy would cut our force in two, enfilade Morrow's and Biddle's brigades, and compel a hasty retreat.

After Hall's battery was driven back, no other artillery occupied the ground for some time, then General Wadsworth borrowed Calef's regular battery from the cavalry, and posted it in rear of the position Hall had occupied. When the remainder of the division came up, Captain Reynolds's Battery "L" of the First New York Artillery, as already stated, was sent to assist Calef in keeping down the fire of two rebel batteries on the ridge to the west; but when Ewell's artillery also opened, the cross fire became too severe. Calef was withdrawn, and Reynolds was severely wounded. The rebel batteries soon after ceased firing for the time being; and at Wadsworth's request, Colonel Wainwright, Chief of Artillery to the First Corps, posted a section of Reynolds's battery, under Lieutenant Wilbur, on Seminary Ridge, south of the railroad cut; Stewart's Battery "B" Fourth United States being on a line north of the cut. Cooper's battery was directed to meet Ewell's attack from the north, and Stevens's Fifth Maine battery was retained behind the Seminary in reserve.

Barlow's division on the right and Schimmelpfennig's on the left, formed somewhat hastily against Ewell, whose line of battle faced south. Barlow rested his right on a wooded knoll, constituting part of the western bank of Rock Creek. As there was an open country to the east he considered that flank secure, for no enemy was in sight there, and if they came from that direction, there would be time to make fresh dispositions. After the formation there was an interval of a quarter of a mile between their left and the First Corps which might have been avoided by placing the two divisions farther apart. This was a serious thing to me, for the attempt to fill this interval and prevent the enemy from penetrating there, lengthened and weakened my line, and used up my reserves. It seems to me that the Eleventh Corps were too far out. It would have been better, in my opinion, if its left had been *echeloned* in rear of the right of the First Corps, and its right had rested on the strong brick buildings with stone foundations at the Almshouse. The enemy then could not have turned the right without compromising the safety of the turning column and endangering his communications ; a movement he would hardly like to make, especially as he did not know what troops might be coming up. Still they had a preponderating force, and as their whole army was concentrating on Gettysburg, it was not possible to keep them back for any great length of time unless the First and Eleventh Corps were heavily reinforced. The position of our forces and those of the enemy, will be best understood by a reference to the map on page 125.

About 2 P.M., after the Eleventh Corps line was formed, General Howard rode over, inspected, and approved it. He also examined my position and gave orders, in case I was forced to retreat, to fall back to Cemetery Hill. I think this was the first and only order I received from him during the day.

Rodes's division of five brigades was formed across Seminary Ridge, facing south, with Iverson on the right, supported by Daniels and O'Neil in the centre, and Dole on the left, Ramseur being in reserve. Iverson was sent to attack the First Corps on Seminary Ridge, and O'Neil and Dole went forward about 2.45 P.M., to keep back the Eleventh Corps. When the two latter became fairly engaged in front, about 3.30 P.M., Early came up with his whole division and struck the Union right. This decided the battle in favor of the enemy.

Barlow had advanced with Von Gilsa's brigade, had driven back Ewell's skirmish line, and with the aid of Wilkinson's battery was preparing to hold the Carlisle road. He was not aware that Early was approaching, and saw Dole's advance with pleasure, for he felt confident he could swing his right around and envelop Dole's left; a manœuvre which could hardly fail to be successful.

Schimmelpfennig now threw forward Von Amberg's brigade to intervene between O'Neil and Dole, and to strike the right flank of the latter; but Dole avoided the blow by a rapid change of front. This necessarily exposed his left to Barlow, who could not take advantage of it as he was unexpectedly assailed by Early's division on his own right, which was enveloped, and in great danger. His men fought gallantly, and Gordon, who attacked them, says, made stern resistance until the rebels were within fifty paces of them. As Barlow was shot down, and their right flank enveloped, they were forced to retreat to the town.   This isolated Von Amberg's brigade, and Dole claims to have captured the greater portion of it.

The retrograde movement of the Eleventh Corps necessarily exposed the right flank of the First to attacks from O'Neil and Ramseur.

Howard sent forward Coster's brigade, of Steinwehr's division, to cover the retreat of the Eleventh Corps; but its force was too small to be effective; its flanks were soon turned by Hays's and Hokes's brigades, of Early's division, and it was forced back with the rest.

We will now go back to the First Corps and describe what took place there while these events were transpiring.

When the wide interval between the First and Eleventh Corps was brought to my notice by Colonel Bankhead of my staff, I detached Baxter's brigade of Robinson's division to fill it. This brigade moved promptly, and took post on Cutler's right, but before it could form across the intervening space, O'Neil's brigade assailed its right flank, and subsequently its left, and Baxter was forced to change front alternately, to meet these attacks. He repulsed O'Neil, but found his left flank again exposed to an attack from Iverson, who was advancing in that direction.[1] He now went forward and took shelter behind a stone fence on the Mummasburg road, which protected his right flank, while an angle in the fence which turned in a southwesterly direction covered his front. As his men lay down behind the fence, Iverson's brigade came very close up, not knowing our troops were there. Baxter's men sprang to their feet and delivered a most deadly volley at very short range, which left 500 of Iverson's men dead and wounded, and so demoralized them, that all gave themselves up as prisoners. One regiment, however, after stopping our firing by putting up a white flag, slipped away and escaped. This destructive effect was not caused by Baxter alone, for he was aided by Cutler's brigade, which was thrown forward on Iverson's right flank, by the fire of our batteries, and the distant fire from Stone's brigade. So long as the latter held his position, his line, with that of Cutler and Robinson's division, constituted a demi-bastion and curtain, and every force that entered the angle suffered severely. Rodes in his report speaks of it as "a murderous enfilade, and reverse fire, to which, in addition to the direct fire it encountered, Daniels's brigade had been subject to from the time it commenced its final advance."

While Iverson was making his attack, Rodes sent one of his reserve brigades—the one just referred to, that of Daniels—against Stone. This joined Davis's brigade of Hill's corps, and the two charged on Stone's three little regiments.

[1] General Robinson states that these changes of front were made by his orders and under his personal supervision:

Stone threw forward one of these—the One Hundred and Forty-ninth Pennsylvania, under Lieutenant-Colonel Dwight, to the railroad cut, where they were partially sheltered. Colonel Dana's regiment, the One Hundred and Forty-third Pennsylvania was posted on the road in rear of Dwight and to the right. When I saw this movement I thought it a very bold one, but its results were satisfactory. Two volleys and a bayonet charge by Dwight drove Daniels back for the time being.[1] In this attack Colonel Stone was severely wounded, and the command of his brigade devolved upon Colonel Wister of the One Hundred and Fiftieth Pennsylvania.

This attack should have been simultaneous with one from the nearest troops of Hill's corps, but the latter were lying down in a sheltered position, and Daniels urged them in vain to go forward.

Not being able to force his way in front on account of Dwight's position in the railroad cut, Daniels brought artillery to enfilade it, and threw the Thirty-second North Carolina across it. The cut being no longer tenable, Dwight retreated to the road and formed on Dana's left.

Daniels had been originally ordered to protect Iverson's right, but Iverson swung his right around without notifying Daniels, and thus dislocated the line.

Ramseur now came forward to aid Iverson, and I sent Paul's brigade of Robinson's division, which was preceded

---

[1] Dwight was a hard fighter, and not averse to plain speaking. Once, when Secretary of War Stanton had determined to grant no more passes to go down to the army, Dwight applied for permission for an old man to visit his dying son. The request was refused; whereupon Dwight said: " *My name is Dwight, Walton Dwight, Lieutenant-Colonel of the One Hundred and Forty-ninth Regiment of Pennsylvania Volunteers. You can dismiss me from the service as soon as you like, but I am going to tell you what I think of you,*" and he expressed himself in terms far from complimentary; whereupon Stanton rescinded the order and gave him the pass.

by Robinson in person, to assist Baxter, and, if possible, to fill the interval between the First and Eleventh Corps, for I feared the enemy would penetrate there and turn my right flank.

When Paul's brigade arrived, Baxter was out of ammunition, but proceeded to refill his cartridge-boxes from those of the dead and wounded.

General Howard has stated that the interval referred to was filled by Dilger's and Wheeler's batteries of the Eleventh Corps, but a glance at the official map will show that, before Paul's advance, these batteries were several hundred yards distant from the First Corps.

Another attack was now made from the north and west by both Daniels's and Davis's brigades.   Colonel Wister faced his own regiment, under Lieutenant-Colonel Huidekoper, to the west, and the other two regiments to the north.   The enemy were again repulsed by two volleys and a gallant bayonet charge, led by Huidekoper, who lost an arm in the fight.   Colonel Wister having been shot through the face, the command devolved upon Colonel Dana, another veteran of the Mexican war.

There had been a great lack of co-ordination in these assaults, for they were independent movements, each repulsed in its turn.   The last attack, however, against Wister was extended by Brockenborough's and Pettigrew's brigades to Morrow's front in the woods, but Morrow held on firmly to his position.

I now sent my last reserve, the One Hundred and Fifty-first Pennsylvania, under Lieutenant-Colonel McFarland, to take post between Stone's and Biddle's brigades.

So far I had done all that was possible to defend my front, but circumstances were becoming desperate.   My line was very thin and weak, and my last reserve had been thrown in. As we had positive information that the entire rebel arr was coming on, it was evident enough that we could not contend any longer, unless some other corps came to our assistance. I had previously sent an aide—Lieutenant Slagle—to ask General Howard to reinforce me from Steinwehr's division, but he declined to do so. I now sent my Adjutant-General, Halstead, to reiterate the request, or to obtain for me an order to retreat, as it was impossible for me to remain where I was, in the face of the constantly increasing forces which were approaching from the west. Howard insisted that Halstead mistook rail fences for troops in the distance. The lorgnettes of his staff finally convinced him of his error; he still, however, refused to order me to retire, but sent Halstead off to find Buford's cavalry, and order it to report to me. The First Corps had suffered severely in these encounters, but by this additional delay, and the overwhelming odds against us, it was almost totally sacrificed. General Wadsworth reported half of his men were killed or wounded, and Rowley's division suffered in the same proportion. Stone reported two-thirds of his brigade had fallen. Hardly a field officer remained unhurt. After five color-bearers of the Twenty-fourth Michigan Volunteers had fallen, Colonel Morrow took the flag in his own hands, but was immediately prostrated. A private then seized it, and, although mortally wounded, still held it firmly in his grasp. Similar instances occurred all along the line. General Robinson had two horses shot under him. He reported a loss of 1,667 out of 2,500. Buford was in a distant part of the field, with Devin's brigade, covering the retreat of the Eleventh Corps, and already had all he could attend to. He expressed himself in unequivocal terms at the idea that he could keep back Hill's entire corps with Gamble's cavalry brigade alone.

As Howard seemed to have little or no confidence in his troops on Cemetery Hill, he was perhaps justified in retaining them in line there for the moral effect they would produce.

About the time the Eleventh Corps gave way on the right, the Confederate forces made their final advance in double lines, backed by strong reserves, and it was impossible for the few men left in the First Corps to keep them back, especially as Pender's large division overlapped our left for a quarter of a mile ; Robinson's right was turned, and General Paul was shot through both eyes in the effort to stem the tide. They could not contend against Ramseur in front, and O'Neil on the flank, at the same time.

Under these circumstances it became a pretty serious question how to extricate the First Corps and save its artillery before it was entirely surrounded and captured.

Biddle, Morrow, and Dana were all forced back from the ridge they had defended so long, which bordered Willoughby's Run. Each brigade was flanked, and Stone's men under Dana were assailed in front and on both flanks. Yet even then Daniels speaks of the severe fighting which took place before he could win the position.

What was left of the First Corps after all this slaughter rallied on Seminary Ridge. Many of the men entered a semi-circular rail entrenchment which I had caused to be thrown up early in the day, and held that for a time by lying down and firing over the pile of rails. The enemy were now closing in on us from the south, west, and north, and still no orders came to retreat. Buford arrived about this time, and perceiving that Perrin's brigade in swinging around to envelop our left exposed its right flank, I directed him to charge. He reconnoitered the position they held, but did not carry out the order ; I do not know why. It was said afterward he found the fences to be an impediment ; but he rendered essential service by dismounting his men and throwing them into a grove south of the Fairfield road, where they opened a severe fire, which checked the rebel advance and prevented them from cutting us off from our direct line of retreat to Cemetery Hill.

The first long line that came on from the west was swept away by our artillery, which fired with very destructive effect, taking the rebel line *en echarpe*.

Although the Confederates advanced in such force, our men still made strong resistance around the Seminary, and by the aid of our artillery, which was most effective, beat back and almost destroyed the first line of Scales's brigade, wounding both Scales and Pender. The former states that he arrived within seventy-five feet of the guns, and adds: "Here the fire was most severe. Every field officer but one was killed or wounded. The brigade halted in some confusion to return this fire." My Adjutant-Generals Baird and Halstead, and my aides Lee, Marten, Slagle, Jones, and Lambdin had hot work carrying orders at this time. It is a marvel that any of them survived the storm of bullets that swept the field.

Robinson was forced back toward the Seminary, but halted notwithstanding the pressure upon him, and formed line to save Stewart's battery north of the railroad cut, which had remained too long, and was in danger of being captured.

Cutler's brigade in the meantime had formed behind the railroad grading to face the men who were pursuing the Eleventh Corps. This show of force had a happy effect, for it caused the enemy in that direction to halt and throw out a skirmish line, and the delay enabled the artillery soon after to pass through the interval between Cutler on the north and Buford's cavalry on the south.

As the enemy were closing in upon us and crashes of musketry came from my right and left, I had little hope of saving my guns, but I threw my headquarters guard, under

Captain Glenn of the One Hundred and Forty-ninth Pennsylvania, into the Seminary and kept the right of Scales's brigade back twenty minutes longer, while their left was held by Baxter's brigade of Robinson's division, enabling the few remaining troops, ambulances, and artillery to retreat in comparative safety.   It became necessary, however, to abandon one gun of Captain Reynolds's battery, as several of the horses were shot and there was no time to disengage them from the piece.   Three broken and damaged caisson bodies were also left behind.   The danger at this time came principally from Hokes's and Hays's brigades, which were making their way into the town on the eastern side, threatening to cut us off from Cemetery Hill.   The troops in front of the Seminary were stayed by the firm attitude of Buford's cavalry, and made a bend in their line, apparently with a view to form square.

I waited until the artillery had gone and then rode back to the town with my staff.   As we passed through the streets, pale and frightened women came out and offered us coffee and food, and implored us not to abandon them.

Colonel Livingston of my staff, who had been sent on a message, came back to the Seminary, not knowing that we had left.   He says the enemy were advancing toward the crest very cautiously, evidently under the impression there was an ambuscade waiting for them there.   They were also forming against cavalry.

On the way I must have met an aide that Howard says he sent to me with orders to retreat, but I do not remember receiving any message of the kind.

I observe that Howard in his account of the battle claims to have handled the First and Eleventh Corps from 11 A.M. until 4 P.M.; but at 11 A.M. his corps was away back on the road, and did not arrive until about 1 P.M.

The map previously given on page 125 demonstrates that we were a mere advance guard of the army, and shows the impossibility of our defending Gettysburg for any length of time.

The First Corps was broken and defeated, but not dismayed. There were but few left, but they showed the true spirit of soldiers. They walked leisurely from the Seminary to the town, and did not run. I remember seeing Hall's battery and the Sixth Wisconsin regiment halt from time to time to face the enemy, and fire down the streets. Both Doles and Ramsey claim to have had sharp encounters there. Many of the Eleventh Corps, and part of Robinson's division, which had been far out, were captured in the attempt to reach Steinwehr's division on Cemetery Hill, which was the rallying point.

When I arrived there I found General Howard, surrounded by his staff, awaiting us at the main gate of the cemetery. He made arrangements to hold the road which led up from the town, and which diverged to Baltimore and Taneytown, by directing me to post the First Corps on the left in the cemetery, while he assembled the Eleventh Corps on the right. Soon after he rode over to ask me, in case his men (Steinwehr's division) deserted their guns, to be in readiness to defend them. General Schurz about this time was busily engaged in rallying his men, and did all that was possible to encourage them to form line again. I understood they were told that Sigel had arrived and assumed command, a fiction thought justifiable under the circumstances. It seemed to me that the discredit that attached to them after Chancellorsville had in a measure injured their morale and *esprit-de-corps*, for they were rallied with great difficulty.

About 3.30 P.M. General Hancock arrived with orders from

General Meade to supersede Howard. Congress had passed
a law authorizing the President to put any general over any
other superior in rank if, in his judgment, the good of the
service demanded it, and General Meade now assumed this
power in the name of the President. Owing to the false
despatch Howard had sent early in the day, Meade must
have been under the impression that the First Corps had
fled without fighting. More than half of them, however, lay
dead and wounded on the field, and hardly a field officer
had escaped.

Hancock being his junior, Howard was naturally unwilling
to submit to his authority and, according to Captain Halstead
of my staff, who was present, refused to do so. Howard stated
in a subsequent account of the battle that he merely regarded Hancock as a staff officer acting for General Meade.
He says "General Hancock greeted me in his usual frank
and cordial manner and used these words, ' General Meade
has sent me to represent him on the field.' I replied, ' All
right, Hancock. This is no time for talking. You take the
left of the pike and I will arrange these troops to the right.'
I noticed that he sent Wadsworth's division, without consult-
ing me, to the right of the Eleventh Corps to Culp's Hill, but
as it was just the thing to do I made no objection." He adds
that Hancock did not really relieve him until 7 P.M. Hancock, however, denies that he told Howard he was merely
acting as a staff officer. He says he assumed absolute command at 3.30 P.M. I know he rode over to me and told
me he was in command of the field, and directed me to
send a regiment to the right, and I sent Wadsworth's division there, as my regiments were reduced to the size of companies.

Hancock was much pleased with the ridge we were on, as
a defensive position, and considered it admirably adapted

for a battle-field. Its gentle slopes for artillery, its stone
fences and rocky boulders to shelter infantry, and its rugged
but commanding eminences on either flank, where far-reach-
ing batteries could be posted, were great advantages. It
covered the principal roads to Washington and Baltimore,
and its convex shape, enabling troops to reinforce with
celerity any point of the line from the centre, or by moving
along the chord of the arc, was probably the cause of our
final success. The enemy, on the contrary, having a concave order of battle, was obliged to move troops much
longer distances to support any part of his line, and could
not communicate orders rapidly, nor could the different
corps co-operate promptly with each other. It was Hancock's recommendation that caused Meade to concentrate
his army on this ridge, but Howard received the thanks of
Congress for selecting the position. He, doubtless, did see
its advantages, and recommended it to Hancock. The latter
immediately took measures to hold it as a battle-ground for
the army, while Howard merely used the cemetery as a
rallying point for his defeated troops. Hancock occupied
all the prominent points, and disposed the little cavalry and
infantry he had in such a way as to impress the enemy with
the idea that heavy reinforcements had come up. By occupying Culp's Hill, on the right, with Wadsworth's brigade,
and posting the cavalry on the left to take up a good deal
of space, he made a show of strength not warranted by the
facts. Both Hill and Ewell had received some stunning
blows during the day, and were disposed to be cautious.
They, therefore, did not press forward and take the heights,
as they could easily have done at this time, but not so
readily after an hour's delay, for then Sickles's corps from
Emmetsburg, and Slocum's corps from Two Taverns, began
to approach the position. The two rebel divisions of Ander-

son and Johnson, however, arrived about dusk, which would have still given the enemy a great numerical superiority.

General Lee reached the field before Hancock came, and watched the retreat of the First and Eleventh Corps, and Hancock's movements and dispositions through his field-glass. He was not deceived by this show of force, and sent a recommendation—not an order—to Ewell to follow us up ; but Ewell, in the exercise of his discretion as a corps commander, did not do so. He had lost 3,000 men, and both he and Hill were under orders not to bring on a general engagement. In fact they had had all the fighting they desired for the time being. Colonel Campbell Brown, of Ewell's staff, states that the latter was preparing to move forward against the height, when a false report induced him to send Gordon's brigade to reinforce Smith's brigade on his extreme left, to meet a supposed Union advance in that direction.

The absence of these two brigades decided him to wait for the arrival of Johnson's division before taking further action. When the latter came up, Slocum and Sickles were on the ground, and the opportunity for a successful attack had passed.

In sending Hancock forward with such ample powers, Meade virtually appointed him commander-in-chief for the time being, for he was authorized to say where we would fight, and when, and how. In the present instance, in accordance with his recommendation, orders were immediately sent out for the army to concentrate on Cemetery Ridge. Two-thirds of the Third Corps, and all of the Twelfth came up, and by six o'clock the position became tolerably secure. Stannard's Second Vermont brigade also arrived, and as they formed part of my command, reported to me for duty ; a very welcome reinforcement to my shattered division. Sickles had taken the responsibility of joining us without orders, knowing that we were hard pressed. His command prolonged the line of the First Corps to the left. Slocum's Corps—the Twelfth—was posted, as a reserve, also on the left.

Hancock now relinquished the command of the field to Slocum and rode back to Taneytown to confer with Meade and explain his reasons for choosing the battle-field.

Longstreet's corps soon arrived and joined Ewell and Hill; so that the whole rebel army was ready to act against us the next morning, with the exception of Pickett's division.

At the close of the day General John Newton rode up and took charge of the First Corps by order of General Meade, and I resumed the command of my division. Several incidents occurred during the severe struggle of the first day which are worthy of record.

Colonel Wheelock of the Ninety-seventh New York was cut off during the retreat of Robinson's division, and took refuge in a house. A rebel lieutenant entered and called upon him to surrender his sword. This he declined to do, whereupon the lieutenant called in several of his men, formed them in line, took out his watch and said to the colonel, "You are an old gray-headed man, and I dislike to kill you, but if you don't give up that sword in five minutes, I shall order these men to blow your brains out." When the time was up *the Colonel still refused to surrender.* A sudden tumult at the door, caused by some prisoners attempting to escape, called the lieutenant off for a moment. When he returned the colonel had given his sword to a girl in the house who had asked him for it, and she secreted it between two mattresses. He was then marched to the rear, but being negligently guarded, escaped the same night and returned to his regiment.

Another occurrence recalls Browning's celebrated poem of "An Incident at Ratisbon." An officer of the Sixth Wisconsin approached Lieutenant-Colonel Dawes, the commander of the regiment, after the sharp fight in the railroad cut. The colonel supposed, from the firm and erect attitude of the man, that he came to report for orders of some kind ; but the compressed lips told a different story. With a great effort the officer said, " *Tell them at home I died like a man and a soldier.*" He threw open his breast, displayed a ghastly wound, and dropped dead at the colonel's feet.

Another incident was related to me at the time, but owing to our hurried movements and the vicissitudes of the battle, I have never had an opportunity to verify it. It was said that during the retreat of the artillery one piece of Stewart's battery did not limber up as soon as the others. A rebel officer rushed forward, placed his hand upon it, and presenting a pistol at the back of the driver, directed him not to drive off with the piece. The latter did so, however, received the ball in his body, caught up with the battery and then fell dead.

We lay on our arms that night among the tombs at the Cemetery, so suggestive of the shortness of life and the nothingness of fame ; but the men were little disposed to moralize on themes like these and were too much exhausted to think of anything but much-needed rest.

CHAPTER V.

THE ridge upon which the Union forces were now assem
bling has already been partially described. In two places
it sunk away into intervening valleys. One between Culps
Hill and Cemetery Hill; the other lay for several hundred
yards north of Little Round Top, as the lesser of the two
eminences on the left was called to distinguish it from the
higher peak called Round Top.

At 1 A.M. Meade arrived from Taneytown. When I saw
him, soon after daylight, he seemed utterly worn out and
hollow-eyed. Anxiety and want of sleep were evidently
telling upon him. At dawn he commenced forming his line
by concentrating his forces on the right with a view to de-
scend into the plain and attack Lee's left, and the Twelfth
Corps were sent to Wadsworth's right to take part in the
movement. It seems to me that this would have been a
very hazardous enterprise, and I am not surprised that
both Slocum and Warren reported against it. The Fifth
and Sixth Corps would necessarily be very much fatigued
after making a forced march. To put them in at once, and
direct them to drive a superior force of Lee's veterans out
of a town where every house would have been loop-holed,
and every street barricaded, would hardly have been judi-
cious. If we had succeeded in doing so, it would simply
have reversed the battle of Gettysburg, for the Confederate

army would have fought behind Seminary Ridge, and we would have been exposed in the plain below. Nor do I think it would have been wise strategy to turn their left, and drive them between us and Washington, for it would have enabled them to threaten the capital, strengthen and shorten their line of retreat, and endanger our communications at the same time. It is an open secret that Meade at that time disapproved of the battle-ground Hancock had selected.

Warren and Slocum having reported an attack against Lee's left as unadvisable, Meade began to post troops on our left, with a view to attack the enemy's right. This, in my opinion, would have been much more sensible. Lee, however, solved the problem for him, and, fortunately for us, forced him to remain on the defensive, by ordering an assault against each extremity of the Union line.

There has been much discussion and a good deal of crimination and recrimination among the rebel generals engaged as to which of them lost the battle of Gettysburg.

I have already alluded to the fact that universal experience demonstrates that columns converging on a central force almost invariably fail in their object and are beaten in detail. Gettysburg seems to me a striking exemplification of this; repeated columns of assault launched by Lee against our lines came up in succession and were defeated before the other parts of his army could arrive in time to sustain the attack. It realized the old fable. The peasant could not break the bundle of fagots, but he could break one at a time until all were gone.

Lee's concave form of battle was a great disadvantage, for it took him three times as long as it did us to communicate with different parts of his line, and concentrate troops. His couriers who carried orders and the reinforcements he sent moved on the circumference and ours on the chord of the arc.

The two armies were about a mile apart. The Confederates—Longstreet and Hill—occupied Seminary Ridge, which runs parallel to Cemetery Ridge, upon which our forces were posted. Ewell's corps, on the rebel left, held the town, Hill the centre, and Longstreet the right.

Lee could easily have manoeuvred Meade out of his strong position on the heights, and should have done so. When he determined to attack, he should have commenced at daybreak, for all his force was up except Pickett's division; while two corps of the Union army, the Fifth and Sixth, were still far away, and two brigades of the Third Corps were also absent.

The latter were marching on the Emmetsburg road, and as that was controlled by the enemy, Sickles felt anxious for the safety of his men and trains, and requested that the cavalry be sent to escort them in. This was not done, however. The trains were warned off the road, and the two brigades were, fortunately, not molested.

There has been a great deal of bitter discussion between Longstreet, Fitz Lee, Early, Wilcox, and others as to whether Lee did or did not order an attack to take place at 9 A.M., and as to whether Longstreet was dilatory, and to blame for not making it. When a battle is lost there is always an inquest, and a natural desire on the part of each general to lay the blame on somebody else's shoulders. Longstreet waited until noon for Laws' brigade to come up, and afterward there was a good deal of marching and countermarching to avoid being seen by our troops. There was undoubtedly too much delay. The fact is, Longstreet saw we had a strong position and was not well pleased at the duty assigned him, for he thought it more than probable his attempt would fail. He had urged Lee to take up a position where Meade would be forced to attack him, and was not in very good humor to find his advice disregarded. The rebel commander, however, finding the Army of the Potomac in front of him, having unbounded confidence in his troops, and elated by the success of the first day's fight, believed he could gain a great victory then and there, and end the war, and determined to attempt it. He was sick of these endless delays and constant sacrifices, and hoped one strong sword-thrust would slay his opponent, and enable the South to crown herself queen of the North American continent.

By 9 A.M. our skirmish line, in front of the Peach Orchard, was actively engaged with that of the enemy, who were making a reconnoissance toward the Emmetsburg road. No serious affair, however, occurred for some hours. Meade, as stated, was forming his lines on the right of the position he afterward occupied. The Fifth Corps, which came up about 1 P.M. was posted, as a reserve, south of the Twelfth Corps, with a view to the attack which has already been referred to. About 3 P.M. the Sixth Corps began to arrive from its long and toilsome march of thirty-four miles, and its tired troops were placed on the Taneytown road in the rear of Round Top, to reinforce the other corps in case our troops made an attack on the left. Lee, however, did not wait for Meade to advance against him, but boldly directed that each flank of the Union army should be assailed at the same time, while constant demonstrations against our centre were to be kept up, to prevent either wing from being reinforced. It was another attempt to converge columns with an interval of several miles between them upon a central force, and, like almost all such enterprises, failed from want of proper co-operation in the different fractions of his line.

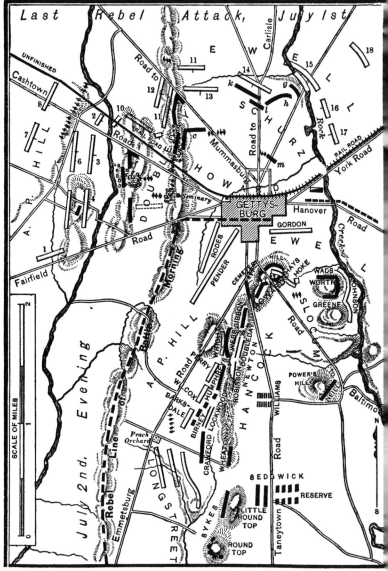

GETTYSBURG.—Final Attack of the First Day, and Battle of the Second Day.[1]

[1] The first day's battle is represented north of the Fairfield and Hanover roads. The second day's battle south of the same roads.

REFERENCES TO THE FIRST DAY'S BATTLE.

Union Troops, ▉.

MAJOR-GENERAL O. O. HOWARD commanding the First and Eleventh Corps.

FIRST CORPS.

MAJOR-GENERAL ABNER DOUBLEDAY commanding.

FIRST DIVISION—MAJOR-GENERAL JAMES S. WADSWORTH commanding.
- *a. First Brigade.* Colonel Henry A. Morrow, 24th Michigan.
- *b. Second brigade.* Brigadier-General Lysander Cutler.

SECOND DIVISION—MAJOR-GENERAL JOHN C. ROBINSON.
- *c. First Brigade.* Brigadier-General Gabriel R. Paul.
- *d. Second Brigade.* Brigadier-General Henry Baxter.

THIRD DIVISION—BRIGADIER-GENERAL THOS. A. ROWLEY.
- *e. First Brigade.* Colonel Chapman Biddle, 121st Pennsylvania.
- *f. Second Brigade.* Colonel Roy Stone, 149th Pennsylvania.

ELEVENTH CORPS.

MAJOR-GENERAL CARL SCHURZ commanding.

FIRST DIVISION—BRIGADIER-GENERAL F. C. BARLOW commanding.
- *g. First Brigade.* Colonel Von Gilsa.
- *h. Second Brigade.* Brigadier-General Adelbert Ames.

SECOND DIVISION—BRIGADIER-GENERAL ALEXANDER SCHIMMELPFENNIG.
- *k. First Brigade.* Colonel Von Arnsberg.
- *l. Second Brigade.* Colonel Kryzanowski.
- *m. Custer's Brigade,* of Steinwehr's Division.

Confederate Troops, ▭.

LIEUTENANT-GENERAL A. P. HILL commanding Third Corps.
MAJOR-GENERAL HENRY HETH commanding Division.

1. Archer's Brigade.
2. Davis's Brigade.
3. Brockenborough's Brigade.
4. Pettigrew's Brigade.

MAJOR-GENERAL W. D. PENDER commanding Division.

6. McGowan's Brigade.
7. Scales's Brigade.
8. Thomas's Brigade.
9. Lane's Brigade.

LIEUTENANT-GENERAL BENJ. EWELL commanding Second Corps.
MAJOR-GENERAL R. E. RODES commanding Division.

10. Daniel's Brigade.
11. Ramseur's Brigade.
12. Iverson's Brigade.
13. O'Neil's Brigade.
14. Dole's Brigade.

MAJOR-GENERAL JUBAL A. EARLY commanding Division.

15. Gordon's Brigade.
16. Hays's Brigade.
17. Hoke's Brigade.
18. Smith's Brigade.

Longstreet's attack was over before Ewell came into action, and although Ewell succeeded in temporarily establishing himself on our extreme right, it was due to an unfortunate order given by General Meade, by which the force in that part of the field was withdrawn just as Ewell advanced against it. But we are anticipating our narrative.

Hood, who commanded the division on the right of Longstreet's corps, complains that he was not allowed to go past Round Top and flank us on the south, as he might have done, but was required by his orders to break in at the Peach Orchard and drive Sickles's line along the Emmetsburg road toward Cemetery Hill; but it seems to me, as he started late in the afternoon, if he had made the detour which would have been necessary in order to attack us on the south, he would have met Sedgwick in front, while Sickles and Sykes might have interposed to cut him off from the main body.

Before describing Longstreet's attack we will give the final disposition made by General Meade when it became necessary to fight a defensive battle. The ridge was nearly in the shape of a horseshoe. The Twelfth Corps was on the extreme right; next came one division of the First Corps on Culps Hill, then the Eleventh Corps on Cemetery Hill, with two divisions of the First Corps at the base; next the Second Corps; then the Third, and the Fifth Corps on the extreme left, the Sixth Corps being posted in rear of Round Top as a general reserve to the army. Sickles, however, denies that any position was ever marked out for him. He was expected to prolong Hancock's line to the left, but did not do so for the following reasons : *First*, because the ground was low, and *second*, on account of the commanding position of the Emmetsburg road, which ran along a cross ridge oblique to the front of the line assigned him, and

which afforded the enemy an excellent position for their
artillery; *third*, because the ground between the valley he
was expected to occupy, and the Emmetsburg road constituted a minor ridge, very much broken and full of rocks and
trees, which afforded excellent cover for an enemy operating
in his immediate front. He had previously held an interview with General Meade and asked that an experienced
staff officer be sent with him to assist in locating a suitable
position for his corps. At his request, General Hunt, the
Chief of Artillery, was sent for that purpose. They rode out
to the ridge and Sickles directed that his troops should be
posted along that road, with his
centre at the Peach Orchard,
which was about a mile from
and nearly opposite to Little
Round Top; his right wing,
under Humphreys, extending
along the road, while his left
wing, under Birney, made a
right angle at the Peach Orchard with the other part of

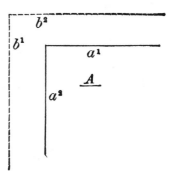

the line, and bent around, so as to cover the front of Little
Round Top at the base. The disadvantages of this position
are obvious enough. It is impossible for any force to hold
its ground when attacked at once on both sides which con-
stitute the right angle. The diagram shows that the force A
will have both its lines a^1 and a^2 enfiladed by batteries at b^1
b^2, and must yield. The ground, however, may be such that
the enemy cannot plant his guns at b^1 or b^2; but under any
circumstances it is a weak formation and the enemy easily
penetrate the angle. When that is the case, and it was so
in the present instance—each side constituting the angle is
taken in flank, and the position is no longer tenable.

If one side of the right angle lies behind a ridge where it cannot be enfiladed, a temporary formation of this kind is sometimes permissible.

Sickles claimed that he acted with the implied sanction of General Meade, who, however, censured the movement afterward. As soon as Sickles took position, General Buford's division of cavalry was sent to the rear at Westminster, to guard the trains there; and Kilpatrick's division was ordered to Hunterstown to attack the rebel left.

Sykes's corps—the Fifth—came up from the right about 5 P.M., soon after Longstreet's attack on Sickles was fairly under way, and formed along the outer base of Little Round Top, with Crawford's Pennsylvania reserves at their right and front.

There had been a Council of War, or Conference of Corps Commanders, called at Meade's headquarters, and it was universally agreed to remain and hold the position. As the Third Corps, in answer to the guns of Clark's battery, was suddenly assailed by a terrible concentrated artillery fire, General Sickles rode back to his command and General Meade went with him. The latter objected to Sickles's line, but thought it was then too late to change it.

The severe artillery fire which opened against the two sides of the angle at the Peach Orchard was a prelude to a furious attack against Ward's brigade on the left. This attack soon extended to the Peach Orchard. The fight became very hot against Birney's division from the left to the centre, but the troops on the right of the centre—Humphreys's division—were not at first actively engaged, and Humphrey reinforced Birney with one of his brigades, and subsequently with a regiment.

The battle which now raged among these trees, rocks, and ravines was so complicated that it is hard to follow and difficult to describe the movements of the contestants. Some idea of it can probably be gained by an examination of the following diagram:

It will be seen that a long line of rebel batteries bears upon A, and that one of them was brought up to enfilade

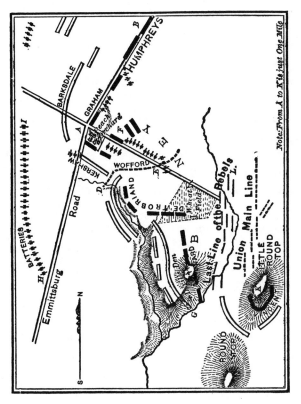

Diagram of the Attack on Sickles and Sykes.

the side AB. The angle at A, attacked by Barksdale on the north and Kershaw on the west, was broken in. In consequence of this, several batteries on the line EF were sacrificed, and Wofford's brigade soon came forward and took the position DE.

The Confederate line being very long, and overlapping Ward's brigade on the left, the latter was forced back, and the exulting rebels advanced to seize Little Round Top. They attacked the force there with great fury, assailing it in front and rear, but they were ultimately repulsed, and finally took up the line GL.   Two divisions of the Fifth Corps and one of the Second Corps were sent in, one after the other, to drive back the strong rebel force posted from D to G, but each one had a bitter contest in front, and was flanked by the rebel line at DE, so that ultimately all were obliged to retreat, although each performed prodigies of valor.   Indeed, Brooks's brigade charged almost up to the enemy's line of batteries, HI.   The rebels gained the position LG, confronting our main line and close to it ; but a fine charge made by Crawford's division of the Pennsylvania Reserves, drove them farther back, and as part of the Sixth Corps came up and formed to support Crawford, the rebels gave up the contest for the night as regards this part of the field.

The attack against Humphreys's division which followed the breaking in of the angle at A will be described further on.   The general result was that Sickles's entire line, together with the reinforcements sent in at different times to sustain it, were all forced back to the ridge which was our main line of battle, with the exception of Crawford's division which maintained a somewhat advanced position.

The details of this contest are full of incident, and too important to be wholly omitted.

About 3.30 P.M. the rebels commenced the movement against our left, by sending a flanking force from Hood's division, formed in two lines, around to attack Sickles's left, held by General J. Hobart Ward's brigade, which occupied the open ground covering the approaches to Little Round

Top; Ward's line passing in front of the mountain, and his flank resting on a rocky depression in the ground called the Devil's Den. The right extended to the minor spur or wooded ridge beyond the wheat-field. The engagement was furious; commencing on the rebel right, it extended to the left, until it reached the Peach Orchard, where it became especially violent. This central point of Sickles's line was held by eleven regiments of Birney's and Humphreys's divisions. Birney's two brigades, commanded by Graham and De Trobriand, held on bravely, for the men who fought with Kearny in the Peninsula were not easily driven; but the line was too attenuated to resist the shock very long, and reinforcements became absolutely necessary to sustain that unlucky angle at the Peach Orchard. Sickles had authority to call on Sykes, whose corps was resting from a long and fatiguing march, but the latter wished his men to get their coffee and be refreshed before sending them in; and as those who are fighting almost always exaggerate the necessity for immediate reinforcements, Sykes thought Sickles could hold on a while longer, and did not respond to the call for three-quarters of an hour.

It would seem that Lee supposed that Meade's main line of battle was on the Emmetsburg pike, and that the flank rested on the Peach Orchard, for he ordered Longstreet to form Hood's division perpendicular to that road, whereas Sickles occupied an advanced line, and Sykes the main line in rear. McLaws says that Lee thought turning the Peach Orchard was turning the Union left. With this idea, he directed Longstreet to form across the Emmetsburg road, and push our troops toward Cemetery Hill. Kershaw, after the minor ridge was taken, reported to Longstreet that he could not carry out these orders without exposing his right flank to an attack from Sykes's Corps.

Ward fought bravely against Benning's and Anderson's brigades on the left, driving back two attacks of the latter, but his line was long and weak, and the enemy overlapped it by the front of nearly two brigades. Being concealed from view, from the nature of the ground they could concentrate against any point with impunity. He attempted to strengthen his force at the Devil's Den by detaching the Ninety-ninth Pennsylvania from his right, and, although De Trobriand had no troops to spare, he was directed by General Birney to send the Fortieth New York, under Colonel Egan, to reinforce that flank. Egan arrived too late to perform the duty assigned him, as Ward had been already driven back, but not too late to make a gallant charge upon the rebel advance.

The fighting soon extended to the Peach Orchard, but as it commenced on the left, we will describe that part of the engagement first.

General Warren, who was on Meade's staff as Chief Engineer, had ridden about this time to the signal station on Little Round Top, to get a better view of the field. He saw the long line of the enemy approaching, and about to overlap Ward's left, and perceived that unless prompt succor arrived Little Round Top would fall into their hands. Once in their possession they would flank our whole line and post guns there to drive our troops from the ridge ; so that this eminence was in reality the key of the battle-field, and must be held at all hazards. He saw Barnes's division, which Sykes had ordered forward, formed for a charge, and about to go to the relief of De Trobriand, who held the centre of Birney's line, and who was sorely beset. Without losing a moment he rode down the slope, over to Barnes, took the

responsibility of detaching Vincent's brigade, and hurried
it back to take post on Little Round Top.   He then sent
a staff officer to inform General Meade of what he had done
and to represent the immense importance of holding this
commanding point.

The victorious column of the enemy was subjected to the
fire of a battery on Little Round Top, and to another farther to the right; but it kept on, went around Ward's brigade and rushed eagerly up the ravine between the two
Round Tops to seize Little Round Top which seemed to be
defenceless.   Vincent's brigade rapidly formed on the crest
of a small spur which juts out from the hill, and not having
time to load, advanced with the bayonet, in time to save the
height.   The contest soon became furious and the rocks
were alive with musketry.   General Vincent sent word to
Barnes that the enemy were on him in overwhelming numbers, and Hazlett's regular battery, supported by the One
Hundred and Fortieth New York under Colonel O'Rorke
of Weed's brigade, was sent as a reinforcement.   The battery was dragged with great labor to the crest of Little
Round Top, and the One Hundred and Fortieth were
posted on the slope on Vincent's right.   They came upon
the field just as the rebels, after failing to penetrate the
centre, had driven back the right.   In advancing to this
exposed position, Colonel O'Rorke, a brilliant young officer who had just graduated at the head of his class at
West Point, was killed and his men thrown into some
confusion, but Vincent rallied the line and repulsed the
assault.   In doing so he exposed himself very much and
was soon killed by a rebel sharpshooter.   General Weed,
who was on the crest with the battery, was mortally
wounded in the same way; and as Hazlett leaned over to
hear his last message, a fatal bullet struck him also and he

dropped dead on the body of his chief. Colonel Rice of the Forty-fourth New York now took command in place of Vincent. The enemy having been foiled at the centre and right, stole around through the woods and turned the left of the line; but Chamberlain's regiment—the Twentieth Maine—was folded back by him, around the rear of the mountain, to resist the attack. The rebels came on like wolves, with deafening yells, and forced Chamberlain's men over the crest; but they rallied and drove their assailants back in their turn. This was twice repeated and then a brigade of the Pennsylvania Reserves and one of the Fifth Corps dashed over the hill. The Twentieth Maine made a grand final charge and drove the rebels from the valley between the Round Tops, capturing a large number of prisoners. Not a moment too soon, for Chamberlain had lost a third of his command and was entirely out of ammunition. Vincent's men in this affair took two colonels, fifteen officers, and five hundred men prisoners, and a thousand stand of arms. Hill in his official report says "Hood's right was held as in a vise."

We will now return to the Peach Orchard. In answer to a shot from Clark's battery a long line of guns opened from the eleven batteries opposite. Graham's infantry were partially sheltered from this iron hail, but the three batteries with him in the beginning, which were soon reinforced by four more from the reserve artillery, under Major McGilvery, were very much cut up; and at last it became necessary to sacrifice one of them—that of Bigelow—to enable the others to retire to a new line in rear. Graham still held the Peach Orchard, although he was assailed on two fronts, by Barksdale's brigade on the north and Kershaw's brigade on the west. A battery was brought forward to enfilade Sickles's line on the Emmetsburg road, and under cover of its fire Barksdale carried the position, but was mortally wounded in doing so.[1] Sickles lost a leg about this time (5.30 P.M.), and Graham, who was also badly wounded, fell into the enemy's hands. The command of the Third Corps now devolved upon General Birney.

The batteries under Major McGilvery, which lined the cross road below the Peach Orchard, were very effective, but were very much shattered. Kershaw captured them at one time but was driven off temporarily by a gallant charge of the One Hundred and Forty-first Pennsylvania of Graham's brigade, who retook the guns, which were then brought off by hand. Bigelow was ordered by Major McGilvery to sacrifice his battery to give the others time to form a new line. He fought with *fixed prolonge* until the enemy were within six feet of him, and then retired with the loss of three officers and twenty-eight men. Phillips's battery, which adjoined his, had a similar experience. McLaws bears testimony to the admirable manner with which this artillery was served. He says one shell killed and wounded thirty men, out of a company of thirty-seven.

The capture of the Peach Orchard necessarily brought the enemy directly on Humphreys's left flank and De Trobriand's right. The disaster then became irremediable, because every force thrown in after this period, had to contend with a direct fire in front, and an enfilading fire from the right.

While the Peach Orchard was assailed, several combats took place in the vicinity, which had a general relation to the defence of Sickles's line. A little stream runs through a ravine parallel to the cross road, and about five hundred yards

---

[1] Barksdale soon after was brought into my lines and died like a brave man, with dignity and resignation. I had known him as an officer of volunteers in the Mexican war. As a member of Congress he was very influential in bringing on the Rebellion.

south of it, and then turns abruptly to the south at the corner of a wheat-field, passing through a rocky wooded country, to empty in Plum Run. De Trobriand held the north
bank of this stream with a very insufficient force—a front of
two regiments—and his contest with Semmes's brigade in
front and Kershaw's brigade, which was trying to penetrate
into the Peach Orchard, on his right, was at very close range
and very destructive. At the same time as Ward's left was
turned and driven back the enemy came in on the left and
rear of De Trobriand, and occupied the wheat-field. Barnes'
division of the Fifth Corps, composed of Sweitzer's and Tilton's brigades, soon came to his assistance. The former, by
wheeling to the left and retaining several lines, kept up the
fight successfully against the enemy who came up the ravine, but the latter was flanked and obliged to give way.
De Trobriand's two regiments in front had a most determined
fight, and would not yield the ground. When relieved by
Zook's force they fell back across the wheat-field. There
Birney used them as a basis of a new line, brought up two
fresh regiments, charged through the field, and drove the
enemy back to the stone fence which bounded it.

Caldwell's division of Hancock's corps now came on to renew the contest. Caldwell formed his men with the brigades of Cross and Kelly in front, and those of Zook and
Brooke in rear. In the advance Colonel Cross was killed,
and the front line being enfiladed in both directions, was
soon so cut up that the rear line came forward in its place,
Zook was killed, but Brooke made a splendid charge, turning Kershaw's right and driving Semmes back through the
supporting batteries. Sweitzer's brigade then came up a
second time to aid Brooks, but it was useless, for there was
still another line of batteries beyond, and as the Peach
Orchard by this time was in possession of the enemy, Brooke's
advanced position was really a disadvantage, for both his

flanks were turned. Semmes's brigade, together with parts
of Benning's and Anderson's brigades, rallied behind a stone
wall, again came forward, and succeeded in retaking the
knoll and the batteries they had lost. Caldwell, under cover
of our artillery, extricated his division with heavy loss, for
both Zook's and Kelly's brigades were completely surrounded.

Then Ayres,[1] who had been at the turning-point of so many
battles, went in with his fine division of regulars, commanded
by Day and Burbank, officers of courage and long experience
in warfare. He struck the enemy in flank who were pursuing
Caldwell, and who would have renewed the attack on Little
Round Top, doubled them up, and drove them back to the
position Caldwell had left; but his line, from the nature of
things, was untenable, for a whole brigade with ample supports had formed on his right rear, so that nothing remained
but to face about and fight his way home again. This was
accomplished with the tremendous loss of fifty per cent. of
his command in killed and wounded. His return was aided
by the artillery on Little Round Top, and by the advance of
part of the Sixth Corps. When the troops were all gone,
Winslow's battery still held the field for a time, and withdrew
by piece.

The enemy, Wofford's, Kershaw's and Anderson's brigades,
now swarmed in the front of our main line between the wheat-
field and Little Round Top. General S. Wiley Crawford,
who commanded a division composed of two brigades of the
Pennsylvania Reserve Corps, was ordered to drive them farther back. This organization, which at one time I had the
honor to command, were veterans of the Peninsula, and were

---

[1] General Ayres, whose service in the war commenced with the first Bull Run
and ended at Appomattox, may almost be called an impersonation of the Army of
the Potomac, as he took part in nearly all its battles and minor engagements.

among the most dauntless men in the army. Crawford called upon them to defend the soil of their native State, and headed a charge made by McCandless' brigade, with the colors of one of the regiments in his hand. The men went forward with an impetus nothing could withstand. The enemy took shelter behind a stone fence on the hither side of the wheat-field, but McCandless stormed the position, drove them beyond the field, and then, as it was getting dark, both sides rested on their arms. The other brigade of Crawford's division—that of Fisher—had previously been sent to reinforce Vincent in his desperate struggle on the slope of Little Round Top. The enemy retired before it, so that it was not engaged, and it then took possession of the main Round Top on the left of Little Round Top and fortified it.

As Crawford charged, two brigades of Sedgwick's corps, those of Nevins and Eustis, formed under Wheaton on the right and below Little Round Top. The sight of the firm front presented by these fresh troops thoroughly discouraged Longstreet, who went forward to reconnoitre, and he gave up all attempts at making any farther advance.

The enemy at night took post at the western base of the ridge, and held a fortified line as far south as the Devil's Den, in which rocky cavern they took shelter.

It remains now to describe the effect of the loss of the Peach Orchard and the wounding of Sickles and Graham— which took place soon after—upon the fate of Humphreys's division, posted on the right along the Emmetsburg road. When Sickles lost his leg, Birney assumed command of the corps, and ordered Humphreys to move his left wing back to form a new oblique line to the ridge, in connection with Birney's division. Humphreys, up to the loss of the Peach Orchard, had not been actively engaged, as the enemy had merely demonstrated along his front; but now he was

obliged, while executing the difficult manœuvre of a change
of front to rear, to contend with Barksdale's brigade of Mc-
Laws's division on his left at the Peach Orchard, and enfilading batteries there also, while his entire front was called
upon to repel a most determined assault from Anderson's
division, which hitherto had not been engaged, and which
now pressed with great force on his right, which still clung
to the road.   Four regiments were thrown in by Hancock to
support that part of the line, but the attack was so sudden
and violent that they only had time to fire a few volleys
before Humphreys received orders to give up his advanced
position and fall back to the ridge itself.   There he turned
at bay.   Hancock, who had been placed in command of the
First, Second, and Third Corps, was indefatigable in his
vigilance and personal supervision, "patching the line"
wherever the enemy was likely to break through.   His
activity and foresight probably preserved the ridge from
capture.   Toward the last Meade brought forward Lockwood's Maryland brigade from the right and sent them in to
cover Sickles's retreat.   Humphreys was followed up by the
brigades of Wilcox, Perry, and Wright—about the best fighting material in the rebel army.   Perry was driven back by
the fire of our main line, and as his brigade was between the
other two, his retreat left each of them in a measure unsupported on the flanks.   Posey's and Mahone's brigades were to
advance as soon as the others became actively engaged, but
failed to do so, and therefore Pender, who was to follow
after them, did not move forward.   Hence the great effort
of Wilcox and Wright, which would have been ruinous to
us if followed up, was fruitless of results.   Both were repulsed for lack of support, but Wright actually reached the
crest with his Georgians and turned a gun, whose cannon-
eers had been shot, upon Webb's brigade of the Second

Corps. Webb gave them two staggering volleys from be-hind a fence, and went forward with two regiments. He charged, regained the lost piece, and turned it upon them. Wright, finding himself entirely isolated in this advanced position, went back again to the main line, and Wilcox did the same. On this occasion Wright did what Lee failed to accomplish the next day at such a heavy expense of life, *for he pierced our centre*, and held it for a short time, and had the movement been properly supported and energetically followed up, it might have been fatal to our army, and would most certainly have resulted in a disastrous retreat. It was but another illustration of the difficulty of success-fully converging columns against a central force. Lee's divisions seemed never to strike at the hour appointed. Each came forward separately, and was beaten for lack of support.

Wright attained the crest and Wilcox was almost on a line with him. The latter was closely followed up and nearly surrounded, for troops rushed in on him from all sides. He lost very heavily in extricating himself from his advanced position. Wilcox claims to have captured tempo-rarily twenty guns and Wright eight.

As they approached the ridge a Union battery limbered up and galloped off. The last gun was delayed and the cannoneer, with a long line of muskets pointing at him with-in a few feet, deliberately drove off the field. The Geor-gians manifested their admiration for his bravery by crying out "Don't shoot," and not a musket was fired at him.[1] I regret that I have not been able to ascertain the man's name.

---

[1] As it is well to verify these incidents, I desire to state that this is a reminis-cence of Dr. J. Robie Wood, of New York, a Georgian, a relative of Wendell Phillips, who was in the charge with Wright. Wood fell struck by six bullets, but recovered.

In the morning General Tidball, who was attached to the cavalry as Chief of Artillery, rode along the entire crest from Little Round Top to Culps Hill to make himself familiar with the lines. As he passed my headquarters he noticed some new troops, the Second Vermont brigade under General Stannard, which formed part of my command. They were a fine-looking body of men, and were drawn up in close column by division, ready to go to any part of the field at a moment's notice. After inquiring to what corps they belonged he passed over to the right. On his return late in the day he saw Sickles's whole line driven in and found Wright's rebel brigade established on the crest barring his way back. He rode rapidly over to Meade's headquarters and found the general walking up and down the room, apparently quite unconscious of the movements which might have been discerned by riding to the top of the hill, and which should have been reported to him by some one of his staff. Tidball said, "General, I am very sorry to see that the enemy have pierced our centre." Meade expressed surprise at the information and said, "Why, where is Sedgwick?" Tidball replied, "I do not know, but if you need troops, I saw a fine body of Vermonters a short distance from here, belonging to the First Corps, who are available." Meade then directed him to take an order to Newton and put the men in at once; the order was communicated to me and I went with my division at double quick to the point indicated. There we pursued Wright's force as it retired, and retook, at Hancock's instigation, four guns taken by Wright earlier in the action. When these were brought in I sent out two regiments, who followed the enemy up nearly to their lines and retook two more guns. I have been thus particular in narrating this incident as Stannard's Vermont brigade contributed greatly to the

victory of the next day and it is worthy of record to state
how they came to be located in that part of the field.

It is claimed that unless Sickles had taken up this
advanced position Hood's division would have turned our
left, have forced us from the shelter of the ridge, and probably have intervened between us and Washington. The
movement, disastrous in some respects, was propitious as
regards its general results, for the enemy had wasted all
their strength and valor in gaining the Emmetsburg road,
which after all was of no particular benefit to them. They
were still outside our main line. They pierced the latter it
is true, but the gallant men who at such heavy expense of
life and limb stood triumphantly on that crest were obliged
to retire because the divisions which should have supported
them remained inactive. I must be excused for thinking
that the damaging resistance these supports encountered on
the first day from the men of my command exerted a be-
numbing influence on the second day.

It is said, that Hood being wounded, Longstreet led the
last advance against Little Round Top in person, but when
he saw Sedgwick's corps coming into line he gave up the
idea of capturing the heights as impracticable. This eminence should have been the first point held and fortified by
us early in the day, as it was the key of the field, but no
special orders were given concerning it, and nothing but
Warren's activity and foresight saved it from falling into the
hands of the enemy.

Meade was considerably startled by the fact that the
enemy had pierced our centre. He at once sent for Pleasonton and gave him orders to collect his cavalry with a view
to cover the retreat of the army. Indeed, in an article on
the "Secret History of Gettysburg," published in the
"Southern Historical Papers," by Colonel Palfrey, of the

Confederate army, he states that the movement to the rear actually commenced, and that Ewell's pickets heard and reported that artillery was passing in that direction. After a short time the noise of the wheels ceased. He also says that in a conversation he had with Colonel Ulric Dahlgren of our cavalry, who had lost a leg, and was a prisoner in Richmond, he was told that while the battle of Gettysburg was going on he (Dahlgren) captured a Confederate scout with a despatch from Jefferson Davis to General Lee, in which the former wrote of the exposed condition of Richmond owing to the presence of a large Union force at City Point. Dahlgren said a retreat had been ordered, but when Meade read this despatch, he looked upon it as a sign indicating the weakness of the enemy, and perhaps thinking it would not do to supplement the probable capture of Richmond by a retreat of the Army of the Potomac, countermanded the order. Sedgwick, who was high in the confidence of General Meade, told one of his division commanders that the army would probably fall back on Westminster. General Pleasonton testifies that he was engaged, by order of General Meade, until 11 P.M. in occupying prominent points with his cavalry, to cover the retreat of the army. Nevertheless it has been indignantly denied that such a movement was contemplated.

Although it was General Lee's intention that both flanks of the Union army should be assailed at the same time, while the intermediate forces made demonstrations against the centre, Ewell did not move to attack the right of our line at Culps Hill until Longstreet's assault on the left had failed. Longstreet attributes it to the fact that Ewell had broken his line of battle by detaching two brigades up the York road. There is always some reason why columns never converge in time. Johnson's division, which was on the extreme left of the rebel army, and had not been engaged, made their way, sheltered by the ravine of Rock Creek, to assail the right at Culps Hill, held by Wadsworth's division of the First Corps, and that part of the line still farther to the right where Geary's division of the Twelfth Corps was posted.

In his desire to reinforce the Fifth Corps at the close of the conflict with Longstreet, General Meade made the sad mistake of ordering the Twelfth Corps to abandon its position on the right and report to General Sykes for duty on the left. General Slocum, sensible that this would be a suicidal movement, reported that the enemy were advancing on his front, and begged permission to keep Geary's division there to defend the position. General Meade finally allowed him to retain Greene's brigade, and no more, and thus it happened that Ewell's troops, finding the works on the extreme right of our line defenceless, had nothing to do but walk in and occupy them. If Meade was determined to detach this large force, there seems no good reason why two of Sedgwick's brigades should not have been sent to take its place, but nothing was done.

Johnson's division, as it came on, deployed and crossed Rock Creek about half an hour before sunset. It suffered so severely from our artillery, that one brigade, that of Jones, fell back in disorder, its commander being wounded. The other, however, advanced against Wadsworth, and Greene on his right ; but as these generals had their fronts well fortified, the attack was easily repulsed. Nevertheless, the left of Johnson's line, not being opposed, took possession of Geary's works about 9 P.M., and thus endangered our communications.

Gregg's division of cavalry which was posted east of Slocum's position saw this movement of Johnson. Gregg opened fire on the column with his artillery and sent out his men dismounted to skirmish on the flank of the enemy. Johnson detached Walker's brigade to meet him, and the contest continued until after dark. Greene, in the meantime, swung his right around on the edge of a ravine, perpendicular to the main line and fortified it, to avoid being flanked. He was an accomplished soldier and engineer, having graduated second in his class at West Point, and knew exactly what ought to be done and how to do it. He held on strongly, and as it was dark, and the enemy did not exactly know where they were, or where our troops were posted, they waited until daylight before taking any further action. Yet they were now but a short distance from General Meade's headquarters, and within easy reach of our reserve artillery. A night attack on the rear of our army, in conjunction with an advance from the opposite side on Hancock's front, would have thrown us into great confusion and must have succeeded.

During the night Ewell sent Smith's brigade to reinforce Johnson. Geary, after all, did not reach Little Round Top or report to Sykes, and if he had done so, his troops would have been of no use, as the battle was over in that part of the field. There was a mystery about his movements which needs to be cleared up.

To supplement this attack on the extreme right, and prevent reinforcements from being sent there, Early's division was directed to carry Cemetery Hill by storm. Before it advanced, a vigorous artillery fire was opened from four rebel batteries on Benner's Hill, to prepare the way for the assault, but our batteries on Cemetery Hill, which were partially sheltered by earthworks, replied and soon silenced those of the enemy. Then Early's infantry moved forth, Hays's brigade on the right, Hoke's brigade on the left, under Colonel Avery, and Gordon's brigade in reserve. It was

supposed Johnson's division would protect Early's left flank,
while Rodes's and Pender's divisions would come forward in
time to prevent any attack against his right.   The enemy
first struck Von Gilsa's brigade, which was posted behind a
stone fence at the foot of the hill.   Still farther to its left, at
the base of the hill, was Ames's brigade, both enclosing
Rickett's and Weidrick's batteries on higher ground above.
Stewart's, Reynolds's and Stevens's batteries, which had been
a good deal cut up on the first day, were now brought
to bear on the approaching enemy.   Colonel Wainwright,
Chief of Artillery to the First Corps, gave them orders not
to attempt to retreat if attacked, but to fight the guns to
the last.   The enemy advanced up the ravine which was
specially commanded by Stevens's battery.   Weidrick, Ricketts, and Stevens played upon the approaching line energetically.   The rebel left and centre fell back, but the right
managed to obtain shelter from houses and undulating
ground, and came on impetuously, charging over Von
Gilsa's brigade, and driving it up the hill, through the
batteries.   In doing so Hays says the darkness and smoke
saved his men from a terrible slaughter.   Weidrick's battery was captured, and two of Ricketts's guns were spiked.
The enemy, in making this movement, exposed their left
flank to Stevens's battery, which poured a terrible fire of
double canister into their ranks.   The Thirty-third Massachusetts also opened a most effective oblique fire.   The batteries were penetrated but would not surrender.   Dearer
than life itself to the cannoneer is the gun he serves, and
these brave men fought hand to hand with handspikes,
rammer, staves, and even stones.   They shouted, " *Death on
the soil of our native State rather than lose our guns.*"   Hancock, all this time should have been kept busy on his own
front repelling an attack from Rodes and Pender, but as

they did not come forward, and as he felt that there was great danger that Howard would lose Cemetery Hill and his own right be turned, he sent Carroll's brigade to the rescue. Carroll was joined by the One Hundred and Sixth Pennsylvania and some reinforcements from Schurz's division. For a few minutes, Hays says, there was an ominous silence and then the tramp of our infantry was heard. They came over the hill and went in with a cheer. The enemy, finding they were about to be overwhelmed, retreated, as no one came to their assistance. When they fell back our guns opened a very destructive fire. It is said that out of 1,750 men of the organization known as "The Louisiana Tigers," only 150 returned. Hays attributes his defeat to the fact that Gordon was not up in time to support him.

The failure to carry the Hill isolated Johnson's division on our extreme right. As it could only be reached by a long circuit it was not easy for Lee to maintain it there, without unduly weakening other parts of his line. That Rodes's division did not reach Cemetery Hill in time to co-operate with Early's attack was not owing to any lack of zeal or activity on the part of that energetic officer. He was obliged to move out of Gettysburg by the flank, then change front and advance double the distance Early had to traverse, and by the time he had done so Early had made the attack and had been repulsed.

The day closed with the rebels defeated on our left, but victorious on our right. Fortunately for us, this incited Lee to continue his efforts. He could not bear to retreat after his heavy losses, and acknowledge that he was beaten. He resolved to reinforce Johnson's division, now in rear of our right, and fling Pickett's troops, the *élite* of his army, who had not been engaged, against our centre. He hoped a simultaneous attack made by Pickett in front and Johnson in rear, would yet win those heights and scatter the Union army to the winds. Kilpatrick, who had been resting the tired men and horses of his cavalry division at Abbotsford after the conflict at Hanover, went on the afternoon of the 2d to circle around and attack the left and rear of the enemy by way of Hunterstown. This plan was foiled, however, by the sudden arrival of Stuart's cavalry from its long march. They reached that part of the field about 4 P.M. After a fierce combat, in which Farnsworth's and Custer's brigades and Estes's squadron were principally engaged against Hampton's brigade supported by the main body, darkness put an end to the fight. Kilpatrick then turned back and bivouacked at Two Taverns for the night.

Gregg's division of cavalry left Hanover and at noon took post opposite and about three miles east of Slocum's Corps on the right. There, as stated, he saw Johnson's division moving to the attack and after throwing some shells into their ranks deployed his own skirmish line and advanced agains' the one they threw out to meet him. At 10 P.M. he withdre and took post on the Baltimore pike where it crosses Cret Run, near Rock Creek. By so doing he guarded the right and rear of the army from any demonstration by Stuart's cavalry.

At night a council of war was held, in which it was unanimously voted to stay and fight it out. Meade was displeased with the result, and although he acquiesced in the decision, he said angrily, " Have it your own way, gentlemen, but Gettysburg is no place to fight a battle in." The fact that a portion of the enemy actually prolonged our line on the right and that our centre had been pierced during the day, made him feel far from confident. He thought it better to retreat with what he had, than run the risk of losing all.[1]

---

[1] Since the above was written, the discussion has been renewed in the public prints as to whether General Meade did or did not intend to leave the field. So far as the drawing up of an order of retreat is concerned, it was undoubtedly right and proper to do so, for it is the duty of a general to be prepared for every emergency. It is easy to criticise, and say what should have been done, after a battle has been fought, after the position of troops is all laid down on the maps, and the plans of every commander explained in official reports; but amid the doubt and confusion of actual combat, where there has been great loss of men and material, it is not always so easy to decide. On the night of the 2d the state of affairs was disheartening. In the combats of the preceding days, the First, Third, and Eleventh Corps had been almost annihilated ; the Fifth Corps and a great part of the Second were shattered, and only the S xth Corps and Twelfth Corps were comparatively fresh. It was possible therefore that the enemy might gain some great success the next day, which would stimulate them to extra exertions, and diminish the spirit of our men in the same proportion. In such a case it was not improbable that the army might be destroyed as an organization, and there is a vast difference between a *destroyed* army and a *defeated* army. By retiring while it was yet in his power to do so, General Meade felt that he would assure the safety of our principal cities, for the enemy were too exhausted to pursue; and being out of ammunition, and far from their base of supplies, were not in a condition to do much further damage, or act very energetically. Whereas our troops could soon be largely reinforced from the draft which had just been established, and, being in the centre of their resources, could be supplied with all that was necessary for renewed effort.

There is no question in my mind that, at the council referred to, General Meade did desire to retreat, and expressed fears that his communications with Taneytown might be endangered by remaining at Gettysburg.

It has also been stated that both General Gibbon and General Newton objected to our position at Gettysburg, but this is an error. They merely recommended some additional precautions to prevent the enemy from turning our left at Round Top, and thus intervening between us and Washington. Hancock, in giving his vote, said the Army of the Potomac had retreated too often, and he was in favor of remaining now to fight it out.

CHAPTER VI.

THE BATTLE OF THE THIRD DAY—JOHNSON'S DIVISION DRIVEN OUT.

At dawn on the 3d the enemy opened on us with artillery, but the firing had no definite purpose, and after some hours it gradually slackened.

The principal interest early in the day necessarily centred on the right, where Johnson's position not only endangered the safety of the army, but compromised our retreat. It was therefore essential to drive him out as soon as possible. To this end batteries were established during the night on all the prominent points in that vicinity. Geary had returned with his division about midnight, and was not a little astonished to find the rebels established in the works he had left. He determined to contest possession with them at daylight. In the meantime he joined Greene and formed part of his line perpendicular to our main line of battle, and part fronting the enemy.

On the other hand, Ewell, having obtained a foothold, swore he would not be driven out, and hastened to reinforce Johnson with Daniels's and O'Neill's brigades from Rodes's division.

As soon as objects could be discerned in the early gray of the morning our artillery opened fire. As Johnson, on account of the steep declivities and other obstacles, had not been able to bring any artillery with him, he could not reply.

It would not do to remain quiet under this fire, and he determined to charge, in hopes of winning a better position on higher ground. His men—the old Stonewall brigade leading—rushed bravely forward, but were as gallantly met by Kane's brigade of Geary's division and a close and severe struggle ensued for four hours among the trees and rocks. Ruger's division of the Twelfth Corps came up and formed on the rebel left, taking them in flank and threatening them in reverse. Indeed, as the rest of our line were not engaged, there was plenty of support for Geary. Troops were sent him, including Shaler's brigade, which took the front, and was soon warmly engaged in re-establishing the line.

At about 11 A.M., finding the contest hopeless, and his retreat threatened by a force sent down to Rock Creek, Johnson yielded slowly and reluctantly to a charge made by Geary's division, gave up the position and withdrew to Rock Creek, where he remained until night.

Our line was once more intact. All that the enemy had gained by dogged determination and desperate bravery was lost from a lack of co-ordination, caused perhaps by the great difficulty of communicating orders over this long concave line where every route was swept by our fire.

Lee had now attacked both flanks of the Army of the Potomac without having been able to establish himself permanently on either. Notwithstanding the repulse of the previous day he was very desirous of turning the left, for once well posted there he could secure his own retreat while interposing between Meade and Washington. He rode over with Longstreet to that end of the line to see what could be done. General Wofford, who commanded a brigade of McLaws's division, writes in a recent letter to General Crawford, United States Army, as follows: "Lee and Longstreet came to my brigade Friday morning before, the artillery opened fire. I told him that the afternoon before, I nearly reached the crest. He asked if I could not go there now. I replied, "No, General, I think not." He said quickly, " Why not?" " Because," I said, "General, the enemy have had all night to intrench and reinforce. I had been pursuing a broken enemy and the situation was now very different."

Having failed at each extremity, it only remained to Lee to retreat, or attack the centre. Such high expectations had been formed in the Southern States in regard to his conquest of the North that he determined to make another effort. He still had Pickett's division, the flower of Virginia, which had not been engaged, and which was full of enthusiasm. He resolved to launch them against our centre, supported on either flank by the advance of the main portion of the army. He had hoped that Johnson's division would have been able to maintain its position on the right, so that the Union centre could be assailed in front and rear at the same time, but Johnson having been driven out, it was necessary to trust to Pickett alone, or abandon the whole enterprise and return to Virginia.

Everything was quiet up to 1 P.M., as the enemy were massing their batteries and concentrating their forces preparatory to the grand charge—the supreme effort—which was to determine the fate of the campaign, and to settle the point whether freedom or slavery was to rule the Northern States.

It seems to me there was some lack of judgment in the preparations. Heth's division, now under Pettigrew, which had been so severely handled on the first day, and which was composed in a great measure of new troops, was designated to support Pickett's left and join in the attack at close quarters. Wilcox, too, who one would think had been pretty well fought out the day before, in his desperate enterprise of attempting to crown the crest, was directed to support the right flank of the attack. Wright's brigade was formed in rear, and Pender's division on the left of Pettigrew, but there was a long distance between Wilcox and Longstreet's forces on the right.

At 1 P.M., a signal gun was fired and one hundred and fifteen guns opened against Hancock's command, consisting of the First Corps under Newton, the Second Corps under Gibbon, the Third Corps under Birney, and against the Eleventh Corps under Howard. The object of this heavy artillery fire was to break up our lines and prepare the way for Pickett's charge. The exigencies of the battle had caused the First Corps to be divided, Wadsworth's division being on the right at Culps Hill, Robinson on Gibbon's right, and my own division intervening between Caldwell on the left and Gibbon on the right. The convex shape of our line did not give us as much space as that of the enemy, but General Hunt, Chief of Artillery, promptly posted eighty guns along the crest—as many as it would hold—to answer the fire, and the batteries on both sides suffered severely in the two hours' cannonade. Not less than eleven caissons were blown up and destroyed; one quite near me. When the smoke went up from these explosions rebel yells of exultation could be heard along a line of several miles. At 3 P.M. General Hunt ordered our artillery fire to cease, in order to cool the guns, and to preserve some rounds for the contest at close quarters, which he foresaw would soon take place.

My own men did not suffer a great deal from this cannonade, as I sheltered them as much as possible under the crest of the hill, and behind rocks, trees, and stone fences.

The cessation of our fire gave the enemy the idea they had silenced our batteries, and Pickett at once moved forward, to break the left centre of the Union line and occupy the crest of the ridge.[1] The other forces on his right and left were expected to move up and enlarge the opening thus made, so that finally, the two wings of the Union Army would be permanently separated, and flung off by this entering wedge in eccentric directions.

This great column of attack, it was supposed, numbered about seventeen thousand men, but southern writers have a peculiar arithmetic by which they always cipher down their forces to nothing. Even on the left, on the preceding day, when our troops in front of Little Round Top were assailed by a line a mile and a half long, they figure it almost out of existence. The force that now advanced would have been larger still had it not been for a spirited attack by Kilpatrick against the left of Longstreet's corps, detaining some troops there which otherwise might have co-operated in the grand assault against our centre.

It necessarily took the rebels some time to form and cross the intervening space, and Hunt took advantage of the opportunity to withdraw the batteries that had been most injured, sending others in their place from the reserve artillery, which had not been engaged. He also replenished the ammunition boxes, and stood ready to receive the foe as he came forward—first with solid shot, next with shell, and lastly, when he came to close quarters, with canister.

General Meade's headquarters was in the centre of this cannonade, and as the balls were flying very thickly there, and killing the horses of his staff, he found it necessary temporarily to abandon the place. Where nothing is to be gained by exposure it is sound sense to shelter men and officers as much as possible. He rode over to Power's Hill,

---

[1] The attack was so important, so momentous, and so contrary to Longstreet's judgment, that when Pickett asked for orders to advance he gave no reply, and Pickett said proudly, " I shall go forward, sir ! "

made his headquarters with General Slocum, and when the firing ceased rode back again. During his absence the

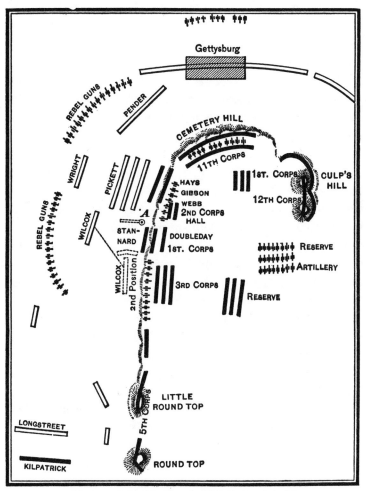

Diagram of the Attack on the Left Centre, July 3d.

charge took place. He has stated that it was his intention to throw the Fifth and Sixth Corps on the flanks of the attacking force, but no orders to this effect were issued, and it is questionable whether such an arrangement would have been a good one. It would have disgarnished the left, where Longstreet was still strong in numbers, and in forming perpendicular to our line of battle the two corps would necessarily have exposed their own outer flanks to attack. Indeed, the rebels had provided for just such a contingency, by posting Wilcox's brigade and Perry's brigade under Colonel Lang on the right, and Pender's division, now under Trimble, on the left, both in rear of the charging column under Pickett and Pettigrew. Owing to a mistake or misunderstanding, this disposition, however, did not turn out well for the enemy. It was not intended by Providence that the Northern States should pass under the iron rule of the slave power, and on this occasion every plan made by Lee was thwarted in the most unexpected manner.

The distance to be traversed by Pickett's column was about a mile and a half from the woods where they started, to the crest of the ridge they desired to attain. They suffered severely from our artillery, which opened on them with solid shot as soon as they came in sight; when half way across the plain they were vigorously shelled; double canisters were reserved for their nearer approach.

At first the direction of their march appeared to be directly toward my division. When within five hundred yards of us, however, Pickett halted and changed direction obliquely about forty-five degrees, so that the attack passed me and struck Gibbon's division on my right. Just here one of those providential circumstances occurred which favored us so much, for Wilcox and Lang, who guarded Pickett's right flank, did not follow his oblique movement, but kept on straight to the front, so that soon there was a wide interval between their troops and the main body, leaving Pickett's right fully uncovered.

The rebels came on magnificently. As fast as the shot and shell tore through their lines they closed up the gaps and pressed forward. When they reached the Emmetsburg road the canister began to make fearful chasms in their ranks. They also suffered severely from a battery on Little Round Top, which enfiladed their line. One shell killed and wounded ten men. Gibbon had directed his command to reserve their fire until the enemy were near enough to make it very effective. Pickett's advance dashed up to the fence occupied by the skirmishers of the Second Corps, near the Emmetsburg road, and drove them back; then the musketry blazed forth with deadly effect, and Pettigrew's men began to waver on the left and fall behind; for the nature of the ground was such that they were more exposed than other portions of the line. They were much shaken by the artillery fire, and that of Hays' division sent them back in masses.[1]

Before the first line of rebels reached a second fence and stone wall, behind which our main body was posted, it was obliged to pass a demi-brigade under Colonel Theodore B. Gates, of the Twentieth New York State Militia, and a Vermont brigade under General Stannard, both belonging to my command. When Pickett's right became exposed in consequence of the divergence of Wilcox's command, Stannard seized the opportunity to make a flank attack, and while his left regiment, the Fourteenth, poured in a heavy oblique fire, he changed front with his two right regiments, the Thirteenth and Sixteenth, which brought them perpendicular to the rebel line of march. In cases of this kind, when struck directly on the flank, troops are more or less unable to defend themselves, and Kemper's brigade crowded in toward the centre in order to avoid Stannard's energetic and deadly attack.

---

[1] The front line of Hays' division, which received this charge, was composed of the Twelfth New Jersey, Fourteenth Connecticut, and First Delaware. The second line was composed of the One Hundred and Eleventh, One Hundred and Twenty-fifth, One Hundred and Twenty-sixth, and Thirty-ninth New York.

They were closely followed up by Gates' command, who continued to fire into them at close range. This caused many to surrender, others to retreat outright, and others simply to crowd together. Simultaneously with Stannard's attack, the Eighth Ohio, which was on picket, overlapping the rebel left, closed in on that flank with great effect. Nevertheless, the next brigade—that of Armistead—united to Garnett's brigade, pressed on, and in spite of death-dealing bolts on all sides, Pickett determined to break Gibbon's line and capture his guns.

Although Webb's front was the focus of the concentrated artillery fire, and he had already lost fifty men and some valuable officers, his line remained firm and unshaken. It devolved upon him now to meet the great charge which was to decide the fate of the day. It would have been difficult to find a man better fitted for such an emergency. He was nerved to great deeds by the memory of his ancestors, who in former days had rendered distinguished services to the Republic, and felt that the results of the whole war might depend upon his holding of the position. His men were equally resolute. Cushing's battery, A, Fourth United States Artillery, which had been posted on the crest, and Brown's Rhode Island Battery on his left, were both practically destroyed by the cannonade. The horses were prostrated, every officer but one was struck, and Cushing had but one serviceable gun left.

As Pickett's advance came very close to the first line, young Cushing, mortally wounded in both thighs, ran his last serviceable gun down to the fence, and said : "*Webb, I will give them one more shot !*" At the moment of the last discharge he called out, "*Good-by !*" and fell dead at the post of duty.

Webb sent for fresh batteries to replace the two that were disabled, and Wheeler's First New York Independent Battery came up just before the attack, and took the place of Cushing's battery on the left.

Armistead pressed forward, leaped the stone wall, waving his sword with his hat on it, followed by about a hundred of his men, several of whom carried battle-flags. He shouted, "Give them the cold steel, boys!" and laid his hands upon a gun. The battery for a few minutes was in his possession, and the rebel flag flew triumphantly over our line. But Webb was at the front, very near Armistead, animating and encouraging his men. He led the Seventy-second Pennsylvania regiment against the enemy, and posted a line of wounded men in rear to drive back or shoot every man that deserted his duty. A portion of the Seventy-first Pennsylvania, behind a stone wall on the right, threw in a deadly flanking fire, while a great part of the Sixty-ninth Pennsylvania and the remainder of the Seventy-first made stern resistance from a copse of trees on the left, near where the enemy had broken the line, and where our men were shot with the rebel muskets touching their breasts.

Then came a splendid charge of two regiments, led by Colonel Hall, which passed completely through Webb's line, and engaged the enemy in a hand-to-hand conflict.[1] Armistead was shot down by the side of the gun he had taken. Dying in the effort to extend the area of slavery over the free States, he may have felt that he had been engaged in an unjust cause; for he said to one of our officers who leaned over him: "Tell Hancock I have wronged him and have wronged my country."

Both Gibbon and Webb were wounded, and the loss in officers and men was very heavy; two rebel brigadier-generals were killed, and more prisoners were taken than twice

---

[1] Colonel Norman J. Hall, commanding a brigade in Hancock's corps, who rendered this great service, was one of the garrison who defended Fort Sumter at the beginning of the war. At that time he was the Second Lieutenant of my company.

Webb's brigade; 6 battle-flags, and 1,463 muskets were also gathered in.[1]

My command being a little to the left, I witnessed this scene, and, after it was over, sent out stretcher-bearers attached to the ambulance train, and had numbers of wounded Confederates brought in and cared for. I was told that there was one man among these whose conversation seemed to indicate that he was a general officer. I sent to ascertain his rank, but he replied: "Tell General Doubleday in a few minutes I shall be where there is no rank." He expired soon after, and I never learned his name.

The rebels did not seem to appreciate my humanity in sending out to bring in their wounded, for they opened a savage fire against the stretcher-bearers. One shell burst among us, a piece of it knocked me over on my horse's neck, and wounded Lieutenant Cowdry of my staff.

When Pickett—the great leader—looked around the top of the ridge he had temporarily gained, he saw it was impossible to hold the position. Troops were rushing in on him from all sides. The Second Corps were engaged in a furious assault on his front. His men were fighting with clubbed muskets, and even banner staves were intertwined in a fierce and hopeless struggle. My division of the First Corps were on his right flank, giving deadly blows there, and the Third Corps were closing up to attack. Pettigrew's forces on his left had given way, and a heavy skirmish line began to accumulate on that flank. He saw his men surrendering in masses, and, with a heart full of anguish, ordered a retreat. Death had been busy on all sides, and few indeed

[1] The spirit of the men was remarkable. Lieutenant Woodruff, of the First United States Artillery, whose battery had been very efficient in repelling the enemy's charge, was leaning against a tree, mortally wounded, when his second in command came to see if he could be of any service. The dying officer told him to go back to his guns, as the fighting there was more important than his own fate.

now remained of that magnificent column which had advanced so proudly, led by the Ney of the rebel army, and these few fell back in disorder, and without organization, behind Wright's brigade, which had been sent forward to cover the retreat. At first, however, when struck by Stannard on the flank, and when Pickett's charge was spent, they rallied in a little slashing, where a grove had been cut down by our troops to leave an opening for our artillery. There two regiments of Rowley's brigade of my division, the One Hundred and Fifty-first Pennsylvania and the Twentieth New York State Militia, under Colonel Theodore B. Gates, of the latter regiment, made a gallant charge, and drove them out. Pettigrew's division, it is said, lost 2,000 prisoners and 15 battle-flags on the left.

While this severe contest was going on in front of Webb, Wilcox deployed his command and opened a feeble fire against Caldwell's division on my left. Stannard repeated the manœuvre which had been so successful against Kemper's brigade by detaching the Fourteenth and Sixteenth Vermont to take Wilcox in flank. Wilcox thus attacked on his right, while a long row of batteries tore the front of his line to pieces with canister, could gain no foothold. He found himself exposed to a tremendous cross fire, and was obliged to retreat, but a great portion of his command were brought in as prisoners by Stannard[1] and battle-flags were gathered in sheaves.

A portion of Longstreet's corps, Benning's, Robertson's, and Law's brigades, advanced against the two Round Tops to prevent reinforcements from being sent from that vicinity to meet Pickett's charge. Kilpatrick interfered with this

---

[1] As Stannard's brigade were new troops, and had been stationed near Washington, the men had dubbed them *The Paper Collar Brigade*, because some of them were seen wearing paper collars, but after this fight the term was never again applied to them.

programme, however, for about 2 P.M. he made his appearance on our left with Farnsworth's brigade and Merritt's
brigade of regulars, accompanied by Graham's and Elder's
batteries of the regular army, to attack the rebel right, with
a view to reach their ammunition trains, which were in that
vicinity. The rebels say his men came on yelling like de-
mons. Having driven back the skirmishers who guarded that
flank, Merritt deployed on the left and soon became engaged there with Anderson's Georgia brigade, which was
supported by two batteries. On the right Farnsworth, with
the First Vermont regiment of his brigade, leaped a fence,
and advanced until he came to a second stone fence, where
he was checked by an attack on his right flank from the
Fourth Alabama regiment of Law's brigade, which came back
for that purpose from a demonstration it was making against
Round Top. Farnsworth then turned and leaping another
fence in a storm of shot and shell, made a gallant attempt to
capture Backman's battery, but was unable to do so, as it
was promptly supported by the Ninth Georgia regiment of
Anderson's brigade. Farnsworth was killed in this charge,
and the First Vermont found itself enclosed in a field, with
high fences on all sides, behind which masses of infantry
were constantly rising up and firing. The regiment was all
broken up and forced to retire in detachments. Kilpatrick
after fighting some time longer without making much progress, fell back on account of the constant reinforcements
that were augmenting the force opposed to him. Although
he had not succeeded in capturing the ammunition train,
he had made a valuable diversion on the left, which doubtless prevented the enemy from assailing Round Top with
vigor, or detaching a force to aid Pickett.

The Confederate General Benning states that the prompt
action of General Law in posting the artillery in the road

and the Seventh and Ninth Georgia regiments on each side, was all that saved the train from capture. "There was nothing else to save it." He also says two-thirds of Pickett's command were killed, wounded, or captured. Every brigade commander and every field officer except one fell. Lee and Longstreet had seen from the edge of the woods, with great exultation, the blue flag of Virginia waving over the crest occupied by the Union troops. It seemed the harbinger of great success to Lee. He thought the Union army was conquered at last. The long struggle was over, and peace would soon come, accompanied by the acknowledgment of the independence of the Southern Confederacy. It was but a passing dream; the flag receded, and soon the plain was covered with fugitives making their way to the rear. Then, anticipating an immediate pursuit, he used every effort to rally men and officers, and made strenuous efforts to get his artillery in position to be effective.

The Confederate General A. R. Wright criticises this attack and very justly says, "The difficulty was not so much in reaching Cemetery Ridge or taking it. My brigade did so on the afternoon of the 2d, but the trouble was to hold it, for the whole Federal army was massed in a sort of horse shoe, and could rapidly reinforce the point to any extent; while the long enveloping Confederate line could not support promptly enough." This agrees with what I have said in relation to the convex and concave orders of battle.

General Gibbon had sent Lieutenant Haskell of his staff to Power's Hill to notify General Meade that the charge was coming. As Meade approached his old headquarters he heard firing on the crest above, and went up to ascertain the cause. He found the charge had been repulsed and ejaculated "Thank God!"

When Lee learned that Johnson had yielded his position

on the right, and therefore could not co-operate with Pickett's advance, he sent Stuart's cavalry around to accomplish the same object by attacking the right and rear of our army. Howard saw the rebel cavalry moving off in that direction, and David McM. Gregg, whose division was near White's Creek where it crosses the Baltimore pike, received orders about noon to guard Slocum's right and rear.

Custer had already been contending with his brigade against portions of the enemy's force in that direction, when Gregg sent forward McIntosh's brigade to relieve him, and followed soon after with J. Irvin Gregg's brigade. Custer was under orders to join Kilpatrick's command, to which he belonged, but the exigencies of the battle soon forced Gregg to detain him. McIntosh, having taken the place of Custer, pushed forward to develop the enemy's line, which he found very strongly posted, the artillery being on a commanding ridge which overlooked the whole country, and covered by dismounted cavalry in woods, buildings, and behind fences below. McIntosh became warmly engaged and sent back for Randol's battery to act against the rebel guns on the crest, and drive the enemy out of the buildings. The guns above were silenced by Pennington's and Randol's batteries, and the force below driven out of the houses by Lieutenant Chester's section of the latter. The buildings and fences were then occupied by our troops. The enemy attempted to regain them by a charge against McIntosh's right flank, but were repulsed. In the meantime Gregg came up with the other brigade, and assumed command of the field. The battle now became warm, for W. H. F. Lee's brigade, under Chambliss, advanced to support the skirmish line, and the First New Jersey, being out of ammunition, was charged and routed by the First Virginia. The Seventh Michigan, a new regiment which came up to sup port it, was also driven in; for the enemy's dismounted line reinforced the First Virginia. The latter regiment, which had held on with desperate tenacity, although attacked on both flanks, was at last compelled to fall back by an attack made by part of the Fifth Michigan. The contending forces were now pretty well exhausted when, to the dismay of our men, a fresh brigade under Wade Hampton, which Stuart had kept in reserve, made its appearance, and new and desperate exertions were required to stem its progress. There was little time to act, but every sabre that could be brought forward was used. As Hampton came on, our artillery under Pennington and Randol made terrible gaps in his ranks. Chester's section kept firing canister until the rebels were within fifty yards of him. The enemy were temporarily stopped by a desperate charge on their flank, made by only sixteen men of the Third Pennsylvania Cavalry, under Captains Treichel and Rogers, accompanied by Captain Newhall of McIntosh's staff. This little band of heroes were nearly all disabled or killed, but they succeeded in delaying the enemy, already shattered by the canister from Chester's guns, until Custer was able to bring up the First Michigan and lead them to the charge, shouting "Come on, you wolverines!" Every available sabre was thrown in. General McIntosh and his staff and orderlies charged into the *mêlée* as individuals. Hampton and Fitz Lee headed the enemy, and Custer our troops. Lieutenant Colonel W. Brooke-Rawle, the historian of the conflict, who was present, says, "For minutes, which seemed like hours, amid the clashing of the sabres, the rattle of the small arms, the frenzied imprecations, the demands to surrender, the undaunted replies, and the appeals for mercy, the Confederate column stood its ground." A fresh squadron was brought up under Captain Hart of the First New Jersey, and the enemy at last gave way and retired.   Both sides still confronted each other, but the battle was over, for Pickett's charge had failed, and there was no longer any object in continuing the contest.

Stuart was undoubtedly baffled and the object of his expedition frustrated ; yet he stated in his official report that he was in a position to intercept the Union retreat in case Pickett had been successful.   At night he retreated to regain his communications with Ewell's left.

This battle being off of the official maps has hardly been alluded to in the various histories which have been written ; but its results were important and deserve to be commemorated.

When Pickett's charge was repulsed, and the whole plain covered with fugitives, we all expected that Wellington's command at Waterloo of " *Up, guards, and at them !* " would be repeated, and that a grand counter-charge would be made.   But General Meade had made no arrangements to give a return thrust.   It seems to me he should have posted the Sixth and part of the Twelfth Corps in rear of Gibbon's division the moment Pickett's infantry were seen emerging from the woods, a mile and a half off.   If they broke through our centre these corps would have been there to receive them, and if they failed to pierce our line and retreated, the two corps could have followed them up promptly before they had time to rally and reorganize.   An advance by Sykes would have kept Longstreet in position.   In all probability we would have cut the enemy's army in two, and captured the long line of batteries opposite us, which were but slightly guarded.   Hancock, lying wounded in an ambulance, wrote to Meade, recommending that this be done.   Meade, it is true, recognized in some sort the good effects of a counter-blow ; but to be effective the movement should have been prepared beforehand. It was too late to commence making preparations for an advance when some time had elapsed and when Lee had rallied his troops and had made all his arrangements to resist an assault. It was ascertained afterward that he had twenty rounds of ammunition left per gun, but it was not evenly distributed and some batteries in front had fired away all their cartridges. A counter-charge under such circumstances is considered almost imperative in war, for the beaten army, running and dismayed, cannot, in the nature of things, resist with much spirit; whereas the pursuers, highly elated by their success, and with the prospect of ending the contest, fight with more energy and bravery. Rodes says the Union forces were so long in occupying the town and in coming forward after the repulse of the enemy that it was generally thought they had retreated. Meade rode leisurely over to the Fifth Corps on the left, and told Sykes to send out and see if the enemy in his front was firm and holding on to their position. A brigade preceded by skirmishers was accordingly sent forward, but as Longstreet's troops were well fortified, they resisted the advance, and Meade—finding some hours had elapsed and that Lee had closed up his lines and was fortifying against him—gave up all idea of a counter-attack.

CHAPTER VII.

GENERAL RETREAT OF THE ENEMY—CRITICISMS OF DISTINGUISHED CONFEDERATE OFFICERS.

LEE was greatly dispirited at Pickett's failure, but worked with untiring energy to repair the disaster.

There was an interval of full a mile between Hill and Longstreet, and the plain was swarming with fugitives making their way back in disorder. He hastened to get ready to resist the counter-charge, which he thought was inevitable, and to plant batteries behind which the fugitives could rally. He also made great personal exertions to reassure and reassemble the detachments that came in. He did not for a moment imagine that Meade would fail to take advantage of this golden opportunity to crush the Army of Virginia and end the war.

The most distinguished rebel officers admit the great danger they were in at this time, and express their surprise that they were not followed up.

The fact is, Meade had no idea of leaving the ridge. I conversed the next morning with a corps commander who had just left him. He said: "Meade says he thinks he can hold out for part of another day here, if they attack him."

This language satisfied me that Meade would not go forward if he could avoid it, and would not impede in any way the rebel retreat across the Potomac. Lee began to make preparations at once and started his trains on the morning of the 4th. By night Rodes's division, which followed them, was in bivouac two miles west of Fairfield. It was a difficult task to retreat burdened with 4,000 prisoners, and a train fifteen miles long, in the presence of a victorious enemy, but it was successfully accomplished as regards his main body. The roads, too, were bad and much cut up by the rain.

While standing on Little Round Top Meade was annoyed at the fire of a rebel battery posted on an eminence beyond the wheat-field, about a thousand yards distant. He inquired what troops those were stationed along the stone fence which bounded the hither side of the wheat-field. Upon ascertaining that it was Crawford's division of the Fifth Corps, he directed that they be sent forward to clear the woods in front of rebel skirmishers, who were very annoying, and to drive away the battery, *but not to get into a fight that would bring on a general engagement.* As Crawford unmasked from the stone fence the battery opened fire on his right. He sent Colonel Ent's regiment, deployed as skirmishers, against the guns, which retired as Ent approached. McCandless, who went forward with his brigade, moved too far to the right, and Crawford ordered him to change front and advance toward Round Top. He did so and struck a rebel brigade in flank which was behind a temporary breastwork of rails, sods, etc. When this brigade saw a Union force apparently approaching from their own lines to attack them in flank, they retreated in confusion, after a short resistance, and this disorder extended during the retreat to a reserve brigade posted on the low ground in their rear. Their flight did not cease until they reached Horner's woods, half a mile distant, where they immediately intrenched themselves. These brigades belonged to Hood's division, then under Law.

Longstreet says, "When this (Pickett's) charge failed, I expected that, of course, the enemy would throw himself against our shattered ranks and try to crush us. I sent my staff officers to the rear to assist in rallying the troops, and hurried to our line of batteries as the only support that I could give them." . . . "I knew if the army was to be saved these batteries must check the enemy." . . . "For unaccountable reasons the enemy did not pursue his advantage."

Longstreet always spoke of his own men as invincible, and stated that on the 2d they did the best three hours' fighting that ever was done, but Crawford's [1] attack seemed to show that they too were shaken by the defeat of Pickett's grand charge.

In regard to the great benefit we would have derived from a pursuit, it may not be out of place to give the opinion of a few more prominent Confederate officers.

Colonel Alexander, Chief of Longstreet's artillery, says in a communication to the "Southern Historical Papers:"

I have always believed that the enemy here lost the greatest opportunity they ever had of routing Lee's army by a prompt offensive. They occupied a line shaped somewhat like a horseshoe. I suppose the greatest diameter of this horseshoe was not more than one mile, and the ground within was entirely sheltered from our observation and fire, with communications by signals all over it, and they could concentrate their whole force at any point and in a very short time without our knowledge. Our line was an enveloping semi-circle, over four miles in development, and communication from flank to flank, even by courier, was difficult, the country being well cleared and exposed to the enemy's view and fire, the roads all running at right angles to our lines, and, some of them at least, broad turnpikes where the enemy's guns could

---

[1] Crawford was also one of those who took a prominent part in the defence of Fort Sumter, at the beginning of the war. We each commanded detachments of artillery on that occasion.

rake for two miles. Is it necessary now to add any statement as to the superiority of the Federal force, or the exhausted and shattered condition of the Confederates for a space of at least a mile in their very centre, to show that a great opportunity was thrown away? I think General Lee himself was quite apprehensive the enemy would *riposte*, and that it was that apprehension which brought him alone out to my guns, where he could observe all the indications.

General Trimble, who commanded a division of Hill's corps, which supported Pickett in his advance, says, "By all the rules of warfare the Federal troops should (as I expected they would) have marched against our shattered columns and sought to cover our army with an overwhelming defeat."

Colonel Simms, who commanded Semmes's Georgia brigade in the fight with Crawford just referred to, writes to the latter, "There was much confusion in our army so far as my observation extended, and I think we would have made but feeble resistance, if you had pressed on, on the evening of the 3d."

General Meade, however, overcome by the great responsibilities of his position, still clung to the ridge, and fearful of a possible disaster would not take the risk of making an advance. And yet if he could have succeeded in crushing Lee's army then and there, he would have saved two years of war with its immense loss of life and countless evils. He might at least have thrown in Sedgwick's corps, which had not been actively engaged in the battle, for even if it was repulsed the blows it gave would leave the enemy little inclination to again assail the heights.

At 6.30 P. M. the firing ceased on the part of the enemy, and although they retained their position the next day, the battle of Gettysburg was virtually at an end.

The town was still full of our wounded, and many of our surgeons, with rare courage, remained there to take charge of them, for it required some nerve to run the risk of being sent to Libby prison when the fight was over, a catastrophe which has often happened to our medical officers. Among the rest, the chief surgeons of the First Corps, Doctor Theodore Heard and Doctor Thomas H. Bache, refused to leave their patients, and in consequence of the hasty retreat of the enemy were fortunately not carried off.

After the battle Meade had not the slightest desire to recommence the struggle. It is a military maxim that to a flying enemy must be given a wall of steel or a bridge of gold. In the present instance it was unmistakably the bridge of gold that was presented. It was hard to convince him that Lee was actually gone, and at first he thought it might be a device to draw the Union army from its strong position on the heights.

Our cavalry were sent out on the 4th to ascertain where the enemy were, and what they were doing. General Birney threw forward a reconnoitering party and opened fire with a battery on a column making their way toward Fairfield, but he was checked at once and directed *on no account to bring on a battle.* On the 5th, as it was certain the enemy were retreating, Sedgwick received orders to follow up the rear of the rebel column. He marched eight miles to Fairfield Pass. There Early, who was in command of the rear guard, was endeavoring to save the trains, which were heaped up in great confusion. Sedgwick, after a distant cannonade, reported the position too strong to be forced. It was a plain, two miles wide, surrounded by hills, and it would not have been difficult to take it, but Sedgwick knew Meade favored the "bridge of gold" policy, and was not disposed to thwart the wishes of his chief. In my opinion Sedgwick should have made an energetic attack, and Meade should have supported it with his whole army, for our cavalry were making great havoc in the enemy's trains in rear;

and if Lee, instead of turning on Kilpatrick, had been forced
to form line against Meade, the cavalry, which was between
him and his convoys of ammunition, in all probability
might have captured the latter and ended the war.   Stuart,
it is true, was following up Kilpatrick, but he took an indirect route and was nearly a day behind.   I do not see
why the force which was now promptly detached from the
garrisons of Washington and Baltimore and sent to Harper's Ferry could not have formed on the Virginia side of
the Potomac opposite Williamsport, and with the co-operation of General Meade have cut off the ammunition of
which Lee stood so much in need.   As the river had risen
and an expedition sent out by General French from Frederick had destroyed the bridge at Falling Waters, everything
seemed to favor such a plan.   The moment it was ascertained that Lee was cut off from Richmond and short of
ammunition the whole North would have turned out and
made a second Saratoga of it.   As it was, he had but few
rounds for his cannon, and our artillery could have opened
a destructive fire on him from a distance without exposing
our infantry.   It was worth the effort and there was little
or no danger in attempting it.   Meade had Sedgwick's
fresh corps and was reinforced by a division of 11,000 men
under General W. F. Smith (Baldy Smith).   French's division of 4,000 at Frederick, and troops from Washington and
Baltimore were also available to assist in striking the final
blow.   The Twelfth Corps was also available, as Slocum
volunteered to join in the pursuit.   Meade, however, delayed moving at all until Lee had reached Hagerstown and
then took a route that was almost twice as long as that
adopted by the enemy.   Lee marched day and night to
avoid pursuit, and when the river rose and his bridge was
gone, so that he was unable to cross, he gained six days

in which to choose a position, fortify it, and renew his supply of ammunition before Meade made his appearance.

In consequence of repeated orders from President Lincoln to attack the enemy, Meade went forward and confronted Lee on the 12th. He spent that day and the next in making reconnoissances and resolved to attack on the 14th; but Lee left during the night, and by 8 A.M. the entire army of the enemy were once more on Virginia soil.

The Union loss in this campaign is estimated by the Count of Paris, who is an impartial observer, at 2,834 killed, 13,709 wounded, and 6,643 missing; total, 23,186.

The rebel loss he puts at 2,665 killed, 12,599 wounded, 7,464 missing; total, 22,728.

Among the killed in the battle on the rebel side were Generals Armistead, Barksdale, Garnett, Pender, and Semmes; and Pettigrew during the retreat.

Among the wounded were Generals G. T. Anderson, Hampton, Jenkins, J. M. Jones, Kemper, and Scales.

Archer was captured on the first day.

Among the killed on the Union side were Major General Reynolds and Brigadier-Generals Vincent, Weed, Zook, and Farnsworth.

Among the wounded were Major-Generals Sickles (losing a leg), Hancock, Doubleday, Gibbon, Barlow, Warren, and Butterfield, and Brigadier-Generals Graham, Stannard, Paul (losing both eyes), Barnes, Brooke, and Webb.

APPENDIX A.

Roster of the Federal Army engaged in the Battle of Gettysburg, Wednesday, Thursday, and Friday, July 1st, 2d, and 3d, 1863.

MAJOR-GENERAL GEO. GORDON MEADE, COMMANDING.

STAFF.

MAJOR-GENERAL DANIEL BUTTERFIELD, Chief of Staff.

BRIG.-GENERAL M. R. PATRICK, Provost Marshal-General.

"   "   SETH WILLIAMS, Adjutant-General.

"   "   EDMUND SCHRIVER, Inspector-General.

"   "   RUFUS INGALLS, Quartermaster-General.

COLONEL HENRY F. CLARKE, Chief Commis'y of Subsistence.

MAJOR JONATHAN LETTERMAN, Surgeon, Chief of Medical Department.

BRIG.-GENERAL G. K. WARREN, Chief Engineer.

MAJOR D. W. FLAGLER, Chief Ordnance Officer.

MAJOR-GENERAL ALFRED PLEASONTON, Chief of Cavalry.

BRIG.-GENERAL HENRY J. HUNT, Chief of Artillery.

CAPTAIN L. B. NORTON, Chief Signal Officer.

————

MAJOR-GENERAL JOHN F. REYNOLDS,[1] Commanding the First, Third, and Eleventh Corps on July 1st.

MAJOR-GENERAL HENRY W. SLOCUM, Commanding the Right Wing on July 2d and July 3d.

MAJOR-GENERAL W. S. HANCOCK, Commanding the Left Centre on July 2d and July 3d.

---

[1] He was killed and succeeded by Major-General O. O. Howard.

FIRST CORPS.

MAJOR-GENERAL JOHN F. REYNOLDS, PERMANENT COMMANDER.
MAJOR-GENERAL ABNER DOUBLEDAY, Commanding on July 1st.
MAJOR-GENERAL JOHN NEWTON, Commanding July 2d and 3d.

FIRST DIVISION.

BRIGADIER-GENERAL JAMES S. WADSWORTH COMMANDING.

First Brigade.—(1) Brigadier-General SOLOMON MEREDITH (wounded); (2) Colonel HENRY A. MORROW (wounded);[2] (3) Colonel W. W. ROBINSON. 2d Wisconsin, Colonel Lucius Fairchild (wounded), Lieut.-Colonel George H. Stevens (wounded), Major John Mansfield (wounded), Captain Geo. H. Otis; 6th Wisconsin, Lieut.-Colonel R. R. Dawes; 7th Wisconsin, Colonel W. W. Robinson; 24th Michigan, Colonel Henry A. Morrow (wounded), Lieut.-Colonel Mark Flanigan (wounded), Major Edwin B. Wright (wounded), Captain Albert M. Edwards; 19th Indiana, Colonel Samuel Williams.

Second Brigade.—Brigadier-General LYSANDER CUTLER Commanding. 7th Indiana, Major Ira G. Grover; 56th Pennsylvania, Colonel J. W. Hoffman; 76th New York, Major Andrew J. Grover (killed), Captain John E. Cook; 95th New York, Colonel George H. Biddle (wounded), Major Edward Pye; 147th New York, Lieut.-Colonel F. C. Miller (wounded), Major George Harney; 14th Brooklyn, Colonel E. B. Fowler.

SECOND DIVISION.

BRIGADIER-GENERAL JOHN C. ROBINSON COMMANDING.

First Brigade.—Brigadier-General GABRIEL R. PAUL Commanding (wounded); Colonel S. H. LEONARD; Colonel RICHARD COULTER. 16th Maine, Colonel Charles W. Tilden (captured), Lieut.-Colonel N. E. Welch, Major Arch. D. Leavitt; 13th Massachusetts, Colonel S. H. Leonard (wounded); 94th New York, Colonel A. R. Root (wounded), Major S. H. Moffat; 104th New York, Colonel Gilbert G. Prey; 107th Pennsylvania, Colonel T. F. McCoy (wounded), Lieut.-Colonel James McThompson (wounded), Captain E. D. Roath; 11th Pennsylvania, Colonel Richard S. Coulter, Captain J. J. Bierer.[1]

Second Brigade.—Brigadier-General HENRY BAXTER Commanding. 12th Massachusetts, Colonel James L. Bates; 83d New York, Lieut.-Colonel Joseph R. Moesch; 97th New York, Colonel Charles Wheelock; 88th Pennsylvania, Major Benezet F. Faust, Captain E. Y. Patterson; 90th Pennsylvania, Colonel Peter Lyle.

THIRD DIVISION.

MAJOR-GENERAL ABNER DOUBLEDAY PERMANENT COMMANDER on July 2d and 3d.
BRIGADIER-GENERAL THOMAS A. ROWLEY, July 1st.

First Brigade.—Brigadier-General THOMAS A. ROWLEY, July 2d and 3d; Colonel CHAPMAN BIDDLE, July 1st. 121st Pennsylvania, Colonel Chapman Biddle, Major Alexander Biddle; 142d Pennsylvania, Colonel Robert P. Cummings (killed), Lieut.-Colonel A. B. McCalmont; 151st Pennsylvania, Lieut.-Colonel George F. McFarland (lost a leg), Captain Walter L. Owens; 20th New York S. M., Colonel Theodore B. Gates.

Second Brigade.—(1) Colonel ROY STONE Commanding (wounded); (2) Colonel LANGHORNE WISTER (wounded); (3) Colonel EDMUND L. DANA. 143d Pennsylvania, Colonel Edmund L. Dana, Major John D. Musser; 149th Pennsylvania, Lieut.-Colonel Walton Dwight (wounded), Captain A. J. Sofield (killed), Captain John Irvin; 150th Pennsylvania, Colonel Langhorne Wister (wounded), Lieut.-Colonel H. S. Huidekoper (wounded), Major Thomas Chamberlain (wounded), Capt. C. C. Widdis (wounded), Captain G. W. Jones.

---

[1] The Eleventh Pennsylvania was transferred from the Second Brigade.
[2] See page 130.

Third Brigade.—Brigadier-General GEO. J. STANNARD Commanding (wounded). 12th Vermont, Colonel Asa P. Blunt (not engaged) ; 13th Vermont, Colonel Francis V. Randall ; 14th Vermont, Colonel William T. Nichols ; 15th Vermont, Colonel Redfield Proctor (not engaged) ; 16th Vermont, Colonel Wheelock G. Veazey.

Artillery Brigade.—Colonel CHARLES S. WAINWRIGHT Commanding. 2d Maine, Captain James A. Hall ; 5th Maine, G. T. Stevens ; Battery B, 1st Pennsylvania, Captain J. H. Cooper ; Battery B, 4th United States, Lieutenant James Stewart ; Battery L, 1st New York, Captain J. A. Reynolds.

[NOTE.—Tidball's Battery of the Second United States Artillery, under Lieutenant John H. Calef, also fought in line with the First Corps. Lieutenant Benj. W. Wilber, and Lieutenant George Breck, of Captain Reynolds's Battery, and Lieutenant James Davison, of Stewart's Battery, commanded sections which were detached at times.]

SECOND CORPS.

MAJOR-GENERAL WINFIELD S. HANCOCK, PERMANENT COMMANDER (wounded).
MAJOR-GENERAL JOHN GIBBON (wounded).
BRIGADIER-GENERAL JOHN C. CALDWELL.

FIRST DIVISION.

BRIGADIER-GENERAL JOHN C. CALDWELL.
COLONEL JOHN R. BROOKE (wounded).

First Brigade.—Colonel EDWARD E. CROSS (killed) ; Colonel H. B. McKEEN. 5th New Hampshire, Colonel E. E. Cross, Lieut.-Colonel C. E. Hapgood ; 61st New York, Lieut.-Colonel Oscar K. Broady ; 81st Pennsylvania, Colonel H. Boyd McKeen, Lieut.-Colonel Amos Stroho ; 148th Pennsylvania, Lieut.-Colonel Robert McFarland.

Second Brigade.—Colonel PATRICK KELLY Commanding. 28th Massachusetts, Colonel Richard Byrnes ; 63d New York, Lieut.-Colonel R. C. Bentley (wounded), Captain Thos. Touhy ; 69th New York, Captain Richard Maroney (wounded), Lieutenant James J. Smith ; 88th New York, Colonel Patrick Kelly, Captain Dennis F. Burke ; 116th Pennsylvania, Major St. Clair A. Mulholland.

Third Brigade.—Brigadier-General S. K. ZOOK Commanding (killed) ; Lieut.-Colonel JOHN FRAZER. 52d New York, Lieut.-Colonel Charles G. Freudenberg (wounded), Captain Wm. Scherrer ; 57th New York, Lieut.-Colonel Alfred B. Chapman ; 66th New York, Colonel Orlando W. Morris (wounded), Lieut. Colonel John S. Hammell (wounded) ; Major Peter Nelson ; 140th Pennsylvania, Colonel Richard P. Roberts (killed), Lieut.-Colonel John Frazer.

Fourth Brigade.—Colonel JOHN R. BROOKE Commanding (wounded). 27th Connecticut, Lieut.-Colonel Henry C. Merwin (killed), Major James H. Coburn ; 64th New York, Colonel Daniel G. Bingham ; 53d Pennsylvania, Colonel J. R. Brooke, Lieut.-Colonel Richard McMichael ; 145th Pennsylvania, Colonel Hiram L. Brown (wounded), Captain John W. Reynolds (wounded), Captain Moses W. Oliver ; 2d Delaware, Colonel William P. Bailey.

SECOND DIVISION.

BRIGADIER-GENERAL JOHN GIBBON, PERMANENT COMMANDER (wounded).
BRIGADIER GENERAL WILLIAM HARROW.

First Brigade—Brigadier-General WILLIAM HARROW Commanding ; Colonel FRANCIS E. HEATH. 19th Maine, Colonel F. E. Heath, Lieut.-Colonel Henry W. Cunningham ; 15th Massachusetts, Colonel George H. Ward (killed), Lieut.-Colonel George C. Joslin ; 82d New York, Colonel Henry W. Huston (killed), Captain John Darrow ; 1st Minnesota, Colonel William Colvill (wounded), Captain N. S. Messick (killed), Captain Wilson B. Farrell, Captain Louis Muller Captain Joseph Periam, Captain Henry C. Coates.

Second Brigade.—Brigadier-General ALEX. S. WEBB Commanding (wounded). 69th Pennsylvania, Colonel Dennis O. Kane (killed), Lieut.-Colonel M. Tschudy (killed), Major James Duffy (wounded), Captain Wm. Davis; 71st Pennsylvania, Lieut.-Colonel Richard Penn Smith ; 72d Pennsylvania, Colonel De Witt C. Baxter ; 106th Pennsylvania, Lieut.-Colonel Theo. Hesser.

Third Brigade.—Colonel NORMAN J. HALL Commanding. 19th Massachusetts, Colonel Arthur F. Devereux ; 20th Massachusetts, Colonel Paul J Revere (killed), Captain H. L. Abbott (wounded) ; 42d New York, Colonel James E. Mallon ; 59th New York, Lieut.-Colonel Max A. Thoman (killed) ; 7th Michigan, Colonel N. J. Hall, Lieut.-Colonel Amos E. Steele (killed), Major S. W. Curtis.

Unattached.—Andrew Sharpshooters.

THIRD DIVISION.

BRIGADIER-GENERAL ALEXANDER HAYS COMMANDING.

First Brigade.—Colonel SAMUEL S. CARROLL Commanding. 4th Ohio, Lieut.-Colonel James H. Godman, Lieut.-Colonel L. W. Carpenter ; 8th Ohio, Colonel S. S. Carroll, Lieut.-Colonel Franklin Sawyer ; 14th Indiana, Colonel John Coons ; 7th West Virginia, Colonel Joseph Snyder.

Second Brigade.—Colonel THOMAS A. SMYTH Commanding (wounded) ; Lieut.-Colonel F. E. PIERCE. 14th Connecticut, Major John T. Ellis ; 10th New York (battalion), Major Geo. F. Hopper : 108th New York, Colonel Charles J. Powers ; 12th New Jersey, Major John T. Hill ; 1st Delaware, Colonel Thomas A. Smyth ; Lieut.-Colonel Edward P. Harris, Captain M. B. Ellgood (killed), Lieutenant Wm. Smith (killed).

Third Brigade.—Colonel GEORGE L. WILLARD Commanding (killed) ; Colonel ELIAKIM SHERRILL (killed) ; Lieut.-Colonel JAMES M. BULL. 39th New York, Lieut.-Colonel James G. Hughes : 111th New York, Colonel Clinton D. McDougall (wounded), Lieut.-Colonel Isaac M. Lusk, Captain A. P. Seeley ; 125th New York, Colonel G. L. Willard (killed), Lieut.-Colonel Levi Crandall ; 126th New York, Colonel E. Sherrill (killed) ; Lieut.-Colonel J. M. Bull.

Artillery Brigade.—Captain J. G. HAZARD Commanding. Battery B, 1st New York, Captain James McK. Roity (killed) ; Battery A, 1st Rhode Island, Lieutenant William A. Arnold ; Battery B, 1st Rhode Island, Lieutenant T. Fred. Brown (wounded) ; Battery I, 1st United States. Lieutenant G. A. Woodruff (killed) ; Battery A, 4th United States, Lieutenant A. H. Cushing (killed).

[NOTE.—Battery C, 4th United States, Lieutenant E. Thomas, was in the line of the Second Corps on July 3d. Some of the batteries were so nearly demolished that there was no officer to assume command at the close of the battle.]

Cavalry Squadron.—Captain RILEY JOHNSON Commanding. D and K, 6th New York.

THIRD CORPS.

MAJOR-GENERAL DANIEL E. SICKLES COMMANDING (wounded). MAJOR-GENERAL DAVID B. BIRNEY.

FIRST DIVISION.

MAJOR-GENERAL DAVID B. BIRNEY PERMANENT COMMANDER.
BRIGADIER-GENERAL J. H. H. WARD.

First Brigade.—Brigadier-General C. K. GRAHAM Commanding (wounded, captured) : Colonel ANDREW H. TIPPIN. 57th Pennsylvania, Colonel Peter Sides, Lieut.-Colonel Wm. P. Neeper ; Captain A. H. Nelson ; 63d Pennsylvania, Lieut.-Colonel John A. Danks ; 68th Pennsylvania, Colonel A. H. Tippin, all the Field Officers wounded ; 105th Pennsylvania, Colonel Calvin A. Craig ;

114th Pennsylvania, Lieut.-Colonel Frederick K. Cavada (captured); **141st Pennsylvania**, Colonel Henry J. Madill, Captain E. R. Brown.[1]

[NOTE.—The Second New Hampshire, Third Maine, and Seventh and Eighth New Jersey also formed part of Graham's line on the 2d.]

Second Brigade.—Brigadier-General J. H. H. WARD Commanding; Colonel H. BERDAN. 1st U. S. Sharpshooters, Colonel H. Berdan, Lieut.-Colonel C. Trapp; 2d U. S. Sharpshooters, Major H. H. Stoughton; 3d Maine, Colonel M. B. Lakeman (captured), Captain William C. Morgan; 4th Maine, Colonel Elijah Walker (wounded), Major Ebenezer Whitcombe (wounded). Captain Edwin Libby; 20th Indiana, Colonel John Wheeler (killed), Lieut.-Colonel William C. L. Taylor; 99th Pennsylvania, Major John W. Moore; 86th New York, Lieut.-Colonel Benjamin Higgins; 124th New York, Colonel A. Van Horn Ellis (killed), Lieut.-Colonel Francis M. Cummings.

Third Brigade.—Colonel PHILIP R. DE TROBRIAND, Commanding. 3d Michigan, Colonel Byron R. Pierce (wounded), Lieut.-Colonel E. S. Pierce; 5th Michigan, Lieut.-Colonel John Pulford (wounded), Major S. S. Matthews; 40th New York, Colonel Thomas W. Egan; 17th Maine, Lieut.-Colonel Charles B. Merrill; 110th Pennsylvania, Lieut.-Colonel David M. Jones (wounded), Major Isaac Rogers.

SECOND DIVISION.
BRIGADIER-GENERAL ANDREW A. HUMPHREYS COMMANDING.

First Brigade.—Brigadier-General JOSEPH B. CARR Commanding. 1st Massachusetts, Colonel N. B. McLaughlin; 11th Massachusetts, Lieut.-Colonel Porter D. Tripp; 16th Massachusetts, Lieut.-Colonel Waldo Merriam; 26th Pennsylvania, Captain Geo. W. Tomlinson (wounded). Captain Henry Goodfellow; 11th New Jersey, Colonel Robert McAllister (wounded), Major Philip J. Kearny (killed), Captain Wm. B. Dunning; 84th Pennsylvania (not engaged), Lieut-. Colonel Milton Opp; 12th New Hampshire, Captain J. F. Langley.

Second Brigade.—Colonel WILLIAM R. BREWSTER Commanding. 70th New York (1st Excelsior), Major Daniel Mahen; 71st New York (2d Excelsior), Colonel Henry L. Potter; 72d New York (3d Excelsior), Colonel Wm. O. Stevens (killed), Lieut.-Colonel John S. Austin; 73d New York (4th Excelsior), Colonel William R. Brewster, Major M. W. Burns; 74th New York (5th Excelsior), Lieut.-Colonel Thomas Holt; 120th New York, Lieut.-Colonel Cornelius D. Westbrook (wounded), Major J. R. Tappen, Captain A. L. Lockwood.

Third Brigade.—Colonel GEORGE C. BURLING Commanding. 5th New Jersey, Colonel William J. Sewall (wounded). Captain Virgel M. Healey (wounded), Captain T. C. Godfrey, Captain H. H. Woolsey; 6th New Jersey, Colonel George C. Burling, Lieut.-Colonel S. R. Gilkyson; 7th New Jersey, Colonel L. R. Francine (killed), Lieut.-Colonel Francis Price; 8th New Jersey, Colonel John Ramsey (wounded), Captain John G. Langston; 115th Pennsylvania, Lieut.-Colonel John P. Dunne; 2d New Hampshire, Colonel Edward L. Bailey (wounded), Major Saml. P. Sayles (wounded).

Artillery Brigade.—Captain GEORGE E. RANDOLPH Commanding. Battery E, 1st Rhode Island, Lieutenant John K. Bucklyn (wounded), Lieutenant Benj. Freeborn; Battery B, 1st New Jersey, Captain A. J. Clark; Battery D. 1st New Jersey, Captain Geo. T. Woodbury; Battery K. 4th U. S., Lieutenant F. W. Seeley (wounded), Lieutenant Robt. James; Battery D, First New York, Captain George B. Winslow; 4th New York, Captain James E. Smith.

FIFTH CORPS.
MAJOR-GENERAL GEORGE SYKES COMMANDING.
FIRST DIVISION.
BRIGADIER-GENERAL JAMES BARNES COMMANDING.

First Brigade.—Colonel W. S. TILTON Commanding. 18th Massachusetts, Colonel Joseph Hayes; 22d Massachusetts, Colonel William S. Tilton, Lieut.-

---

[1] Colonel Madill commanded the 114th and 141st Pennsylvania.

Colonel Thomas Sherman, Jr.; 118th Pennsylvania, Colonel Charles M. Prevost; 1st Michigan, Colonel Ira C. Abbot (wounded), Lieut.-Colonel W. A. Throop.

Second Brigade.—Colonel J. B. SWEITZER Commanding. 9th Massachusetts, Colonel Patrick R. Guiney; 32d Massachusetts, Col. Geo. L. Prescott (wounded), Lieut.-Colonel Luther Stephenson (wounded), Major J. Cushing Edmunds; 4th Michigan, Colonel Hamson H. Jeffords (killed), Lieut.-Colonel George W. Lombard; 62d Pennsylvania, Colonel J. B. Sweitzer, Lieut.-Colonel James C. Hull.

Third Brigade.—Colonel STRONG VINCENT Commanding (killed); Colonel JAMES C. RICE. 20th Maine, Colonel Joshua L. Chamberlain; 44th New York, Colonel James C. Rice, Lieut.-Colonel Freeman Conner; 83d Pennsylvania, Major William H. Lamont, Captain O. E. Woodward; 16th Michigan, Lieut.-Colonel N. E. Welch.

SECOND DIVISION.

BRIGADIER-GENERAL ROMAYN B. AYRES COMMANDING.

First Brigade.—Colonel HANNIBAL DAY, 6th U. S. Infantry, Commanding. 3d U. S. Infantry, Captain H. W. Freedley (wounded), Captain Richard G. Lay; 4th U. S. Infantry, Captain J. W. Adams; 6th U. S. Infantry, Captain Levi C. Bootes; 12th U. S. Infantry, Captain Thomas S. Dunn; 14th U. S. Infantry, Major G. R. Giddings.

Second Brigade.—Colonel SIDNEY BURBANK, 2d U. S. Infantry, Commanding. 2d U. S. Infantry, Major A. T. Lee (wounded), Captain S. A. McKee; 7th U. S. Infantry, Captain D. P. Hancock; 10th U. S. Infantry, Captain William Clinton; 11th U. S. Infantry, Major De L. Floyd Jones; 17th U. S. Infantry, Lieut.-Colonel Durrell Green.

Third Brigade.—Brigadier-General S. H. WEED (killed); Colonel KENNER GARRARD. 140th New York, Colonel Patrick H. O'Rorke (killed), Lieut.-Colonel Louis Ernst; 146th New York, Colonel K. Garrard, Lieut.-Colonel David T. Jenkins; 91st Pennsylvania, Lieut.-Colonel Joseph H. Sinex; 155th Pennsylvania, Lieut.-Colonel John H. Cain.

THIRD DIVISION.

BRIGADIER-GENERAL S. WILEY CRAWFORD COMMANDING.

First Brigade.—Colonel WILLIAM McCANDLESS Commanding. 1st Pennsylvania Reserves, Colonel William Cooper Talley; 2d Pennsylvania Reserves, Colonel William McCandless, Lieut.-Colonel George A. Woodward; 6th Pennsylvania Reserves, Colonel Wellington H. Ent; 11th Pennsylvania Reserves, Colonel S. M. Jackson; 1st Rifles (Bucktails), Colonel Charles J. Taylor (killed), Lieut.-Colonel A. E. Niles (wounded), Major William R. Hartshorn.

Second Brigade.—Colonel JOSEPH W. FISHER Commanding. 5th Pennsylvania Reserves, Colonel J. W. Fisher, Lieut.-Colonel George Dare; 9th Pennsylvania Reserves, Lieut.-Colonel James McK. Snodgrass; 10th Pennsylvania Reserves, Colonel A. J. Warner; 12th Pennsylvania Reserves, Colonel M. D. Hardin.

Artillery Brigade.—Captain A. P. MARTIN Commanding. Battery D, 5th United States, Lieutenant Charles E. Hazlett (killed), Lieutenant B. F. Rittenhouse; Battery I, 5th United States, Lieutenant Leonard Martin: Battery C, 1st New York, Captain Albert Barnes: Battery L, 1st Ohio, Captain N. C. Gibbs; Battery C, Massachusetts, Captain A. P. Martin.

Provost Guard.—Captain H. W. RYDER. Companies E and D, 12th New York.

SIXTH CORPS.

MAJOR-GENERAL JOHN SEDGWICK.

FIRST DIVISION.

BRIGADIER-GENERAL H. G. WRIGHT COMMANDING.

First Brigade.—Brigadier-General A. T. A. TORBERT Commanding. 1st New Jersey, Lieut.-Colonel William Henry, Jr.; 2d New Jersey, Colonel Samuel L. Buck; 3d New Jersey, Colonel Henry W. Brown; 15th New Jersey, Colonel William H. Penrose.

Second Brigade.—Brigadier-General J. J. BARTLETT Commanding. 5th Maine, Colonel Clark S. Edwards; 121st New York, Colonel Emory Upton; 95th Pennsylvania, Lieut.-Colonel Edward Carroll; 96th Pennsylvania, Lieut.-Colonel William H. Lessig.

Third Brigade.—Brigadier-General D. A. RUSSELL Commanding. 6th Maine, Colonel Hiram Burnham; 49th Pennsylvania, Colonel William H. Irvin; 119th Pennsylvania, Colonel P. C. Elimaker; 5th Wisconsin, Colonel Thomas S. Allen.

SECOND DIVISION.

BRIGADIER-GENERAL A. P. HOWE COMMANDING.

Second Brigade.—Colonel L. A. GRANT Commanding. 2d Vermont, Colonel J. H. Walbridge; 3d Vermont, Colonel T. O. Seaver; 4th Vermont, Colonel E. H. Stoughton; 5th Vermont, Lieut.-Colonel John R. Lewis; 6th Vermont, Lieut.-Colonel Elisha L. Barney.

Third Brigade —Brigadier-General T. H. NEILL Commanding. 7th Maine, Lieut.-Colonel Seldon Conner; 49th New York, Colonel D. D. Bidwell; 77th New York, Colonel J. B. McKean; 43d New York, Colonel B. F. Baker; 61st Pennsylvania, Major Geo. W. Dawson.

THIRD DIVISION.

BRIGADIER-GENERAL FRANK WHEATON COMMANDING.

First Brigade. —Brigadier-General ALEXANDER SHALER Commanding. 65th New York, Colonel J. E Hamblin; 67th New York, Colonel Nelson Cross; 122d New York, Lieut.-Colonel A. W. Dwight; 23d Pennsylvania, Lieut.-Colonel John F. Glenn; 82d Pennsylvania, Colonel Isaac Bassett.

Second Brigade.—Colonel H. L. EUSTIS Commanding. 7th Massachusetts, Lieut.-Colonel Franklin P. Harlow; 10th Massachusetts, Lieut.-Colonel Jefford M. Decker; 37th Massachusetts, Colonel Oliver Edwards; 2d Rhode Island, Colonel Horatio Rogers.

Third Brigade.—Colonel DAVID I. NEVIN Commanding. 62d New York, Colonel D. I. Nevin, Lieut.-Colonel Theo. B. Hamilton; 102d Pennsylvania,[1] Colonel John W. Patterson; 93d Pennsylvania, Colonel James M. McCarter; 98th Pennsylvania, Major John B. Kohler; 139th Pennsylvania, Lieut.-Colonel William H. Moody.

Artillery Brigade.—Colonel C. H. TOMPKINS Commanding. Battery A, 1st Massachusetts, Captain W. H. McCartney; Battery D, 2d United States, Lieutenant E. B. Williston; Battery F, 5th United States, Lieutenant Leonard Martin; Battery G, 2d United States, Lieutenant John H. Butler; Battery C, 1st Rhode Island, Captain Richard Waterman; Battery G, 1st Rhode Island, Captain George W. Adams; 1st New York, Captain Andrew Cowan; 3d New York, Captain William A. Harn.

Cavalry Detachment.—Captain WILLIAM L. CRAFT Commanding. H, 1st Pennsylvania; L, 1st New Jersey.

ELEVENTH CORPS.

MAJOR-GENERAL OLIVER O. HOWARD PERMANENT COMMANDER.
MAJOR-GENERAL CARL SCHURZ, July 1st.

FIRST DIVISION.

BRIGADIER-GENERAL FRANCIS C. BARLOW COMMANDING (wounded).
BRIGADIER-GENERAL ADELBERT AMES.

First Brigade.—Colonel LEOPOLD VON GILSA Commanding. 41st New York, Colonel L. Von Gilsa, Lieut.-Colonel D. Von Einsiedel; 54th New York, Colonel Eugene A. Kozlay; 68th New York, Colonel Gotthilf Bourny de Ivernois; 153d Pennsylvania, Colonel Charles Glanz.

---

[1] Not engaged.

Second Brigade.—Brigadier-General ADELBERT AMES Commanding; Colonel ANDREW L. HARRIS. 17th Connecticut, Lieut.-Colonel Douglass Fowler (killed), Major A. G. Brady (wounded); 25th Ohio, Lieut.-Colonel Jeremiah Williams (captured), Lieutenant William Maloney (wounded), Lieutenant Israel White; 75th Ohio, Colonel Andrew L. Harris (wounded), Lieut.-Colonel Ben Morgan (wounded), Major Charles W. Friend; 107th Ohio, Captain John M. Lutz.

SECOND DIVISION.

BRIGADIER-GENERAL A. VON STEINWEHR COMMANDING.

First Brigade.— Colonel CHARLES R. COSTER Commanding. 27th Pennsylvania, Lieut.-Colonel Lorenz Cantador; 73d Pennsylvania, Captain Daniel F. Kelly; 134th New York, Colonel Charles R. Coster, Lieut.-Colonel Allan H. Jackson; 154th New York, Colonel Patrick H. Jones.

Second Brigade.—Colonel ORLANDO SMITH Commanding. 33d Massachusetts, Lieut.-Colonel Adin B. Underwood; 136th New York, Colonel James Wood, Jr.; 55th Ohio, Colonel Charles B. Gambee; 73d Ohio, Colonel Orlando Smith, Lieut.-Colonel Richard Long.

THIRD DIVISION.

MAJOR-GENERAL CARL SCHURZ PERMANENT COMMANDER.
BRIGADIER-GENERAL ALEXANDER SCHIMMELPFENNIG Commanding on July 1st.

First Brigade.—Brigadier-General A. VON SCHIMMELPFENNIG Commanding (captured): Colonel GEORGE VON ARNSBURG. 45th New York, Colonel G. Von Arnsburg, Lieut.-Colonel Adolphus Dobke; 157th New York, Colonel Philip P. Brown, Jr.; 74th Pennsylvania, Colonel Adolph Von Hartung (wounded), Lieut.-Colonel Von Mitzel (captured), Major Gustav Schleiter; 61st Ohio, Colonel S. J. McGroarty; 82d Illinois, Colonel J. Hecker.

Second Brigade.—Colonel WALDIMIR KRYZANOWSKI Commanding. 58th New York, Colonel W. Kryzanowski, Lieut.-Colonel August Otto, Captain Emil Koenig, Lieut.-Colonel Frederick Gellman; 119th New York, Colonel John T. Lockman, Lieut.-Colonel James C. Rogers; 75th Pennsylvania, Colonel Francis Mahler (wounded), Major August Ledig; 82d Ohio, Colonel James S. Robinson (wounded), Lieut.-Colonel D. Thomson; 26th Wisconsin, Colonel Wm. H. Jacobs.

Artillery Brigade.—Major THOMAS W. OSBORN Commanding. Battery I, 1st New York, Captain Michael Wiedrick; Battery I, 1st Ohio, Captain Hubert Dilger; Battery K, 1st Ohio, Captain Lewis Heckman; Battery G, 4th United States, Lieutenant Bayard Wilkeson (killed), Lieutenant E. A. Bancroft; 13th New York, Lieutenant William Wheeler.

Unattached.—I and K, 1st Indiana Cav.; 8th New York Inf., one company.

TWELFTH CORPS.

BRIGADIER-GENERAL ALPHEUS S. WILLIAMS COMMANDING.

FIRST DIVISION.

BRIGADIER-GENERAL THOMAS H. RUGER COMMANDING.

First Brigade.—Colonel ARCHIBALD L. McDOUGALL Commanding. 5th Connecticut, Colonel Warren W. Packer; 20th Connecticut, Lieut.-Colonel William B. Wooster; 123d New York, Colonel A. L. McDougall, Lieut.-Colonel James C. Rogers; 145th New York, Colonel E. L. Price; 46th Pennsylvania, Colonel James L. Selfridge; 3d Maryland, Colonel J. M. Sudsburg.

Second Brigade.[1]—Brigadier-General HENRY H. LOCKWOOD Commanding. 150th New York, Colonel John H. Ketcham; 1st Maryland (P. H. B.), Colonel William P. Maulsby; 1st Maryland (E. S.), Colonel James Wallace.

---

[1] Unassigned during progress of battle; afterward attached to First Division as Second Brigade.

Third Brigade.—Colonel SILAS COLGROVE Commanding. 2d Massachusetts, Colonel Charles R. Mudge (killed), Lieut.-Colonel Charles F. Morse; 107th New York, Colonel Miron M. Crane; 13th New Jersey, Colonel Ezra A. Carman (wounded), Lieut.-Colonel John R. Fesler; 27th Indiana, Colonel Silas Colgrove, Lieut.-Colonel John R. Fesler; 3d Wisconsin, Lieut.-Colonel Martin Flood.

SECOND DIVISION.

BRIGADIER-GENERAL JOHN W. GEARY, COMMANDING.

First Brigade.—Colonel CHARLES CANDY Commanding. 28th Pennsylvania, Captain John Flynn; 147th Pennsylvania, Lieut.-Colonel Ario Pardee, Jr.; 5th Ohio, Colonel John H. Patrick; 7th Ohio, Colonel William R. Creighton; 29th Ohio, Captain W. F. Stevens (wounded), Captain Ed. Hays; 66th Ohio, Colonel C. Candy, Lieut.-Colonel Eugene Powell.

Second Brigade.—(1) Colonel GEORGE A. COBHAM, JR.; (2) Brigadier-General THOMAS L. KANE. 29th Pennsylvania, Colonel William Rickards; 109th Pennsylvania, Captain Fred. L. Gimber; 111th Pennsylvania, Lieut.-Colonel Thomas M. Walker, Lieut.-Colonel Frank J. Osgood.

Third Brigade.—Brigadier-General GEORGE S. GREENE Commanding. 60th New York, Colonel Abel Godard; 78th New York, Lieut.-Colonel Herbert Von Hammerstein; 102d New York, Lieut.-Colonel James C. Lane (wounded); 137th New York, Colonel David Ireland; 149th New York, Colonel Henry A. Barnum, Lieut.-Colonel Charles B. Randall.

Artillery Brigade.—Lieutenant EDWARD D. MUHLENBERG Commanding. Battery F, 4th United States, Lieutenant E. D. Muhlenberg, Lieutenant S. T. Rugg; Battery K, 5th United States, Lieutenant D. H. Kinsie; Battery M, 1st New York, Lieutenant Charles E. Winegar; Knap's Pennsylvania Battery, Lieutenant Charles Atwell.

Headquarter Guard.—Battalion 10th Maine.

CAVALRY CORPS.

MAJOR-GENERAL ALFRED PLEASONTON COMMANDING.

FIRST DIVISION.

BRIGADIER-GENERAL JOHN BUFORD COMMANDING.

First Brigade.—Colonel WILLIAM GAMBLE Commanding. 8th New York, Colonel Benjamin F. Davis; 8th Illinois, Colonel William Gamble, Lieut.-Colonel D. R. Clendenin; two squadrons 12th Illinois, Colonel Amos Voss; three squadrons 3d Indiana, Colonel George H. Chapman.

Second Brigade.—Colonel THOMAS C. DEVIN Commanding. 6th New York, Colonel Thomas C. Devin, Lieut.-Colonel William H. Crocker; 9th New York, Colonel William Sackett; 17th Pennsylvania, Colonel J. H. Kellogg; 3d West Virginia (detachment).

Reserve Brigade.—Brigadier-General WESLEY MERRITT Commanding. 1st United States, Captain R. S. C. Lord; 2d United States, Captain T. F. Rodenbough; 5th United States, Captain J. W. Mason; 6th United States, Major S. H. Starr (wounded), Captain G. C. Cram; 6th Pennsylvania, Major James H. Hazeltine.

SECOND DIVISION.

BRIGADIER-GENERAL D. McM. GREGG COMMANDING.

(HEADQUARTER GUARD—Company A, 1st Ohio.)

First Brigade.—Colonel J. B. McINTOSH Commanding. 1st New Jersey, Major M. H. Beaumont; 1st Pennsylvania, Colonel John P. Taylor; 3d Pennsylvania, Lieut.-Colonel Edward S. Jones; 1st Maryland, Lieut.-Colonel James M. Deems; 1st Massachusetts at Headquarters Sixth Corps.

Second Brigade.[1]—Colonel PENNOCK HUEY Commanding. 2d New York, 4th New York, 8th Pennsylvania, 6th Ohio.

Third Brigade.—Colonel J. I. GREGG Commanding. 1st Maine, Colonel Charles H. Smith; 10th New York, Major W. A. Avery; 4th Pennsylvania, Lieut.-Colonel W. E. Doster; 16th Pennsylvania, Lieut.-Colonel John K. Robison.

THIRD DIVISION.

BRIGADIER-GENERAL JUDSON KILPATRICK COMMANDING.

(HEADQUARTER GUARD—Company C, 1st Ohio.)

First Brigade.—(1) Brigadier-General E. J. FARNSWORTH; (2) Colonel N. P. RICHMOND. 5th New York, Major John Hammond; 18th Pennsylvania, Lieut.-Colonel William P. Brinton; 1st Vermont, Colonel Edward D. Sawyer; 1st West Virginia, Colonel H. P. Richmond.

Second Brigade.—Brigadier-General GEORGE A. CUSTER Commanding. 1st Michigan, Colonel Charles H. Town; 5th Michigan, Colonel Russell A. Alger · 6th Michigan, Colonel George Gray; 7th Michigan, Colonel Wm. D. Mann.

HORSE ARTILLERY.[2]

First Brigade.—Captain JOHN M. ROBERTSON Commanding. Batteries B and L, 2d United States, Lieutenant Edw. Heaton; Battery M, 2d United States, Lieutenant A. C. M. Pennington; Battery E, 4th United States, Lieutenant S. S. Elder; 6th New York, Lieutenant Jos. W. Martin; 9th Michigan, Captain J. J. Daniels.

Second Brigade.—Captain JOHN C. TIDBALL Commanding. Batteries G and E, 1st United States, Captain A. M. Randol; Battery K, 1st United States, Captain Wm. M. Graham; Battery A, 2d United States, Lieutenant John H. Calef; Battery C, 3d United States, Lieutenant Wm. D. Fuller.

ARTILLERY RESERVE.

(1) BRIGADIER-GENERAL R. O. TYLER (disabled).
(2) CAPTAIN JOHN M. ROBERTSON.

First Regular Brigade.—Captain D. R. RANSOM Commanding (wounded). Battery H, 1st United States, Lieutenant C. P. Eakin (wounded); Batteries F and K, 3d United States, Lieutenant J. C. Turnbull; Battery C, 4th United States, Lieutenant Evan Thomas; Battery C, 5th United States, Lieutenant G. V. Weir.

First Volunteer Brigade.—Lieut.-Colonel F. McGILVERY Commanding. 15th New York, Captain Patrick Hart; Independent Battery Pennsylvania, Captain R. B. Ricketts; 5th Massachusetts, Captain C. A. Phillips; 9th Massachusetts, Captain John Bigelow.

Second Volunteer Brigade.—Captain E. D. TAFT Commanding. Battery B, 1st Connecticut;[1] Battery M, 1st Connecticut;[1] 5th New York, Captain Elijah D. Taft; 2d Connecticut, Lieutenant John W. Sterling.

Third Volunteer Brigade.—Captain JAMES F. HUNTINGTON Commanding. Batteries F and G, 1st Pennsylvania, Captain R. B. Ricketts; Battery H, 1st Ohio, Captain Jas. F. Huntington; Battery A, 1st New Hampshire, Captain F. M. Edgell; Battery C, 1st West Virginia, Captain Wallace Hill.

---

[1] Not engaged.
[2] A section of a battery attached to the Purnell Legion was with Gregg on the 3d.

Fourth Volunteer Brigade.—Captain R. H. FITZHUGH Commanding. Battery B, 1st New York, Captain Jas. McRorty (killed); Battery G, 1st New York, Captain Albert N. Ames; Battery K, 1st New York (11th Battery attached), Captain Robt. H. Fitzhugh; Battery A, 1st Maryland, Captain Jas. H. Rigby; Battery A, 1st New Jersey, Lieutenant Augustin N. Parsons; 6th Maine, Lieutenant Edwin B. Dow.

Train Guard.—Major CHARLES EWING Commanding. 4th New Jersey Infantry.

Headquarter Guard.—Captain J. C. FULLER Commanding. Battery C, 32d Massachusetts.

DETACHMENTS AT HEADQUARTERS ARMY OF THE POTOMAC.

Command of the Provost-Marshal-General.—Brigadier General M. R. PATRICK Commanding. 93d New York,[1] 8th United States,[1] 1st Massachusetts Cavalry, 2d Pennsylvania Cavalry, E and I, 6th Pennsylvania Cavalry, Detachment Regular Cavalry, United States Engineer Battalion,[1] Captain George H. Mendel, United States Engineers.

Guards and Orderlies.—Captain D. P. MANN Commanding. Independent Company Oneida, N. Y., Cavalry.

[1] Not engaged.

APPENDIX B.

Organization of the Army of Northern Virginia, June 1, 1863.

GENERAL ROBERT E. LEE COMMANDING.

STAFF.

COLONEL W. H. TAYLOR, Adjutant-General.
" C. S. VENABLE, A.D.C.
" CHARLES MARSHALL, A.D.C.
" JAMES L. CORLEY, Chief Quartermaster.
" R. G. COLE, Chief Commissary.
" B. G. BALDWIN, Chief of Ordnance.
" H. L. PEYTON, Assistant Inspector-General.
GENERAL W. N. PENDLETON, Chief of Artillery.
DOCTOR L. GUILD, Medical Director.
COLONEL W. PROCTOR SMITH, Chief Engineer.
MAJOR H. E. YOUNG, Assistant Adjutant-General.
" G. B. COOK, Assistant Inspector-General.

FIRST CORPS.

LIEUTENANT-GENERAL JAMES LONGSTREET COMMANDING.

McLAWS'S DIVISION.

MAJOR-GENERAL L. McLAWS COMMANDING.

Kershaw's Brigade.—Brigadier-General J. B. KERSHAW Commanding. 15th South Carolina Regiment, Colonel W. D. De Saussure; 8th South Carolina Regiment, Colonel J. W. Mamminger; 2d South Carolina Regiment, Colonel John D. Kennedy; 3d South Carolina Regiment, Colonel James D. Nance; 7th South Carolina Regiment, Colonel D. Wyatt Aiken; 3d (James's) Battalion South Carolina Infantry, Lieut.-Colonel R. C. Rice.

Benning's Brigade.—Brigadier-General H. L. BENNING Commanding. 50th Georgia Regiment, Colonel W. R. Manning; 51st Georgia Regiment, Colonel W. M. Slaughter; 53d Georgia Regiment, Colonel James P. Somms; 10th Georgia Regiment, Lieut.-Colonel John B. Weems.

Barksdale's Brigade.—Brigadier-General Wm. BARKSDALE Commanding. 13th Mississippi Regiment, Colonel J. W. Carter; 17th Mississippi Regiment, Colonel W. D. Holder; 18th Mississippi Regiment, Colonel Thomas M. Griffin; 21st Mississippi Regiment, Colonel B. G. Humphreys.

Woffard's Brigade.—Brigadier-General W. T. WOFFARD Commanding. 18th Georgia Regiment, Major E. Griffs; Phillips's Georgia Legion, Colonel W. M. Phillips; 24th Georgia Regiment, Colonel Robert McMillan; 16th Georgia Regiment, Colonel Goode Bryan; Cobb's Georgia Legion, Lieut.-Colonel L. D. Glewn.

PICKETT'S DIVISION.

MAJOR-GENERAL GEORGE E. PICKETT COMMANDING.

Garnett's Brigade.—Brigadier-General R. B. GARNETT Commanding. 8th Virginia Regiment, Colonel Eppa Hunton; 18th Virginia Regiment, Colonel R. E. Withers; 19th Virginia Regiment, Colonel Henry Gantt; 28th Virginia Regiment, Colonel R. C. Allen; 56th Virginia Regiment, Colonel W. D. Stuart.

Armistead's Brigade.—Brigadier-General L. A. ARMISTEAD Commanding. 9th Virginia Regiment, Lieut.-Colonel J. S. Gilliam; 14th Virginia Regiment, Colonel J. G. Hodges; 38th Virginia Regiment, Colonel E. C. Edmonds; 53d Virginia Regiment, Colonel John Grammer; 57th Virginia Regiment, Colonel J. B. Magruder.

Kemper's Brigade—Brigadier-General J. L. KEMPER Commanding. 1st Virginia Regiment, Colonel Lewis B. Williams, Jr.; 3d Virginia Regiment, Colonel Joseph Mayo, Jr.; 7th Virginia Regiment, Colonel W. T. Patton; 11th Virginia Regiment, Colonel David Funston; 24th Virginia Regiment, Colonel W. R. Terry.

Toombs's Brigade.—Brigadier-General R. TOOMBS Commanding. 2d Georgia Regiment, Colonel E. M. Butt; 15th Georgia Regiment, Colonel E. M. DuBose; 17th Georgia Regiment, Colonel W. C. Hodges; 20th Georgia Regiment, Colonel J. B. Cummings.

Corse's Brigade.—Brigadier-General M. D. CORSE Commanding. 15th Virginia Regiment, Colonel T. P. August; 17th Virginia Regiment, Colonel Morton Marye; 30th Virginia Regiment, Colonel A. T. Harrison; 32d Virginia Regiment, Colonel E. B. Montague.

HOOD'S DIVISION.

MAJOR-GENERAL J. B. HOOD.

Robertson's Brigade.—Brigadier-General J. B. ROBERTSON Commanding. 1st Texas Regiment, Colonel A. T. Rainey; 4th Texas Regiment, Colonel J. C. G. Key; 5th Texas Regiment, Colonel R. M. Powell; 3d Arkansas Regiment, Colonel Van H. Manning.

Laws's Brigade.—Brigadier-General E. M. LAWS Commanding. 4th Alabama Regiment, Colonel P. A. Bowls; 44th Alabama Regiment, Colonel W. H. Perry; 15th Alabama Regiment, Colonel James Canty; 47th Alabama Regiment, Colonel J. W. Jackson; 48th Alabama, Colonel J. F. Shepherd.

Anderson's Brigade.—Brigadier-General G. T. ANDERSON Commanding. 10th Georgia Battalion, Major J. E. Rylander; 7th Georgia Regiment, Colonel W. M. White: 8th Georgia Regiment, Lieut.-Colonel J. R. Towers; 9th Georgia Regiment, Colonel B. F. Beck; 11th Georgia Regiment, Colonel F. H. Little.

Jenkins's Brigade.—Brigadier-General M. JENKINS Commanding. 2d South Carolina Rifles, Colonel Thomas Thompson; 1st South Carolina Regiment, Lieut.-Colonel David Livingstone; 5th South Carolina Regiment, Colonel A. Coward; 6th South Carolina Regiment, Colonel John Bratton; Hampton's Legion, Colonel M. W. Gary.

ARTILLERY OF THE FIRST CORPS.

COLONEL J. B. WALTON COMMANDING.

Battalion.—Colonel H. C. CABELL; Major HAMILTON. Batteries: McCarty's, Manly's, Carlton's, Fraser's.

Battalion.—Major DEARING; Major REED. Batteries: Macon's, Blount's, Stribling's, Caskie's.

Battalion.—Major HENRY. Batteries: Bachman's, Rielly's, Latham's, Gordon's.

Battalion.—Colonel E. P. ALEXANDER; Major HUGER. Batteries: Jordan's, Rhett's, Moody's, Parker's, Taylor's.

Battalion.—Major ESHLEMAN. Batteries: Squires's, Miller's, Richardson's, Norcom's.

Total number of guns, Artillery of the First Corps, 83.

SECOND CORPS.

LIEUTENANT-GENERAL R. S. EWELL.

EARLY'S DIVISION.

MAJOR-GENERAL J. A. EARLY COMMANDING.

Hays's Brigade.—Brigadier-General H. S. HAYS Commanding. 5th Louisiana Regiment, Colonel Henry Forno; 6th Louisiana Regiment, Colonel William Monaghan; 7th Louisiana Regiment, Colonel D. B. Penn; 8th Louisiana Regiment, Colonel Henry B. Kelley; 9th Louisiana Regiment, Colonel A. L. Stafford.

Gordon's Brigade.—Brigadier-General J. B. GORDON Commanding. 13th Georgia Regiment, Colonel J. M. Smith; 26th Georgia Regiment, Colonel E. N. Atkinson; 31st Georgia Regiment, Colonel C. A. Evans; 38th Georgia Regiment, Major J. D. Matthews; 60th Georgia Regiment, Colonel W. H. Stiles; 61st Georgia Regiment, Colonel J. H. Lamar.

Smith's Brigade.—Brigadier-General WILLIAM SMITH Commanding. 13th Virginia Regiment, Colonel J. E. B. Terrill; 31st Virginia Regiment, Colonel John S. Hoffman; 49th Virginia Regiment, Colonel Gibson; 52d Virginia Regiment, Colonel Skinner; 58th Virginia Regiment, Colonel F. H. Board.

Hoke's Brigade.—Colonel J. E. AVERY Commanding (General R. F. HOKE being absent, wounded). 5th North Carolina Regiment, Colonel J. E. Avery; 21st North Carolina Regiment, Colonel W. W. Kirkland; 54th North Carolina Regiment, Colonel J. C. T. McDowell; 57th North Carolina Regiment, Colonel A. C. Godwin; 1st North Carolina Battalion, Major R. H. Wharton.

RODES'S DIVISION.

MAJOR-GENERAL R. E. RODES COMMANDING.

Daniel's Brigade.—Brigadier-General JUNIUS DANIEL Commanding. 32d North Carolina Regiment, Colonel E. C. Brabble; 43d North Carolina Regiment, Colonel Thomas S. Keenan; 45th North Carolina Regiment, Lieut.-Colonel Saml. H. Boyd; 53d North Carolina Regiment, Colonel W. A. Owens; 2d North Carolina Battalion, Lieut.-Colonel H. S. Andrew.

Doles's Brigade.—Brigadier-General GEORGE DOLES Commanding. 4th Georgia Regiment, Lieut.-Colonel D. R. E. Winn; 12th Georgia Regiment, Colonel Edward Willis; 21st Georgia Regiment, Colonel John T. Mercer; 44th Georgia Regiment, Colonel S. P. Lumpkin.

Iverson's Brigade.—Brigadier-General ALFRED IVERSON Commanding. 5th North Carolina Regiment, Captain S. B. West; 12th North Carolina Regiment, Lieut.-Colonel W. S. Davis; 20th North Carolina Regiment, Lieut.-Colonel N. Slough; 23d North Carolina Regiment, Colonel D. H. Christie.

Ramseur's Brigade.—Brigadier-General S. D. RAMSEUR Commanding. 2d North Carolina Regiment, Major E. W. Hurt; 4th North Carolina Regiment, Colonel Bryan Grimes; 14th North Carolina Regiment, Colonel R. T. Bennett; 30th North Carolina Regiment, Colonel F. M. Parker.

Rodes's Brigade.—Colonel E. A. O'NEAL Commanding. 3d Alabama Regiment, Colonel C. A. Battle; 5th Alabama Regiment, Colonel J. M. Hall; 6th Alabama Regiment, Colonel J. N. Lightfoot; 12th Alabama Regiment, Colonel S. B. Pickens; 26th Alabama Regiment, Lieut.-Colonel J. C. Goodgame.

JOHNSON'S DIVISION.

MAJOR-GENERAL ED. JOHNSON COMMANDING.

Steuart's Brigade.—Brigadier General GEO. H. STEUART Commanding. 10th Virginia Regiment, Colonel E. T. H. Warren ; 23d Virginia Regiment, Colonel A. G. Taliaferro; 27th Virginia Regiment, Colonel T. V. Williams ; 1st North Carolina Regiment, Colonel J. A. McDowell ; 3d North Carolina Regiment, Lieut.-Colonel Thurston.

"Stonewall" Brigade.—Brigadier-General JAMES A. WALKER Commanding. 2d Virginia Regiment, Colonel J. Q. A. Nadenbousch ; 4th Virginia Regiment, Colonel Charles A. Ronald ; 5th Virginia Regiment, Colonel J. H. S. Funk, 27th Virginia Regiment, Colonel J. K. Edmondson ; 33d Virginia Regiment, Colonel F. M. Holladay.

Jones's Brigade.—Brigadier-General JOHN M. JONES Commanding. 21st Virginia Regiment, Captain Moseley; 42d Virginia Regiment, Lieut.-Colonel Withers: 44th Virginia Regiment, Captain Buckner ; 48th Virginia Regiment, Colonel T. S. Garnett ; 50th Virginia Regiment, Colonel Vandeventer.

Nicholls's Brigade.—Colonel J. M. WILLIAMS Commanding (General F. T. Nicholls being absent, wounded). 1st Louisiana Regiment, Colonel William R. Shirers; 2d Louisiana Regiment, Colonel J. M. Williams ; 10th Louisiana Regiment, Colonel E. Waggaman ; 14th Louisiana Regiment, Colonel Z. York ; 15th Louisiana Regiment, Colonel Edward Pendleton.

ARTILLERY OF THE SECOND CORPS.

COLONEL S. CRUTCHFIELD, COMMANDING.

Battalion.—Lieut.-Colonel Thomas H. Carter ; Major Carter M. Braxton. Batteries: Page's, Fry's, Carter's, Reese's.

Battalion.—Lieut.-Colonel H. P. JONES ; Major BROCKENBOROUGH. Batteries: Carrington's, Garber's, Thompson's, Tanner's.

Battalion.—Lieut.-Colonel S. ANDREWS ; Major LATIMER. Batteries: Brown's, Dermot's, Carpenter's, Raine's.

Battalion.—Lieut.-Colonel NELSON ; Major PAGE. Batteries: Kirkpatrick's, Massie's, Millege's.

Battalion.—Colonel J. T. BROWN ; Major HARDAWAY. Batteries: Dance's, Watson's, Smith's, Huff's, Graham's.

Total number of guns, Artillery of the Second Corps, 82.

THIRD CORPS.

LIEUT.-GENERAL A. P. HILL, COMMANDING.

R. H. ANDERSON'S DIVISION.

Wilcox's Brigade.—Brigadier-General C. M. WILCOX Commanding. 8th Alabama Regiment. Colonel T. L. Royster ; 9th Alabama Regiment, Colonel S. Henry ; 10th Alabama Regiment, Colonel W. H. Forney; 11th Alabama Regiment, Colonel J. C. C. Saunders ; 14th Alabama Regiment, Colonel L. P. Pinkhard.

Mahone's Brigade.—Brigadier-General WILLIAM MAHONE Commanding. 6th Virginia Regiment, Colonel G. T. Rogers ; 12th Virginia Regiment, Colonel D. A. Weisiger; 16th Virginia Regiment, Lieut.-Colonel Joseph H. Ham ; 41st Virginia Regiment, Colonel W. A. Parham ; 61st Virginia Regiment, Colonel V. D. Groner.

Posey's Brigade.—Brigadier-General CANOT POSEY Commanding. 46th Mis-sissippi Regiment. Colonel Jos. Jayne ; 16th Mississippi Regiment, Colonel Saml. E. Baker ; 19th Mississippi Regiment, Colonel John Mullins ; 12th Mississippi Regiment, Colonel W. H. Taylor.

Wright's Brigade.—Brigadier-General A. R. WRIGHT Commanding. 2d Georgia Battalion, Major G. W. Ross ; 3d Georgia Regiment, Colonel E. J. Walker ; 22d Georgia Regiment, Colonel R. H. Jones ; 48th Georgia Regiment, Colonel William Gibson.

Perry's Brigade.—Brigadier-General E. A. PERRY Commanding. 2d Florida Regiment, Lieut.-Colonel S. G. Pyles ; 5th Florida Regiment, Colonel J. C. Hately ; 8th Florida Regiment, Colonel David Long.

HETH'S DIVISION.

First, Pettigrew's Brigade.—42d, 11th, 26th, 44th, 47th, 52d, and 17th North Carolina Regiments.

Second, Field's Brigade.—40th, 55th, and 47th Virginia Regiments.

Third, Archer's Brigade.—1st, 7th, and 14th Tennessee, and 13th Alabama Regiments.

Fourth, Cook's Brigade.—15th, 27th, 46th, and 48th North Carolina Regiments.

Fifth, Davis's Brigade.—2d, 11th, 42d Mississippi, and 55th N. Carolina Reg'ts.

PENDER'S DIVISION.

First, McGowan's Brigade.—1st, 12th, 13th, and 14th North Carolina Regiments.

Second, Lane's Brigade.—7th, 18th, 28th, 33d, and 37th Georgia Regiments.

Third, Thomas's Brigade.—14th, 35th, 45th, and 49th Georgia Regiments.

Fourth, Pender's Old Brigade.—13th, 16th, 22d, 34th, and 38th North Carolina Regiments.

ARTILLERY OF THE THIRD CORPS.

COLONEL R. LINDSEY WALKER COMMANDING.

Battalion.—Major D. G. McINTOSH ; Major W. F. POAGUE. Batteries : Hurt's Rice's, Luck's, Johnson's.

Battalion.—Lieut.-Colonel GARNETT ; Major RICHARDSON. Batteries : Lewis's, Maurin's, Moore's, Grandy's.

Battalion.—Major CUTSHAW. Batteries : Wyatt's, Woolfolk's, Brooke's.

Battalion.—Major WILLIE P. PEGRAM. Batteries : Brunson's, Davidson's, Crenshaw's, McGraw's, Marye's.

Battalion. — Lieut.-Colonel CUTTS ; Major LANE. Batteries : Wingfield's, Ross's, Patterson's.

Total number of guns, Artillery of the Third Corps, 83.

Total number of guns, Army of Northern Virginia, 248.

LIEUT.-GENERAL J. E. B. STUART'S CAVALRY CORPS.

Brigadier-General Wade Hampton's Brigade.
Brigadier-General Fitz Hugh Lee's Brigade.
Brigadier-General W. H. F. Lee's Brigade, under Colonel Chambliss.
Brigadier-General B. H. Robertson's Brigade.
Brigadier-General William E. Jones's Brigade.
Brigadier-General J. D. Imboden's Brigade.
Brigadier-General A. G. Jenkins's Brigade.
Colonel White's Battalion.
Baker's Brigade.

[NOTE —The regimental roster of this Cavalry Corps is unfortunately unobtainable.]

INDEX.

NOTE.—*Regiments, batteries, etc., are indexed under the names of their States, excepting batteries called by their captain's or by some other special name. These are indexed under* BATTERIES.

ABERCROMBIE, division of, 105
Adjutant-General at Richmond, 112
Alabama, regiment of : Fourth, 198
Alabama, the, 77
Alden, his " History of the Great Rebellion," 71, 72
Aldie Gap, 100, 101
Aldie, Va., 100, 102 et seq.
Alexander, Captain (U. S.), 90
Alexander, Colonel, Chief of Longstreet's artillery, 65, 206
Ames, Brigadier-General Adelbert, brigade of, 82, 161, 182
Anderson, brigade of, 168. 173 ; Georgia brigade, 198
Anderson, Gen. R. H., commander of Third Division of Hill's corps, 2; begins to fortify Tabernacle Church, 8; joined by Jackson there, 11; pressed by Pleasonton's cavalry, 11; reinforces McLaws, 13, 17; checks Williams, 24, 34; makes a junction with Stuart, 49 et

seq. ; detached against Sedgwick, 51, 54, 59 et seq.; reinforces McLaws, 63 et seq., 72 ; on the Chambersburg Road, 120, 138,152; at Peach Orchard, 175
Anderson, General G. T., wounded, 210
Applebie Ridge. 91
Appomattox, 173
Archer, brigade of, 38, 46, 126, 129, 131 ; taken prisoner, 132; brigade of, 133, 161. 210
Armistead, General, brigade of, 193, 194 ; shot down, 195, 210
Ashby's Gap, 99 et seq.
Ashland, 70
Author (see Doubleday, General)
Averill, 4, 7, 40; supplanted by Pleasonton, 69
Avery, Colonel, 181
Ayers, General, 173

BACHE, Dr. Thos. H., 208
Backman, battery of, 198
Baird, Gen. A., at Chickamauga, 53

Baird, Adjutant-General, 148

Baltimore, Md., 80, 107, 108, 112, 115 et seq., 134, 150, 152, 184, 200, 209

Baltimore and Ohio Railroad, 80, 92, 105, 110

Bankhead, Colonel, on Reynolds's staff, 142

Bank's Ford, Va., 1, 4, 10 et seq., 42, 44, 47, 57, 61, 63 et seq., 79

Barksdale, General, 10, 58, 168, 170 et seq., 175; wounded, 210

Barlow, General F. C., 23, 25, 32, 33, 38; takes command of Schurz's division, 137 et seq., 140; shot down, 142, 161, 210

Barnes, General, division of, 168 et seq., 172, 210

Bartlett, brigade of, 60, 61, 64

Bassett, Colonel, regiment of, 58

Bath, W. Va., 94

Batteries: Alexander's, 65, 90; Backman's, 198; Best's, 48; Bigelow's, 170, 171; Brown's, 194; Butler's, 66; Calef's, 135, 140; Clark's, 23, 164, 170; Cooper's, 135, 136, 140; Cushing's, 194; Dilger's, 145; Dimick's, 35, 40; Elder's, 198; Ewell's, 140; Graham's, 198; Hall's, 128, 129, 140, 150; Hazlett's, 169; Huntingdon's, 46; Knap's, 17; Livingston's, 23; McGilvery's, 171; McIntosh's, 137; Martin's, 36; Pegram's, 134, 137; Pennington's, 200, 201; Phillip's, 171; Pleasonton's, 36; Randolph's, 23; Randol's, 200, 201; Reynolds's, 135, 140, 149, 182; Ricketts's, 182; Stevens's, 135, 182; Stewart's, 135, 140, 145, 148, 155;

Stuart's, 182; Weed's, 52; Weidrick's, 182; Wheeler's, 145, 194; Wilkeson's, 142; Williston's, 60; Winslow's, 35, 173

Baxter, Brig.-Gen. Henry, brigade of, 142 et seq., 145, 149, 161

Bealton, 95

Beauregard, 107

Benham, General H. W., Engineer Corps, 61, 65, 66

Benner's Hill, 181

Benning, General, brigade of, 168, 173, 197 et seq.

Berdan, sharpshooters of, 23

Berry, reserve forces under, 26; division of, 35, 38, 41, 42, 44, 45; death of, 49

Berryville, Va., 89, 90

Best, Captain, 38, 44, 45, 47, 48

Best, Colonel, Chief of Artillery to Twelfth Corps, 36

Beverly Ford, 81 et seq.

Biddle, Colonel Chapman, brigade of, 136, 139 et seq., 145; forced back from the ridge, 147, 161

Bigelow, battery of, 170 et seq.

Birney, General, commander of Third Corps, 16, 22, 23, 34, 38, 44, 45, 113, 163; division of, 164, 167 et seq.; takes command of Third Corps, 171 et seq.; assumes Sickles's command, 174, 189, 208

Bixby, Captain, 102, 103

Bloody Run, 94

Blue Ridge, 84, 87, 99, 100, 106

Boonsborough, Md., 108

Bottom's Bridge, Va., 100

Bowling Green Road, 44, 56

Bowman, Colonel, 47

Brandy Station, Va., 7; battle of 81 et seq., 88, 101, 111

Brockenborough, brigade of, 126, 145, 161

Brooke, Colonel John R., brigade of, 165, 172, 210

Brooke-Rawle, Lieut.-Col. W., 201

Brooks, Adjutant E. P., 133

Brookeville, 112

Brooklyn, L. I., 128

Brooklyn, regiment of: Fourteenth, 128, 129

Brooks, Major-General Wm. T. H., division of, 9, 59 et seq., 64 et seq., 97

Brown, Colonel Campbell, on Ewell's staff, 153

Buckland, 110

Buford, General, 4, 82 et seq., 103; division of, 113, 115; brigades of, 118, 122; at Gettysburg, 124 et seq., 130, 133; cavalry of, 146, 149, 164

Bullock's House, 52

Bull Run, 100, 102, 173, 195

Bunker Hill Monument, 112

Bunker Hill, Va., 90

Burbank, 173

Burnham, Colonel, 58

Burnside, General, 1, 3, 58

Buschbeck, Colonel Adolph, 29, 30, 33, 34, 36, 41

Butler, battery of, 66

Butterfield, General, remonstrance of, 114, 210

CALDWELL, division of, 172 et seq., 189, 197

Calef, battery of, 135, 140

Carlisle, Penn., 97, 107, 108, 111 et seq., 120 et seq., 138, 142

Carolinas, the, 112

Carpenter, Major J. E., statement of, 37

Carroll, brigade of, 48, 183

Carter, Colonel, 49

Cashtown, Penn., 118, 120, 122

Catlett's Station, 80, 95, 100

Cedarsville, 89

Cemetery Ridge, Penn., 126 et seq., 138, 141, 146, 148, 150, 153, 156, 158, 162, 181, 183, 199

Centreville, Va., 98, 100, 102, 103

Central Railroad, 108

Chambersburg, Penn., 96, 106 et seq., 112, 115, 118 et seq., 123, 130, 134 et seq., 138

Chancellorsville House, Va., 12, 21, 35, 46, 50, 53, 54

Chancellorsville, Va., 1, 7 et seq., 13 et seq., 34, 36, 39, 42 et seq., 50, 52, 53, 56, 59, 62, 64, 68; losses at, 71, 72, 76, 79, 87, 121, 146, 150

Chambliss, 200

Chester Gap, 88

Chester, Lieutenant, 200 et seq.

Chickahominy, 70, 100

Chickamauga, 53

City Point, 179

Clark, battery of, 23, 164, 170

Colston, division of, 27, 34, 38

Columbia, Penn., 113

Columbia, Va., canal at, 70

Congressional Committee on the Conduct of the War, unreliable investigations, 32

Connecticut, regiments of: Fourteenth, 193; Seventeenth, 29, 30; Twenty-seventh, 50

Cookesville, 112

Cooper, battery of, 135, 140

"Copperheads," 77, 111

Coster, Colonel Charles R., 142

Couch, Major-General Darius M., 4, 11, 14, 16, 21, 30, 35, 45;

succeeds to command after Hooker is wounded, 53 et seq., 55, 68; succeeded by Hancock in command of Second Army Corps, 9; placed under Meade's orders, 116

Cox's house, 60

Crampton's Gap, Md., 108

Crawford, General S. Wiley, division of, 105, 164, 166; heads a gallant charge, 173 et seq.; letter from Wofford to, 187; division of, 205 et seq.

Cress Run, 184

Cross, Colonel, killed, 172

Crutchfield, Colonel, 37

Culpeper, Va., 4, 7, 79, 80, 83, 95, 99, 107

Culp's Hill, 151 et seq.; 156, 162, 177, 179 et seq., 189

Cumberland, 105

Cumberland Valley, 106, 107, 116

Curtin, Governor, of Pennsylvania, 98, 111

Cushing, brave death of, 194

Custer, General, 121; brigade of, 184, 200 et seq.

Cutler, Brigadier-General Lysander, brigade of, 128, 130 et seq., 135 et seq., 139, 143, 148, 161

DAHLGREN, Captain Ulric, 55; successful raid of, 123; a prisoner, 179

Dana, Colonel, 144; takes Wister's command, 145; forced back from ridge, 147

Daniels, brigade of, 141, 143 et seq., 147, 161, 186

Davis, brigade of, 126, 128 et seq., 132 et seq., 143, 145, 161

Davis, Colonel Hasbrouck, 70

Davis Jefferson, 76, 77, 99, 100, 107, 111, 113; despatch from, 179

Dawes, Lieutenant-Colonel R. R., 131 et seq., 155

Day, 173

Delaware, regiment of: First Cavalry, 117, First, 193

De Peyster, General, 53

De Peyster, Major J. Watts, 65

De Trobriand, 48; brigade of, 167 et seq., 172

Devens, brigade of, 27, 29, 30, 33

Devil's Den, 167 et seq., 174

Devin, Colonel, cavalry brigade of, 123 et seq., 128, 138, 146

Dilger, battery of, 145

Dimick, battery of, 40; bravery of, 40, note

Dix, General, 80, 99, 119

Doles, brigade of, 46, 48, 141 et seq., 150, 161

Doubleday, General Abner, 5, 9, 21, 27; left temporarily in charge of First Corps, 42, 55; letter of, 73; takes command of First Army Corps, 95, 98; at Middletown, 113; takes command of First Corps, 124, 128; his instructions from Reynolds, 130; assumes command of battlefield, 132; receives orders from General Howard, 141; asks for reinforcements, 146; fight and retreat from the seminary, 149 et seq.; receives orders from Hancock, 151; resumes command of his division, 154, 161, 189, 192; his attention to Confederate wounded, 196, 210

Dover, 100, 107

Dowdall's Tavern, Va., 12, 33, 39, 41
Dragon River, 74
Drainsville, 112
Duffie, Colonel, 82, 83, 101 et seq.
Dumfries, Va., 95
Dwight, Lieutenant-Colonel Walton, defends the railroad cut, 144

Early, General Jubal A., 44, 56, 57, 59, 60, 63 et seq.; repulsed, 64, 65, 91, 92, 94, 107, 108, 111, 112; levies a contribution on York, 113, 119 et seq., 138, 141 et seq. ; discussions of, 158, 161, 181 et seq.; endeavors to save the trains, 208
Edwards's Ferry, 106, 108
Egan, Colonel, 168
Elder, battery of, 198
Elley's Ford, 7, 8, 40, 43, 69
Elliot, General, 90, 92, 93
Ely, Colonel, 90 et seq.
Emmetsburg, Md., 115, 118 et seq., 122, 125, 130, 152, 158 et seq., 162 et seq., 167, 170, 174, 178, 193
England, partiality of, toward the Confederacy, 76, 77
Ent, Colonel, 205
Estes, squadron of, 184
Eustis, Colonel H. L., 57, 174
Ewell, General Benj., 78 et seq., 88 et seq., 91, 94 et seq., 97, 99, 103, 106 et seq., 111 et seq.; at Heidlersburg, 120 et seq. ; corps of, 128, 138 et seq., 142, 152 ; receives suggestion from Lee, 153 et seq. ; holds Gettysburg, 158, 161 et seq. ; pickets of, 179 et seq. ; persistency of, 186, 202

Fairchild, Colonel, 131
Fairfax Court House, Va., 98
Fairfield, Penn., 115, 118 et seq., 130, 147, 205, 208
Fairview, 15, 35, 36, 38, 45 et seq.
Falling Waters, 209
Falmouth, Va., 4, 44, 67, 74
Farmer, Captain Geo. E., testimony in regard to Howard's misconduct, 31; defence of, 31
Farnsworth, brigade of, 121, 184; killed, 198
Fayetteville, Penn., 115, 118, 120
Fisher, brigade of, 174
Fleetwood, battle of (see Brandy Station, battle of)
Fleetwood Hill, 81, 84
Flint Hill, 88
Flint Ridge, 91
Forbes, Lieut.-Colonel W. E., 2
Fortress Monroe, Va., 99
Fort Sims, 29
Fort Sumter, 195, 206, notes
Foundry, 23
Fountaindale Gap, Md., 122
Fowler, Colonel, 129, 132 et seq.
Franklin, Colonel, 47
Frederick, Md., 103, 112 et seq., 119, 209
Fredericksburg, Va., 1, 3 et seq., 8 et seq., 20, 44, 56, 58 et seq., 63 et seq., 74, 78, 87, 89, 95
Fredericksburg and Richmond Railroad, 40, 68
Fredericksburg Railroad, 4, 24, 70
French, General, 11, 14, 16, 26, 38, 45, 48, 50, 54, 111, 115 ; moves from Harper's Ferry, 209
French Government, partiality toward the Southern States, 77

Frick, Colonel, gives orders for destruction of bridge, 113

Frizzelburg, Md., 119

Front Royal, Va., 88 et seq.

Furnace, the, 24, 34, 36

Gaines's Cross Roads, 88

Gainesville, Va., 110

Gamble, brigade of, 122, 124, 128, 146

Garnett, General, brigade of, 193, 210

Gates, Colonel Theodore B., 139, 193, 197

Geary, division of, 17, 24, 34, 49, 51, 180 et seq., 186 et seq.

Georgia, regiments of: Seventh, 199; Ninth, 198, 199; Twenty-third, 23

Germania Ford, 7, 8

Getty, General, 99, 100

Gettysburg, Penn., 53; battle of, 87 et seq., 107; map of, 109; 116, 118 et seq., 121 et seq.; "secret history" of, 178, 179; et seq.

Gibbon, General, brigade of, 4, 56, 57, 59, 63, 185, 189, 192 et seq.; wounded, 196, 199, 202, 210

Glenn, Captain, 149

Gloucester Point, 70, 74

Goose Creek, 103, 106

Gordon, 66; brigade of, 113, 119, 142, 153, 161, 181, 183

Gordonsville, Va., 4, 7, 21, 22, 26, 69

Grant, brigade of, 66

Graham, Brigadier-General, brigade of, 16, 41, 45 et seq., 50, 167, 170; wounded and taken prisoner, 171 et seq., 174, 210

Graham, Lieut.-Col., battery, 198

Greene, General Geo. S., brigade of, 180 et seq., 186

Greenwood, Pa., 108, 118, 120, 138

Gregg, Gen. D. McM., 70, 82, 83, 84, 101 et seq., 108; division of, 115, 117; divisions of, 125, 184, 200

Gregg, J. Irvin, brigade of, 200

Griffin, division of, 11, 12

Guest's House, 59

Guilford, Va., 107

Guiney's Station, 40, 68

Gum Springs, 107, 110

Hagerstown, Md., 109, 111, 130, 209

Hall, battery of, 128; retreat of, 129, 133, 140, 150

Hall, Colonel Norman J., charge of, 195

Halleck, General, 80, 88; refuses Hooker's request, 114, 116, 119; arrests Hooker, 116

Hall, Major, aide to General Howard, 126

Halstead, Major, 130, 146, 148, 151

Hamblin, Colonel, 56

Hamilton's Crossing. 2

Hammond, Major, 121

Hampton, Wade, General, brigade of, 81, 104, 121, 184, 201, 210

Hancock, General Winfield S., 113 et seq., 16, 17, 21, 22, 24, 34, 45, 49, 50, 53, 54; succeeds Couch in command of Second Army Corps, 96, 110; given command of First Corps, 138; supersedes Howard, 150 et seq.; virtually appointed commander-in-chief, 153; turns over command of field to Slocum, 154; Meade disapproves his battle-ground, 157, 162, 172; vigilance of, 175, 177, 181 et seq., 189, 195; wounded, 202, 210

Hancock, Md., 94

Hanover Junction, Pa., 70, 99, 121, 125, 184

Harper's Ferry, W. Va., 89 et seq., 94 et seq., 102, 106, 108, 111, 113 et seq., 192, 209

Harrisburg, Penn., 96, 98, 107, 110, 112, 113, 115 et seq., 118 et seq.

Hart, Captain, 201

Hartwood Church, 12

Haskell, Lieutenant, on Gibbon's staff, 199

Hayman, brigade of, 41, 46, 50

Haymarket, 110

Hays, General Wm., brigade of, 38; taken prisoner, 51

Hays, Confederate general, brigade of, 57, 59, 65, 142, 149, 161, 181, 182 et seq.

Hays, General Alexander, division of, 193 et seq.

Hazel Grove, Va., 15, 24, 30, 36, 41, 43 et seq., 56, 72

Hazel Run, Va., 58, 81

Hazlett, division of, 169; killed, 170

Heard, Dr. Theodore, 208

Heidlersburg, Penn., 120, 128, 138

Heintzelman, General, 80, 105, 106

Heth, General Henry, 47, 118, 124; division of, 125, 128, 133 et seq., 136 et seq., 161, 188

Hill, Lieutenant-General A. P., 27; at Chancellorsville, 39;

wounded, 40, 46 et seq.; sends for reserves, 48; at Fredericksburg, 79; starts for Culpeper, 95; relieves Longstreet there, 99 et seq.; at Winchester, 104, 106; crosses the Potomac at Shepherdstown, 107; unites with Longstreet at Hagerstown, 111; at Chambersburg, 112, 114; at Fayetteville, 115, 118; at Cashtown and Mummasburg, 120, 122; at Gettysburg, 124, 128, 138 et seq., 143 et seq., 146; losses of, 152 et seq.; occupies Seminary Ridge, 157, 161; report of, 170; distance from Longstreet, 204, 207

Hokes, brigade of, 65, 142, 149, 161, 181

Hood, General, 78, 162; division of, 166 et seq., 170, 178, 205

Hood's Mill, Md., 116

Hooker, Major-General Joseph, plans of, 1; force of, 2; popularity of, 3; plan of, 4, 5, 8, 9; delays action, 10; attacks Lee, 11, 12 et seq.; receives General Birney's report, 22; order to Generals Slocum and Howard 22, 25, 26; sanctions Sickles's movements, 23; irresolution of, 24, 28; Hooker deceived as to Jackson's plan of attack, 31; investigation of his conduct by Congressional Committee, 32; Hooker's defence of himself, 32; plans for protecting Eleventh Corps, 34; failure to rally the Eleventh Corps, 35; discouragement of, 38, 43; orders to Sickles, 41;

conference with General Reynolds, 42; order to Sedgwick, 44, 45; refuses to send reinforcements, 51; wounded, 53; succeeded by Couch, 54; orders from Lincoln, 55; misinformed as to Sedgwick's position, 56; represented by Warren, 57; resumes command, 64, 66; order to Sedgwick, 67; losses of, 68; order to Averell, 69; causes of his defeat, 71; letter to Lincoln, 78; his plans, 78, 79, 80; displaces Stoneman in favor of Pleasonton, 80, 82, 84, 87, 88, 89, 91; starts north, 95; plans of, 98 et seq.; his resignation accepted, 114; wisdom of his later policy, 116

Hopewell Gap, 102, 103

Horner's Woods, 205

Howard, General O. O., commander of Eleventh Corps, 3, 5, 11, 15 et seq., 18, 20, 22; order from Hooker, 22, 24, 25; neglect of, 26 et seq., 72; conduct investigated by Congressional Committee, 32; his defence, 32; fruitless exertions of, 34, 41 et seq., 68, 71, 72; at Boonsborough, 113, 126 et seq.; at Gettysburg, 134; despatch to Meade, 135; assumes command of left wing, 137 et seq., 145; Doubleday asks him for reinforcements, 146; says he sent orders to Doubleday to retreat, 149 et seq.; superseded by Hancock, 151; receives thanks of Congress, 152, 161, 183, 189, 200

Howe, division of, 44, 57, 58, 61, 64 et seq., 78

Huidekoper, Lieutenant-Colonel, gallant bayonet charge of, 145

Humphreys, General A. A., 11, 25, 48, 50, 163, division of, 164, 166 et seq., 171, 174 et seq.

Hungary Station, 70

Hunt, General, chief of artillery, 163, 189 et seq.

Hunterstown, 122, 164, 184

Hunting Creek, 43

Huntingdon, battery of, 36, 38, 46

ILLINOIS, regiment of, Twelfth, 70

Imboden, cavalry of, 92, 105, 110

Iverson, brigade of, 48, 141, 143 et seq., 161

JACKSON, General Thomas J. ("Stonewall"), 2, 5, 9, 10, 13, 17, 20 et seq.; preparations for attack, 27; advance of, 28; advance temporarily stopped by Germans in Eleventh Corps, 29; advance continued, 30 et seq., 33; attack of, 34; pursuit of Eleventh Corps, 35 et seq.; halt of, 38; death of, 39, 41; his corps commanded by Stuart, 46, 47, 63, 71; his rout of Eleventh Corps, 72, 187

Jenkins, General, 90, 94; exactions of, 96; occupies Carlisle, 97, 99, 106, 107, 112; within sight of Harrisburg, 118, 122, 210

Johns, Colonel, attacks Marye's Hill, 57 et seq.; wounded, 58

Johnson, division of, 91 et seq.; prisoners, horses, etc., captured by, 94; at Chambersburg, 107; marches on Gettysburg, 119 et seq., 138 et seq., 153, 179 et seq., 186 et seq., 200

Jones, General J. M., brigade of, 81, 103, 110, 122, 180, 210

Jones, Meredith L., Doubleday's aide, 130, 148

KANE, brigade of, 186

Kearney, General Philip, 167

Keenan, Major Peter, 36; death of, 37

Keifer, Colonel, 82

Kelly, brigade of, 172 et seq.

Kelly's Ford, Va., 3, 5, 7, 82

Kemper, General, brigade of, 193, 197, 210

Kershaw, 165, 167; brigade of, 170 et seq., 173

Keys, General, 100

Kilpatrick, General, 70, 74, 101, 103; division of, 115, 117, 120 et seq.; divisions of, 125, 164; at Hunterstown and Two Taverns, 184; spirited attack of, 190, 197 et seq., 209

Kingston, 112

Knap, battery of, 17

Kress, Lieut.-Col., 126, note

Kryzanowski, Colonel, 161

LAMBDIN, aide of Doubleday, 148

Lane, brigade of, 47, 137, 161

Lang, Colonel, 192

Laws, General, brigade of, 158, 197 et seq., 205

Lee, Doubleday's aide, 148

Lee, Fitz-Hugh, 7, 8, 12, 21, 27, 69, 81, 100, 101, 103; discussions of, 158, 201

Lee, General Robert E., 2, 4, 5, 7; at Fredericksburg, 8 et seq., attacked by Hooker, 11, 15, 17, 18, 20, 21, 24, 26, 27, 32; attack of, 34, 40, 44, 52, 53, 56, 63 et seq.; despondency of, 76; reasons for his northward march, 77, 78, 79, 84; plans of, 87 et seq., 91, 98; invades Pennsylvania, 104, 106 et seq.; his lack of information as to Hooker's movements, 108; continues his advance, 113 et seq.; turns back, 115; concentrates his troops at Gettysburg, 118 et seq.; forces of, 123, 134; sends a recommendation to Ewell, 153, 156 et seq., 167, 176; intentions of, 179, 183, 187; plans of, 188; his plans thwarted, 192; disappointment, 199; rallies his troops, 203; discouragement of, 204, 207 et seq.

Leesburg, Va., 102, 105 et seq.

Lee, W. H. F., 7, 8, 69, 81, 100, 102, 103; capture of, 111; brigade of, 200

Lewis Creek, Va., 11, 23

Libby Prison, 111, 208

Lincoln, President Abraham, 54, 75; letter from Hooker to, 78; calls for 120,000 men, 97, 151; orders from, 210

Little River, 102

Little Round Top, 156, 163 et seq., 168 et seq., 173 et seq., 177, 181, 190, 193, 197, 205

Littlestown, Penn., 115, 117, 120 et seq.

Livingston, battery of, 23

Livingston, Colonel, on Doubleday's staff, 149

Lockwood, brigade of, 106, 175
Locust Grove, Va., 79
Longstreet, General, his corps, 2, 10 ; rejoins Lee at Fredericksburg, 73 et seq., 78 ; at Locust Grove, 79, 91 ; leaves Culpeper, 99 et seq. ; at Ashley's Gap, 104 ; leaves Chambersburg, 118 et seq. ; joins Ewell and Hill, 154 ; occupies Seminary Ridge, 157 ; attack of, 162, 164 ; his instructions from Lee, 167 ; discouragement of, 174 ; leads advance against Little Round Top, 178 ; assault of, 179, 187 ; distance from Wilcox, 189, 190 ; at the Round Tops, 197 ; disappointment of, 199, 202 et seq. ; distance from Hill, 204 ; report of, 206
Loudon and Hampshire Railroad, 107
Loudon County, 101, 104
Louisa Court House, 4, 7, 69
Louisiana, regiment of : Eighth, 66

McCANDLESS, brigade of, 174, 205
McClellan, Major, 81 et seq.
McConnellsburg, Penn., 119
McFarland, Lieut.-Col., 145
McGilvery, Major, 170 ; batteries of, 171
McGowan, brigade, 47, 137, 161
McIntosh, General, artillery of, 137 ; brigade of, 200 et seq.
McLaws, Major-General, Lafayette, commander of Fourth Division of Longstreet's corps, 2, 10, 12 et seq., 23, 34, 46, 50, 54, 59 et seq., 63, 64, 78, 167, 171, 175, 187

McReynolds, Colonel, 89 et seq., 94
McVicar, Lieutenant - Colonel, death of, 8
Mahone, brigade of, 8, 13, 48, 175
Maine, regiments of : First, 70, 101 ; Twelfth, 170 ; Twentieth, 170 ; Batteries of : Second, 128, 129, 140, 150 ; Fifth, 140, 182
Manassas, Va., 98
Manchester, England, active aid to the Confederates, 77
Manchester, Md., 119, 120, 125
Maps : operations on the 1st of May, 6, 19 ; Sedgwick's position, 62 ; country from the Potomac to Harrisburg, 109 ; Gettysburg and vicinity, 125, 129, 133, 136, 160 ; Little Round Top, 165 ; Gettysburg, 191
Marsh Creek, 119, 122, 125
Marten, aide of Doubleday, 148
Martin, battery of, 36
Martinsburg, W. Va., 90, 92, 93, 94
Marye's Hill, Va., 57 ; Union loss in capture of, 58, 59
Maryland Heights, 95, 106, 111
Maryland, invasion of, 2, 84 ; Governor of, 97 ; troops of, 106
Maryland, regiments of : First, 70 ; Third, 49 ; Sixth, 90
Massachusetts, regiments of : First, 40 ; Fifth, 58 ; Seventh, 57 ; Thirty-third, 182
Massaponax Creek, 11
Mattapony River, 70
Meade, Gen. Geo. G., commander Fifth Corps, 5, 11, 13, 16 et seq., 21, 31, 35, 48, 54, 55, 68 ; assigned command of the Army of the Potomac, 114 et seq. :

a favorite of General Halleck, 116 ; at Pipe Creek, 119 et seq.; forces of, 123 ; despatches from, 125, 133 : at Taneytown, 134 ; misled by Howard's despatch, 135, 137 ; orders Hancock to supersede Howard, 150 et seq. ; appoints Hancock to act for him, 153 et seq., 156 ; disapproves of Hancock's battle-ground, 157, 158 et seq. ; unfortunate order of, 162 et seq. ; censures Sickles's movement, 164, 167, 169, 175 ; interview with Tidball, 177, 178 et seq. ; displeasure of, 184 et seq., 187, 190, 199, 202 et seq. ; inactivity of, 204, 207 et seq.

Meadow Bridge, 70
Mechanicstown, Md., 118
Melford Ford, 81
Meredith, General, brigade of, 128, 131
Merritt, brigade of, 198
Mexico, war with, 1, 131
Michigan, regiments of : First, 201; Fifth, 121, 201 ; Sixth, 121 ; Seventh, 200 ; Twenty-fourth, 5, 130, 131, 146, 161
Middleburg, Md., 100 et seq., 118, 120
Middletown, Md., 108
Miles, Colonel, 50
Mill Creek, 91
Millwood, Va., 89
Milroy, 88 et seq. ; perilous situation of, 93, 94, 95
Mine Road, 60
Mississippi River, 76
Mobile, Ala., 29
Monocacy, Md., 84
Monongahela, Department of, 97
Morris, Major, 90

Morrow, Colonel Henry A., 5, 130 et seq., 136, 139 et seq., 145 et seq. ; forced back from ridge, 147, 161
Morton's Ford, Va., 7
Moss Creek, 9
Mott, General, 42, 47 ; wounded, 49
Mott Run, Va., 11, 45, 50
Mummasburg, Penn., 120, 123, 143

Napoleon, 2, 27
Neil, General, 66
Nevins, brigade of, 174
Newhall, Captain, on McIntosh's staff, 201
New Jersey, regiments of : First, 70, 200, 201 ; Fifth, 48 ; Seventh, 47 ; Twelfth, 193, 196
New Kent Court House, 100
Newton, General John, 56 et seq., 61, 64 et seq.; given command of First Corps, 138 ; takes charge of First Corps, 154, 177, 185, 189
New Windsor, Md., 115, 118
New York, 99, 107
New York, Artillery of : First, 145, 194 ; Second, 135, 140, 149, 182
New York, Governor of, 97
New York, regiments of : First Cavalry, 90 ; Second, 70 ; Fifth, 121 ; Sixth, 8, 32, 36, 38 ; Twentieth Militia, 139, 193, 197 ; Thirty-sixth, 58 ; Thirty-ninth, 193 ; Fortieth, 41, 168 ; Forty-fourth, 170 ; Sixty-first, 50; Sixty-seventh, 58 ; Seventy-third, 40 ; Seventy-sixth, 30, 128 ; Ninety-fifth, 128, 129 ; Ninety-seventh, 154; One Hundred and Eleventh, 193 ; One Hundred and Twenty-first, 193; One Hundred and Twenty-

fifth, 193 ; One Hundred and Twenty-sixth, 193 ; One Hundred and Fortieth, 169 ; One Hundred and Forty-seventh, 128, 133

Nichols, brigade of, 48

Noble, General, statement of, 28, 29

North Anna, 99

North Carolina, regiment of: Thirty-second, 144

Northern Central Railroad, 112

Northern Virginia, Army of, number of, 2

OAK Hill, 139

Ohio, regiments of : Eighth, 194 ; One Hundred and Tenth, 92, 93 ; One Hundred and Twenty-second, 93

Old Guard, 27

Old Point Comfort, Va., 80

O'Neil, brigade of, 48, 141 et seq., 147, 161, 186

Opequan Creek, 90

Orange Court House, Plank Road, 31

Orders : to Slocum and Howard, from Hooker, 22, 25, 26 ; from Hooker to Sickles, 41 ; from Hooker to Sedgwick, 44, 45, 67 ; from Hooker to Averill, 69

O'Rorke, Colonel, killed, 169

Osborne, Major, 138

Owens, General J. T., 17, 61

PALFREY, Colonel, 178

Pamunkey River, 4, 70

Paris, Count of, 123, 210

Paul, General Gabriel R., 144 et seq.; shot through both eyes, 147, 210

Paxton, brigade of, 49

Payne, Captain, 15

Peach Orchard, 159, 163 et seq., 167 et seq., 170 et seq., 174 et seq.

Pegram, artillery of, 134, 137

Pender, General W. D., 40, 47, 134 ; division of, 137, 147 ; wounded, 148, 161, 175, 182, 189, 192, 210

Pennington, battery of, 200, 201

Pennsylvania, Governor of, 97 ; invasion of, 104

Pennsylvania, regiments of : Eighth Cavalry, 16, 37 ; Eighth, 92 ; Eleventh, 111 ; Seventeenth, 36, 38 ; Fifty-first, 197 ; Fifty-sixth, 128 ; Sixty-first, 58 ; Sixty-ninth, 195 ; Seventy-first, 195 ; Seventy-Second, 195 ; Eighty-second, 58 ; Eighty-seventh, 92 ; Ninety-ninth, 168 ; One Hundred and Sixth, 183 ; One Hundred and Tenth, 38 ; One Hundred and Twenty-first, 161 ; One Hundred and Forty-first, 171 ; One Hundred and Forty-third, 144 ; One Hundred and Forty-ninth, 131 ; One Hundred and Fiftieth, 144 ; One Hundred and Fifty-first, 145

Perrin, brigade of, 137, 147

Perry, brigade of, 17, 175, 192

Petersburg, 120

Pettigrew, General, brigade of, 122, 126, 130, 145, 161, 188 et seq., 192 et seq. ; retreat of, 196 ; loss of 197, 210

Philadelphia, Penn., 98, 99, 110, 112 et seq., 118 et seq.

Philemont, 103

Phillips, battery of, 171

Phillips, Wendell, note, 176

Pickett, division of, 119 et seq. ;

conspicuous by his absence, 154, 158 ; sent against Union centre, 183 et seq., 188 et seq.; suffers from Union artillery, 192, 193 et seq. ; retreat of, 196 et seq., 200, 202 ; failure of his charge, 204, 206 et seq.

Piedmont, Va., 100

Pillow, General Gideon J., 1

Pipe Creek, Md., 120

Pittsburg, Pa., 97

Plank Road, 11, 16, 17, 24, 34 et seq., 41, 44 et seq., 57, 59, 63

Pleasonton, Major-General Alfred, force of, note, 2 ; directed to report to Slocum, 7, 8, 10 ; cavalry of, 11, 23, 24 ; spies of, 28, 31 ; at Hazel Grove, 36 et seq. ; fortifies it, 44 ; supplants Averill, 69 ; at Culpoper, 79 ; succeeds Stoneman, 80, 81 et seq., 88 ; cavalry of, 98 ; success at Aldie Gap, 100 et seq. ; 103 et seq. ; ordered to occupy Gettysburg, 118 ; forces of, 123, 178, 179

Plum Run, 172

Poolesville, Md., 84, 106, 122

Port Conway, 5

Port Royal, 2, 5

Posey, brigade of, 8, 175

Potomac, Army of, position of, 1, 106, 107

Potomac River, 1, 94, 102, 106, 107, 108, 112, 204

Power's Hill, 190, 199

Pughtown, 91, 92

RACCOON Ford, Va., 7

Ramseur, brigade of, 13, 48, 51, 141 et seq., 144. 147, 161

Ramsey, 150

Randol, battery of, 200 et seq.

Randolph, battery of, 23

Rapidan River, 7, 52

Rapidan Station, 7, 69

Rappahannock River, 4, 7, 16, 52, 64, 81, 87, 100

Rector's Cross Roads, 102

Rectortown, 100

Revere, General, retreats without authority, 49

Reynolds, Captain, battery of, 135, 137, 149, 182

Reynolds, Major-General, at Fredericksburg, 8 ; ordered to join Hooker, 21, 42 et seq. ; his eagerness for action, 54 et seq., 68 ; placed in command of left wing of army, 95, 108 ; at Frederick, 113 ; halts the First Corps at Marsh Creek, 119 ; his anxiety for Pennsylvania, 122 ; gives command of First Corps to Doubleday, 124 ; directs Howard to bring his corps forward, 126 et seq. ; his instructions to Doubleday, 130 ; death of, 131, 133 et seq., 137, 139, 210

Rhode Island, regiment of : First, 103 ; battery of : Brown's, 194

Rice, Colonel, takes Vincent's command, 170

Richmond, Va., 4, 15, 32, 59, 65, 67, 68, 70, 76, 79, 94, 98, 99, 103, 107, 108, 110, 112, 119, 179, 204

Ricketts, battery of, 182

Rivanna, 70

River Road, 60

Robertson, 81, 100, 103, 110 ; brigade of, 122, 197

Robinson, Colonel W. W., 130

Robinson, General J. C., 9, 136, 142 et seq. ; 147 et seq. ; retreat of, 154, 189

Rock Creek, 140, 180, 184, 187

Rockville, Md., 112, 117

Rodes, General R. E., division of, 13 ; statement of, 31; division of, 34, 38, 46; report of, 51 ; division of, 89 et seq., 94, 99, 107 ; division of, 119 et seq., 138, 141 ; report of, 143, 161, 181 et seq., 186, 203, 205

Rogers, Captain, 201

Romney, W. Va., 91, 92

Rosengarten, Lieutenant, 127

Round Top, 156, 159, 162, 170, 174, 185, 195, 198, 205

Rowley, Brigadier-General Thos. A., 136, 161, 197

Ruger, division of, 187

Russell, brigade of, 60, 64, 82

Russia, willingness to assist the Union, 77

Saint James's Church, 83

Salem Church, Va., 59 et seq.

Salem, Va., 100

Scales, General, brigade of, 137 ; wounded, 148 ; brigade of, 149, 161, 210

Schenck, General, troops of, 80 ; orders of, 88 et seq. ; skirmishers of his command, 104 et seq.

Schimmelpfennig, General Alexander, 29, 138, 140, 142, 161

Schurz, Major-General Carl, 26, 28, 29, 33, 137; tries to rally his men, 150, 161, 185

Scott's Dam, Va., 15, 61

Sedgwick, Major-General, 3 ; below Fredericksburg, 8 et seq.; order from Hooker, 44, 46, 51 et seq., 56 et seq.; at Salem Church, 61 et seq. ; attack on force of, 63 et seq. ; order from Hooker, 67 ; losses of, 71, 73; report of, 78, 79, 95, 162, 174, 177 et seq., 207 et seq.

Seminary Ridge, Penn., 129, 136, 138, 140 et seq., 147 ɩt seq., 157 et seq.

Semmes, General, brigade of, 60, 172 et seq., 207, 210

Shaler, General, brigade of, 56, 58, 187

Shawl, Colonel, 93

Shenandoah River, 104

"Sheanandoah," the, 77

Shenandoah, Valley of the, 80, 88, 92, 95, 105

Shepherdstown, W. Va., 94, 107

Sherman, General, 131

Sickles, General, commander of Third Corps at Chancellorsville, 8 et seq., 12, 14, 16 ; his suggestion to Hooker, 21 ; attacks Jackson's corps, 23 et seq. ; reinforced by Barlow, 25, 28, 30 et seq.; his instructions to Pleasonton, 36, 38 ; fights his way back, 41 et seq.; wounded, 50, 54 ; an attack on force of, 63 ; votes a retreat, 68, 108, 152 ; requests aid, 158, 162 et seq. ; his movement censured by Meade, 164 ; forced back, 166 et seq., 170 ; loses a leg, 171, 174 ; retreat of, 175, 177 et seq.

Sigel, General Franz, withdrawn from command of Eleventh Corps, 3, 150

Simms, Colonel, 207

Slagle, Lieut., 146, 148

Slocum, Major-General, commander of Twelfth Corps, crosses the Rappahannock, 3; commands three corps, 5, 7 et seq.; moves to attack Lee, 11, 13 et seq., 16 et seq., 21; order from Hooker, 22, 24, 35, 44 et seq., 68, 72; sent to Harper's Ferry, 108; not permitted to join Hooker, 114; ordered to join the main army, 115; at Two Taverns, 137, 152 et seq.; reports against attacking Lee's left, 156 et seq.; begs permission to keep Geary's division, 180, 184, 191, 200, 209

Smith, brigade of, 153, 161, 181

Smithfield, 94

Smith, General W. F., 121, 209

Snicker's Gap, 99 et seq.

South Anna River, 70, 99

South Mountain, 106, 107

Spear, Colonel, Eleventh Pennsylvania, 111, 119

Spear, Colonel, Sixty-first Pennsylvania, killed, 58

Sperryville, 95

Spottsylvania, 8

Stafford Hills, 95

Stahl, cavalry of, 98

Stannard, General, brigade of, 98, 153, 177, 194, 197, 210

Stanton, Secretary of War, note, 144

Steinwehr, division of, 29, 33, 138, 142, 146, 150

Stevens, battery of, 135, 182

Stevensburg, 83

Stewart, battery of, 135, 140, 148, 155, 182

Stone, Colonel Roy, 55, 135, 139 et seq., 143; wounded, 144, 145 et seq., 161

Stoneman, directed to make a raid on Lee, 4 et seq.; at Culpeper, 7 et seq.; operations of his cavalry, 68 et seq., 74; displaced by Hooker in favor of Pleasonton, 80

Strasburg Road, 90 et seq.

Stuart, Major-General J. E. B., at Brandy Station, 7 et seq.; attacks Slocum's corps, 17 et seq., 20, 26, 31; assigned command of Jackson's corps, 40, 46; Anderson makes a junction with, 49 et seq., 53 et seq., 72; at Brandy Station, 81 et seq., 89, 99 et seq., 107; injudicious raid of, 108; driven off by Hancock, 110; crosses the Potomac, 112; burns bridge at Sykesville, 117; at Hanover, 120 et seq.; forces of, 123, 184, 200 et seq.; follows up Kilpatrick, 209

Suffolk, 74

Summit Point, 90

Sumter Fort (see Fort Sumter)

Susquehanna, Department of, 96, 97; river, 108

Sweitzer, brigade of, 172

Sykes, division of, 11, 13, 162, 164; delays reinforcing Sickles, 167, 168, 180 et seq., 202 et seq.

Sykesville, 117

Tabernacle Church, Va., 8, 10, 12

Talley's, 15

Taneytown, Md., 118 et seq., 125, 134, 150, 154, 156, 159, 185

Taylor's Hill, Va., 64, 67
Thomas, brigade of, 47, 137, 161
Thomas, General George H., 131
Thompson, Colonel C., statement of, 37
Thompson's Cross Roads, 69
Thoroughfare Gap, 100, 102, 105, 110
Tidball, General, chief of artillery, 177
Tilton, brigade of, 172
Todd's Tavern, 8, 11, 14
Toll Gate, 59
Toll House, Va., 61
Toombs, Senator, of Georgia, 112
Torbert, brigade of, 64
Treichel, Captain, 201
Tremaine, General, 54, 55
Trimble, General, 207
Tunstall's Station, 70
Turner's Gap, Md., 108
Two Taverns, Penn., 125, 137, 152, 184
Tyler, Colonel, 94
Tyler, General, 95

UNION, 102 et seq.
Union Mills, Md., 117, 119
Uniontown, 118, 119
United States, batteries of : Third, 131 ; B—Fourth, 135, 140, 145, 148, 155, 194 ; L—Fifth, 92; Calef's, 135, 140 ; Hazlett's, 169
United States Ford, 8, 21, 26, 42, 79
Upperville, 102, 104
Urbanna, 74

VAN ALLEN, Brigadier-General Jas. H., aide-de-camp to Hooker, 22

Vermont, regiments of : First, 198; Second, 98, 153, 177, 193 ; Thirteenth, 193 ; Fourteenth, 193, 197 ; Sixteenth, 193, 197
Vicksburg, Tenn., 76
Vincent, Brigadier-General, killed, 169, 174, 210
Virginia Central Railroad, 7, 21, 69
Virginia, regiments of : First, 200, 201 ; Eleventh, 13 ; Fifteenth, 100
Von Arnsberg, Colonel, brigade of, 142, 161
Von Gilsa, Colonel, brigade of, 33, 142, 161, 182

WADSWORTH, Captain, 43
Wadsworth, General James S., 5, 9; at Gettysburg, 125 et seq. ; orders Cutler's withdrawal, 132, 135 et seq., 139 et seq. ; report of, 146, 151 et seq., 156, 161, 180, 189
Wainwright, Colonel, Chief of Artillery, 140, 182
Wainwright, General, 30
Walker, brigade of, 181
Walsh, Colonel, rallies John's men in attack on Marye's Hill, 58
Ward, General J. H. H., brigade of, 41, 46, 49, 164, 166 et seq., 172
Warren, General, Chief Engineer on Hooker's staff, 14; takes charge of batteries, 30, 35 et seq. ; urges an assault, 57, 62, 73 ; reports against attacking Lee's left, 157 et seq. ; on Meade's staff, 168 ; saves Little Round Top, 168, 177; activity of, 178, 210

Warrenton, 80, 98, 100, 104

Washington, D. C., 5, 79, 87, 88, 95, 98, 99, 102, 105, 107, 108, 112, 114 et seq., 134, 152, 157, 178, 185, 187, 207, 209

Waynesborough, P .nn., 107

Web, General Alexander S., 54, 175 et seq. ; b:av ry of, 194 et seq. ; wounde , 6, 197, 210

Weed, General, artillery of, 52 · mortally wounded, 169, 210

Weidrick, battery of, 182

Welford House, 23

Westminster, Md.,115, 117, et seq., 164, 179

West Point, N. Y., 57, 66, 131, 169, 181

West Virginia, Governor of, 97

Wheaton, brigade of, 57, 61, 65, 66, 174,

Wheeler, battery of, 145, 194

Wheelock, Colonel, 154

Whipple, General, division of, 23, 38, 41, 44 et seq. ; killed, 63

White, battalion of, 110, 122

White House, Va., 99, 100

White Plains, 103

White's Creek, 200

Wickham, cavalry of, 17

Wilbur, Lieutenant, 140

Wilcox, General Cadmus, brigade of, 12, 57, 59 ; fierce charge of, 60 et seq. ; discussion of, 158 ; brigade, 175 et seq., 188 et seq., 192 et seq.

Wilderness, 72

Wilderness Tavern, 39

Wilkinson, Adjutant, 29

Wilkeson, battery of, 142

Williams, division of, 24, 26, 34, 38, 41, 44, 49

Williamsport, Md., 94, 96 et seq., 99, 108, 115, 209

Williston, battery of, 60

Willoughby's Run, Penn., 127, 131 et seq., 136, 147

Winchester, Va., 88 et seq., 94, 96, 104

Winslow, battery of, 35, 173

Wisconsin, regiments of : Second, 132 ; Sixth, 131, 150, 155

Wister, Colonel, takes command of Stone's brigade, 144 ; shot through the face, 145

Wofford, brigade of, 165, 173 ; letter from, 187

Wood, Dr. J. Robie, 176, note

Wright, General A. R., brigade of, 8, 14, 17, 175 et seq., 189, 197, 199

Wrightsville, Penn., 108, 113, 119

Wyndham, Colonel, 70

York, Penn., 107, 108, 111 et seq., 118, 120 et seq., 134, 138, 179

Yorktown, 99

Zook, General, brigade of, 172 et seq.; killed, 171, 210